THE COMMON GLUE

AN ALTERNATIVE WAY OF TRANSCENDING DIFFERENCES TO UNLEASH COMPETITIVE PERFORMANCE

INTERNATIONAL BUSINESS AND MANAGEMENT SERIES

Series Editor: **Pervez N. Ghauri**

Published:

European Union and the Race for Foreign Direct Investment in Europe
Oxelheim & Ghauri

Strategic Alliances in Eastern and Central Europe
Hyder & Abraha

Intellectual Property and Doing Business in China
Yang

Alliances and Co-operative Strategies
Contractor & Lorange

Relationships and Networks in International Markets
Gemünden, Ritter & Walter

International Business Negotiations
Ghauri & Usunier

Critical Perspectives on Internationalisation
Havila, Forsgren & Håkansson

Managing Cultural Differences
Morosini

Network Dynamics in International Marketing
Naude & Turnbull

The Global Challenge for Multinational Enterprises
Buckley & Ghauri

Business Network Learning
Håkansson & Johanson

Managing International Business Ventures in China
Li

Forthcoming titles include:

Global Competitive Strategies
Hennart & Thomas

Non-Business Actors in a Business Network
Hadjikhani & Thilenius

Other titles of interest:

International Trade in the 21st Century
Fatemi

Globalization, Trade and Foreign Direct Investment
Dunning

International Trade and the New Economic Order
Moncarz

Contemporary Issues in Commercial Policy
Kreinin

Related journals — sample copies available on request:

European Management Journal
International Business Review
International Journal of Research in Marketing
Long Range Planning
Scandinavian Journal of Management

For full details of all IBM titles published under the Elsevier imprint please go to:

http://www.elsevier.com/locate/series/ibm

THE COMMON GLUE

AN ALTERNATIVE WAY OF TRANSCENDING DIFFERENCES TO UNLEASH COMPETITIVE PERFORMANCE

BY

PIERO MOROSINI

2005

ELSEVIER

Amsterdam – Boston – Heidelberg – London – New York – Oxford
Paris – San Diego – San Francisco – Singapore – Sydney – Tokyo

ELSEVIER B.V.	ELSEVIER Inc.	**ELSEVIER Ltd**	ELSEVIER Ltd
Radarweg 29	525 B Street, Suite 1900	**The Boulevard, Langford Lane**	84 Theobalds Road
P.O. Box 211, 1000 AE	San Diego, CA 92101-4495	**Kidlington, Oxford OX5 1GB**	London WC1X 8RR
Amsterdam, The Netherlands	USA	**UK**	UK

First edition 2005

British Library Cataloguing in Publication Data
A catalogue record is available from the British Library.

ISBN: 0-08-044610-8

♾ The paper used in this publication meets the requirements of ANSI/NISO Z39.48-1992 (Permanence of Paper).
Printed in The Netherlands.

To Leonardo.
My son, my friend,
my inspiration.

Contents

Piero Morosini

Piero Morosini, an Adjunct Professor of strategy and leadership at the European School of Management and Technology (esmt), Berlin, is the founding president of PAYA Sàrl, Lausanne, a leadership institute that helps organizations build a strong Common Glue® for successful performance across cultural, professional and organizational boundaries.

A keynote speaker in cross-cultural leadership, mergers and acquisitions, innovation strategies and knowledge management, Piero has studied at the Wharton School, Philadelphia (Ph.D., 1994) and has graduated in Economics at the Universidad del Pacifico, Lima in 1984. He has previously been: a full-time Professor at the International Institute for Management Development (IMD), Lausanne; a strategy consultant at Accenture in Milan and at McKinsey & Company in Madrid and London; and an executive in JP Morgan and at Robert Fleming in Milan.

He has been selected as one of the world's next generation thought leaders in management (*Next Generation Business Handbook,* Wiley, 2004), and is a former thought leadership award winner worldwide at Accenture. His original research work has been published in books (*Managing Complex Mergers,* Financial Times — Prentice-Hall, U.K., 2004; *Managing Cultural Differences,* Pergamon Press, U.K., 1998), book chapters, video cases, case studies and articles in leading international journals.

e-mail: piero.morosini@commonglue.com

Preface

> All metaphors are sexual...
>
> Norman O. Brown[1]

A thought occurred to me in the a sudden and unexpected way that inspirational ideas often arrive. For months I had examined most well-established managerial taxonomies only to realize that none would portray my new research findings suitably. I was growing disappointed and uneasy by the day. But then, during a break at an international women's conference in Lausanne, the thought arrived swiftly to my mind. The Harmonic Fusion of the Two Great Powers: the male and the female — the oldest archetype known to humankind — would provide the powerful metaphor I was looking for. I had in fact discovered evidence that only when an organization blends its male and female characteristics harmoniously — at the individual, group and organizational level — does it become capable of transcending cultural, geographic and organizational boundaries and of achieving lasting and superior competitive performance. This book contains this evidence unveiled in a 5-year research project spanning scores of organizations and company executives worldwide, together with an account of its far-reaching implications for any entity or individual person who has an interest in *what really drives* the competitive performance of organizations in today's increasingly multicultural milieu.

The idea that organizations ought to integrate harmoniously their male and female characteristics is not an entirely new one. Already in 1990, a management pundit suggested that, "new theories of entrepreneurship that incorporate the experiences of both men and women [...] are needed."[2] Many people then saw this as a sign of the times. However, the new managerial theories this author asked for did not materialize over the ensuing decade. This volume is a first attempt to fulfill this aspiration. Based on rigorous research methods, it provides a theory grounded in hard empirical data portraying the fundamental link between an organization's male and female characteristics and its competitive performance.

Understanding this link is crucial for *all* organizations striving to perform within complex and international environments.

For a few such organizations that already are quite "female" in their approach, the findings in this book will help them incorporate more "male" managerial aspects into focus. However, the vast majority of organizations will find in this book evidence that will encourage them to integrate "female" managerial approaches to a much greater extent than they have done so far. Most of this book is in fact devoted to readers that subscribe to the prevailing "male" managerial approach, either in mindset or in practice — or in *both*. In chapter after chapter, these readers will find a compelling portrayal of a new and female-like business paradigm that I call the "Common Glue®", as well as hard data suggesting a positive link between the practical application of such paradigm and the superior competitive performance of multinational organizations.

My choice of focus should surprise nobody. In fact, the challenge of harmoniously blending an institution's "female" and "male" characteristics, in itself calls for organizational traits that behavioral scientists have identified as being *female* such as: the ability to integrate efforts across dividing lines, the social use of conversations for the realization of shared initiatives, the nurturing of transformational partnerships across diverse groups of people, and a focus on interpersonal skills. Even though I found these types of capabilities to be crucial for blending the diverse organizational characteristics that drive performance, most companies I studied either had these capabilities in a barely functioning state or found it very difficult to recognize and develop them within the organization. Once more, this should be of little surprise to the reader. For, although men and women are different, today we still live in a man's world. In politics, sciences, finance and elsewhere, male professionals typically dominate their female counterparts and promote their own rules of the game. Being male often implies "alpha" behavior such as boldness, command-and-control style management, and attempt at a victory at all costs. In corporate hierarchy such attitudes have been largely responsible for upward professional movement of both men and women over the whole of the 20th century. On the other hand, being female typically implies empathy, management through engaging, flat structures, and attempt at positive-sum outcomes. It is only lately that such attitudes have begun to attract a positive resonance in the Anglo-Saxon workplace.[4]

My focus on certain organizational traits that can be termed 'female' is therefore to be set within the context of the need to *harmoniously integrate* them with 'male' traits in order to unleash fully the performance of organizations. This is an important point and one that the reader ought to recognize from the outset. The approach of this book in fact differs *profoundly* from a certain kind of literature that has portrayed "fraternalistic", "transformational" or "partnership" approaches to leadership as being both "female" *and* desirable over the prevailing "male" approaches.[3] These kinds of authors seem to criticize the one-sided application of "male" leadership within organizations, only to introduce — more or less explicitly — an equally one-sided agenda to replace those approaches with supposedly "female" ones. To justify the attractiveness of such a proposition, these authors offer evidence which has been called into question.[5]

By contrast, I found neither one-sided "male" nor exclusively "female" organizational approaches at work in the better performing companies I examined. Rather, what I observed in these organizations were leadership cadres blending harmoniously and relentlessly *both* of their organization's male and female characteristics at all levels: individual, group, team, cross-functional and organization-wide. In doing so they achieved a rare kind of fulfillment, and — equally importantly — they managed to consistently outperform their competitors over time and across cultural, geographic and organizational boundaries.

This book thus attempts to balance the "male" managerial approaches that are predominant today by creating a "female" theory of strategic management and corporate leadership that is grounded in hard data and empirical evidence. The central tenet of this theory is constituted by the notion I call: *the blending power of organizations*. This *blending power* harnesses the harmony and diversity of organizations to unleash performance across boundaries. It is made up of two mutually reinforcing elements: a strategic dimension and a transformational aspect. The strategic dimension is constituted by an organization's ability to design what I call *blending* strategies and *blending* approaches to top-line growth. The transformational aspect is about an organization's capability to nurture a strong Common Glue that enables it to attain challenging strategic goals across all sorts of cultural, organizational and professional boundaries. I found that only when an organization has both the ability to craft *blending* strategies and *blending* approaches to growth, together with the capability to nurture a strong Common Glue, does it become able to harness its *blending power* fully to direct differences toward achieving positive organizational transformations and superior competitive performance.

The notion of *blending strategies* moves the debate within organizations from the choice of *one* clear *competitive* strategy out of a limited number of supposedly conflicting strategic options (i.e. "overall cost leadership" vis-à-vis "differentiation"), to the issue of: harmoniously *blending* those seemingly conflicting strategic options depending on context. For example, the better-performing organizations I looked at *simultaneously* pursued the twin goals of delighting the customer via product and service differentiation, while gaining cost advantages over their competitors through continuous innovation and knowledge sharing. Similarly, from a tactical perspective, most of these successful organizations pursued a mix of both cooperative and competitive strategic options at any given point of time. Likewise, top-line growth was described by these organizations as a balanced combination of external (i.e., through mergers, acquisitions, joint ventures and alliances) as well as internal — i.e. organic — growth approaches. Still, these *blending* strategies and approaches to growth were portrayed by the managers I interviewed as being just specific dimensions of the far broader blending power at work of the Common Glue.

The Common Glue represents the social capabilities that build *cohesive* and *co-operative* leadership harmoniously within organizations. More precisely, it stands for the way in which cohesive and co-operative relationships between a company's key executive cadres should be created, nurtured and *transformed* harmoniously into valuable products and services in the marketplace. The Common Glue consists of the following five ingredients or *social capabilities*: boundary-spanning leadership, company-wide building blocks, communication rituals, knowledge interactions and cross-boundary rotations. The interplay between these five ingredients is of an organic, rather than a mechanistic nature. Moreover, within the organizations I studied, the Common Glue is nurtured as an intrinsically holistic phenomenon: each of its constituent ingredients is related to one another, and none works by itself. Only when all five are in place, does a firm attain the Common Glue and becomes capable of transcending geographic, cultural, and organizational boundaries and of unleashing superior competitive performance (see Figure 1).

The first ingredient, *boundary-spanning leadership*, stands for the extent to which the key leadership cadre of a multinational organization — typically numbering a few hundred executives from many nationalities — is able to avoid preconceived mental models, possesses humility to accept others and courage to go beyond its comfort zone, works patiently on creating a company-wide common language and understanding, coaches its subordinates, follows its statements with actions, and is comfortable in using both co-operative and confrontational tactics depending on circumstance. In short, it describes leadership character traits and suggests that the road to success in this realm lies in blending "male" and "female" characteristics harmoniously.

The second ingredient, which I named *company-wide building blocks*, addresses the ability of an organization's members to craft a common language, instill shared beliefs around a common company mission, and establish unified performance measurements within the organization. In the case of language, for example, company-wide building blocks act as a dictionary of terms with meanings that are common to all organizational members, providing them with a communication and a cohesion tool. Given that the same word may have different meaning or implications in different cultures, even if translated properly (for example, "logistics" often stands for transportation/delivery in the U.S. and for the entire supply chain in Europe), company-wide building blocks amount to firm-specific ISO standards that are *enacted* by the members of the organization.

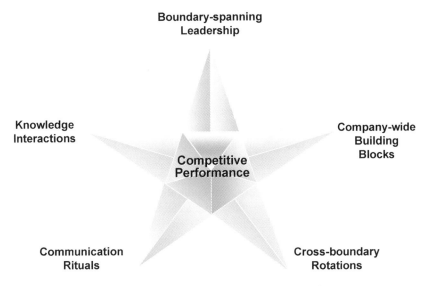

Boundary-spanning
Leadership

Knowledge
Interactions

Company-wide
Building
Blocks

Competitive
Performance

Communication
Rituals

Cross-boundary
Rotations

Figure 1: Five ingredients of the Common Glue.

They define what the most important aspects of a firm's operations are, what priority the organization places on them and how the performance in each area should be evaluated.

The third ingredient, *communication rituals*, explains *how* communication within an organization must be conducted. In order to develop cohesion among the organization's key leadership cadres, its members must have the ability to create lines of communication that are short in length, direct in transmission and frank in quality. Employees must have the ability to talk about both positive and negative experiences and to develop face-to-face communication networks to promote a shared understanding and mutual trust across the cultural and professional boundaries that span the organization. Within the better performing organizations I studied, transparent and factual communications were brought to life by its top leaders' habit of 'walking-the-talk', in other words, by demonstrating the values of cohesiveness and co-operation across boundaries through their daily behavior, interactions and concrete actions. As a result, some of these daily events and actions became powerful and visible communications rituals within the organization.

The fourth ingredient, induced *knowledge interactions*, suggests that successful intra-organizational knowledge flows are conditional on a firm's ability to stimulate "all hands" involvement in the process. Initiation and enactment of a "company-wide business case" helps a firm to better process information, codify know-how and knowledge-sharing channels, and transform knowledge into valuable output. Equally important, "company-wide business cases" are also central to bringing the organization passionately together. This is one of the important findings of my research. For a number of decades, a vast managerial literature has postulated that what keeps a company together are common business values, a strong corporate culture and the like. However, my findings demonstrated that common corporate values are not just what keeps an organization together. A "company-wide business case" — an exciting business initiative with very clear and challenging goals that has an impact throughout and involves passionately everyone in the entire organization — is equally crucial to driving a strong sense of organizational cohesiveness. "Company-wide business cases" also illustrate that there is much more than corporate cultural values to the Common Glue. Corporate cultural values can be considered as an important part of the building blocks described above, but a company's Common Glue also includes other building blocks, as well as four other social capabilities.

The fifth and final ingredient of the Common Glue, *cross-boundary rotations*, describes a company's ability to develop and implement global personnel policies such as equitable expatriate and repatriate programs, as well as global career development tracks and reward incentives. Comprehensive global personnel management standards help a firm create valuable formal and informal networks by fostering the smooth and continual rotation of its key executives across geographic, organizational and cultural boundaries. The informal social networks that are created through these cross-boundary rotations provide the organization with a much more compact network of social relationships that allows for a much faster transmission of ideas and resources than the formal organizational structure does.

As a leadership theory, the Common Glue proposes that for a global enterprise to succeed, it must first uncover the boundaries facing a firm, as well as their roots and source of power, and then proceed with tearing down these barriers whilst nurturing the richness of a firm's social and cultural endowments. At its core, the Common Glue views organizations as social entities that specialize in the transformation of individual and group knowledge into products and services that are valuable in the marketplace. This transformation is of a social character, and can only take place within each firm's unique social milieu. The transformational capacity requires a number of co-ordination and communication capabilities to occur, and represents the main reason why certain economic activities are better carried out *within* a firm's boundaries rather than externally, in the marketplace.

A number of factors, however, may impede this transformational capacity in multinational enterprises. Chief amongst these is the boundaries that can inhibit — or even prevent — the social transformation of knowledge. There are several types of boundaries to be found in the global arena, first and foremost being the boundaries of mind. For example, managers operating internationally might be conditioned to view their and others' actions through the prism of their domestic culture, thus creating an obstacle to co-operation and co-ordination both within and across firms. Such boundaries are the most insidious as they often are the least visible and hardest to identify.

Then there are linguistic barriers. Even among groups of managers sharing a common national language, functional or professional languages emerge powerfully, establishing invisible — yet enduring — dividing lines. Various groups of employees can also form and cluster within a company on the basis of mutual interest, informal contacts social or professional status and the like. In this case, different professional codes and diverse functional practices, processes routines and repertoires can act as organizational boundaries that establish a strong sense of belonging and determine who is to remain inside and outside the group. Also in existence are "classical" national-cultural boundaries that every multinational organization encounters. The list could go on and on, as the boundaries facing these types of organizations are manifold (see Figure 2).

Most of the existing literature portrays the many boundaries that organizations face in a negative light, describing them as only inhibiting factors to the performance of multinational firms. By contrast, from the Common Glue perspective, if an organization develops the capability to handle these boundaries successfully, they then become a lasting source of internal strength and of superior competitive performance. As mentioned, my research findings suggest that the way in which a

Figure 2: Some of the multiple boundaries that organizations face.

multinational firm can go about turning its boundaries into performance advantages is by developing a strong Common Glue, that is: a set of five social capabilities that generate a powerful degree of organizational co-operation and internal cohesiveness.

As a theory, Common Glue draws inspiration from seven areas: neuroscience, genetic research, psychology, behavioral science, cultural anthropology, management and economics. Research from the first five fields is used to explain the differences between the "male" and the "female" archetypal elements, their emergence across disciplines and cultures, and to then build the foundation of a "female" approach to corporate leadership and strategic management that blends both male and female elements together within organizations. From economics and management I utilize the theories of social organization, knowledge management and the multinational enterprise. The first set of theories explains the types, sources and implications of organizational boundaries; the second set describes how knowledge is acquired and utilized within organizations; the third addresses implications of globalization and internationalization of enterprise for boundary reduction and knowledge management. Common Glue then integrates the implications of the abovementioned theories to develop a higher-order framework, which describes elements a company can use to create and test collective corporate understanding and then transform this understanding into superior results.

It is hard to exaggerate the central relevance of these findings in today's global business milieu. Indeed, an overwhelming number of empirical studies carried out over the last three decades of the 20th century suggested that multinational firms' inability to work consistently across geographic, cultural and organizational boundaries was one of the most important reasons behind the dismal performance record of cross-border mergers, acquisitions, alliances, large-scale change programs, outsourcing efforts and restructuring and re-engineering initiatives.[6] While these kinds of corporate initiatives made the business environment more global than ever before, in the aftermath of these radical — often unsuccessful — undertakings, many multinational company executives were left wondering: what is it that keeps us together? The research findings reported in this book suggest that what keeps a multinational company together is precisely what gives that company a competitive edge in today's global marketplace. Looking at a company's Common Glue — my research findings suggest — can have potentially radical implications for an organization that wants to improve its competitive performance across geographic, organizational and cultural boundaries.

In a nutshell, the plan of this book is as follows. The first two chapters elicit the theoretical tenets behind the notion of: the harmonic fusion of the "male" and "female". This archetype is central to this work, and builds the foundation of my approach to corporate leadership and strategic management. Since an examination of the prevailing management theories explaining organizational performance reveals an overwhelmingly "male" perspective, developing a "female" approach seemingly provides a much-needed complementary viewpoint. Supporting this, Chapter 3 provides some compelling real-life examples of organizations that blend competitive and co-operative strategies harmoniously, and nurture a strong Common Glue to unleash superior competitive performance within their sectors of activity. These ideas are rigorously tested in Chapter 4, through the development of an empirical methodology and a series of hypothesized relationships between "male" and "female" organizational characteristics and competitive performance. Once more, the focus here is largely on the "female" side of things, as much of the previous literature has already examined with a certain amount of detail the relationship between "male" organizational characteristics and competitive performance (which is not always — as it turns out — favorable). Chapter 5 provides the empirical results of this research, reporting the main statistical findings obtained on the basis of a large sample of executives from an array of very diverse multinational organizations. As it turns out, the empirical evidence strongly support the ideas and relationships hypothesized in the previous chapters. Finally, in the last chapter I summarize some of the profound implications that my research results might represent for academics, practitioners, managers and other professionals alike whose activities take place within — or close to — the realm of multinational organizations.

More specifically, in chapter 1 I look at evidence from diverse scientific fields — ranging from neurology to genetics to cultural anthropology — to characterize the "female" and "male" elements of the archetypal framework developed in this book. It turns out that the archetype suggesting the harmonic fusion of the "male" and "female" transcends time, space and cultural differences, constituting a sort of spontaneous and organic knowledge that is inherent to all human beings. As such, the "male" and "female" elements of the archetype provide the best conceptual framework for the organic, holistic and social approach to organizational performance that I observed at play in the organizations I studied.

Having established the "male" and "female" archetypal framework in detail, in chapter 2 I apply it to specific areas of the management science that in the past have advanced theories explaining differences in the competitive performance of organizations. From this analysis it emerges that many of these managerial theories are largely "male" in character, content and approach. However, a few of these managerial approaches can be portrayed as "female", and these resonate strongly with the empirical observations I carried out across a series of diverse multinational organizations. This "female" managerial approach is explored further in chapter 3, where the notion of "male" vis-à-vis "female" strategies as well as the Common Glue with its constituent social capabilities, are examined in more detail. We look at a few examples of companies undertaking various "female" strategies, we are able to distil some of the central components of the Common Glue, and to make a case for a series of links between "male" and "female" strategies, the Common Glue and competitive performance.

In chapter 4, we set up a number of formal propositions and hypotheses, link- ing *blending* strategies, *blending* approaches to top-line growth, the Common Glue and competitive performance. The empirical methodology and the underly- ing structural equation model developed to test the hypothesized links are also described in this chapter. Statistical support for these hypotheses is found and pre- sented in chapter 5, based on a large-scale survey of executives from leading multinational organizations representing a broad diversity of countries, indus- tries, functions and many other key characteristics. These results suggest that, in addition to *blending* organizational strategies and approaches to top-line growth, the Common Glue is a phenomenon of central importance to explain why some multinational organizations perform better than their competitors over time, and across cultural, geographic and organizational boundaries.

Finally, in the last chapter I describe some of the most important implications of my findings for academics, practitioners and other professionals interested in discovering what really drives the superior competitive performance of organiza- tions, as well as for executives of multinational institutions that operate within complex and multicultural environments. These implications are both wide-rang- ing in scope, profound in character and potentially radical in their application. However, they might contribute to a deeper understanding of organizational per- formance in a way that might increasingly become the norm in the future. A way that blends both "male" and "female" organizational characteristics within a uni- fying paradigm that is rigorous in its analytical power and at the same time organic, social and holistic in its practical application.

References

[1] Brown, N.O. (1966) *Love's Body,* University of California Press, Berkeley.
[2] Stevenson, L. (1990) "Some Methodological Problems Associated With Researching Women Entrepreneurs," *Journal of Business Ethics* 9(4–5): 439.
[3] Rosener, J. B. 1990. "Ways Women Lead," *Harvard Business Review* 68(6): 119–125.
[4] Besides the fact that we might have lived in a man's world for *too long,* there is an addi- tional number of factors that can explain the surge of interest towards "female" manage- ment characteristics. First and foremost it is the increasing empowerment of women that started at the end of the 19th century and bloomed fully at the end of the 20th. While slightly over a hundred years ago Charles Eliot, then president of Harvard University,

refused to admit women into his school as not to "waste" the university's "precious resources," by 2003 women had started to dominate U.S. higher education, earning around 57 percent of all bachelor's and 58 percent of all master's degrees (Conlin, M. 2003. "The New Gender Gap," *Business Week*, Issue 3834, May 26, 2003, pp. 74–80). In the same year, Conlin reported that by 2020 the ratio of women-to-men earning their bachelor's degrees in the U.S. was expected to be 1.56-to-1 (Conlin, 2003). Similar trends were taking place at the graduate education levels, with an increasing amount of women obtaining M.D. and Ph.D. degrees in the U.S. and operating more and more businesses. From 1972 to 1987, female-owned businesses in that country grew from less than 5% to 28% of the total (Buttner, E. H. 1995. "Female entrepreneurs: How far have they come?" *Business Horizons*, March-April 1995, p. 59). In 1990, the number of sole proprietorships run by women in the U.S. stood at 5.6 million, or 33.5% of the total; by 1998, it increased to 7.1 million, or 36.8% (U.S. Small Business Administration, 2003. "Dynamics of women-operated sole proprietorships, 1990–1998," *Research Bulletin*, March 2003). Over the same period, sales of female-owned small businesses grew by 2.8%, and net income by 4.6% (U.S. Small Business Administration, 2003). The trend toward female empowerment is not specific to the U.S. In fact, during the 1980s and 1990s it started to look like a universal trend. In Germany, for example, female participation in creating new enterprises rose from 10% in 1975 to 33% in 1984.[8] By the 1990s women made up 26% of the total number of German entrepreneurs (Chirikova, A. 2001. "Woman as a Company Head: Problems of establishing female entrepreneurship in Russia," *Russian Social Science Review*, 42(4): 65). In Hong Kong, from 1991 to 1996 the number of female entrepreneurs grew by 44% (Chu, P. 2000. "The characteristics of chinese female entrepreneurs: Motivation and personality," *Journal of Enterprising Culture* 8(1): 68.). In Russia, by the late 1990s the growth rates of female entrepreneurship exceeded the growth rates of male entrepreneurship by the factor of 1.3 to 1.5 (Chirikova, 2001). The second factor that brought attention to "female" management characteristics is globalization. As the business milieu became increasingly global in scope, cultural differences in managerial approaches became evident. With them came the realization that the command-and-control management paradigm is not always suitable within the new international realities. Previously unthinkable combines such as the DaimlerChrysler merger or the Renault-Nissan alliance highlighted, for example, that Northern European countries tend to emphasize *stakeholder* rather than *shareholder* perspective in their business activities, and that the Japanese often place an emphasis on *collaborative* rather than *competitive* efforts. While globalization made some barriers to entry disappear across several industries, some other sectors saw new boundaries in place, perhaps stimulated by the protective instincts of certain national governments. The 1990s also saw a surge of *cooperative* forms of institutional organization, such as joint ventures and alliances. These were seen as a way to achieve strategic positioning, generate value, reduce transaction costs, transfer organizational knowledge, set technology standards and hedge bets for new product developmental efforts. In 1995, 55% of the U.S. fastest growing companies were involved in an average of three alliances (Han Chan, S., J. W. Kensinger, A. J. Keown and J. D. Martin. 1997. "Do strategic alliance create value?" *Journal of Financial Economics*

46(2): 199–221). In 1999, alliances accounted for between 6 and 15% of the market value of a typical company, and represented more than 20 percent of the revenue generated by the top 2,000 U.S. and European firms (C. Kalmbach Jr. and C. Roussel. 1999. "Dispelling the myth of alliances," *Outlook Special Edition*, Accenture, October, p.5; Harbison, J. R. , P. Pekar Jr., D. Moloney, and A. Viscio (2000) "The Alliance Enterprise: Breakout strategy for the new millennium," *Viewpoints Series on Alliances*, Booz, Allen and Hamilton, Number 5, p. 1). During the 1998–1999 period, more than 20,000 alliances were formed worldwide with the expected return on investment of nearly seventeen percent for the top 2,000 firms (Harbison, J. R. , P. Pekar Jr., D. Moloney, and A. Viscio. 2000. "The alliance enterprise: Breakout strategy for the new millennium," *Viewpoints Series on Alliances*, Booz, Allen and Hamilton, Number 5, p. 3). In the light of these developments, the question arises as to whether one-sided "male" approaches to management should be reconsidered. A careful examination is clearly required as to which of its premises are beneficial and which are unproductive and should be replaced. In 1991, Schwartz, for example, noted that, "the command-and-control leadership style of men was suitable to a manufacturing economy. As we move towards an information-service, I believe we will find an interactive mode [to be] more effective" (Schwartz, F. 1991. "Debate: Ways men and women lead," *Harvard Business Review* 69(1): 154). During the same year, Cohen echoed this sentiment by pointing out that "the command-and-control style of leadership is increasingly less appropriate for either men or women since rapid changes require greater utilizations of all talents and views of people of all levels of organizations. The more traditional leadership style presumes that the leader knows what to command and can predict events well enough to control everyone's behavior closely. Not only that is seldom true anymore, but also more employees are educated and expect to have a voice in decisions" (Cohen, A. 1991. "Debate: Ways men and women lead," *Harvard Business Review* 69(1): 158).

[5] Epstein, C. F. (1991) "Debate: Ways men and women lead," *Harvard Business Review* 69(1): 150–158.

[6] Morosini, P. (2004) "Competing on social capabilities". In: *Next Generation Business Handbook,* S. Chowdhury (Ed.), Wiley, New York, p. 248–271.

Acknowledgments

Love will be lost
if you sit too long
at a friend's fire

Hávamál, *ca.* 700 AD

This book comes as a result of over a decade of reflection and practice as a teacher, a researcher and an executive in multinational organizations. During this time period, I matured the thoughts and ideas that gradually took shape into the Common Glue theory of organizational performance, a paradigm grounded in the experiences of hundreds of leaders and managers from all around the globe. I owe these individuals many of the best ideas and inspiration behind this work and, although naming them would make it too long a list, I nevertheless express to each of them my whole-hearted gratitude for their generosity in sharing their thoughts and experiences with me. There are some individuals, however, that I would like to name and thank for their valuable contributions to the present volume.

First of all, I thank Marianna Kozintseva and Olivier Renaud, who co-authored specific parts of this book together with me. Marianna Kozintseva's excellent research notes — prepared under my guidance while she was in the latter stages of her doctoral studies — provided the main content for Chapter 2, and for the six sub-sections in Chapter 1 under the section entitled: 'scientific evidence for the archetype.' I also included many of Marianna's insightful descriptions of the Common Glue in the preface of this book. During August to December 2004, Olivier Renaud developed at my request a set of statistical models to empirically examine the series of hypothesized relationships I had elicited in Chapter 4, and carried out statistical tests based on a large-scale sample of data I had previously gathered. Olivier's statistical write-up became the main basis for the three sub-sections in Chapter 4 under the section entitled: 'developing a statistical model to test the hypotheses', and for chapter 5.

I am also indebted to Sophie Linguri, whose invaluable research work, editing support and enthusiasm throughout the entire research and writing stages of this book were very important to me, and to Dinesh Sonak, whose friendship, encouragement and assistance were also fundamental during the early phases of this research project. I also express my gratitude to Erling Chr. Nøttaasen, Erik Næss and Ruth Jouanne for their enormous help and inspiration throughout the research project leading to the present volume. In particular, Erling's boundless enthusiasm for the Common Glue was instrumental to get Erik and Ruth on board of a series of most enjoyable and useful workshops we shared together in Paris, Verona and Copenhagen, where many of the ideas that sprung out found its way in important parts throughout the book.

Needless to say, any flaws and inaccuracies found in this book are exclusively the author's responsibility.

Chapter 1

The Archetype of the Harmonic Fusion

Work is the great gateway to experiencing the cosmic harmony
Kichua adage in ancient Peru

The notion of 'archetype' is central to the theories developed in this book, and the origin of the word is crucial to understanding its meaning. It was coined from the Greek term *archon* denoting an Athenian magistrate in antiquity, and the Latin word *tipo,* meaning the general set of relationships linking a collection of forms, models or species. The word 'archetype' therefore signifies *the prime set of general relationships linking a collection of forms, models or species.* The ancient Romans noticed that this concept lent itself beautifully to describe all sorts of notions related to the building of static and *mechanical* structures. The master of a team of builders was thus called an 'architect', and some of the fundamental linkages of any edifice — such as the curved constructions connecting and distributing the weight of the building — were named *arcus,* which is of course the Latin word from which the English term 'arch' derives from.

More than 27 centuries later, the term *archetype* started to be applied systematically to the realm of *organic* and living forms. This was the result of the pioneering work of psychologists and anthropologists such as Carl Jung and Claude Lévi-Strauss, who used the term 'archetype' to describe the *prime set of general relationships linking a range of phenomena of the collective human mind.* The former described human archetypes as the timeless and universal 'prime images' of the collective unconscious, from which much of mankind's cultural creations stem from:

> Jung defined the archetypes as *primordial images* of the collective unconscious, stemming from a common atavic (and probably pre-conscious) past. They are also sometimes associated with a sort of ancient race memory from prehistoric stages of mankind. According to Jung, an unsuspected amount of human creativity – i.e. the artistic, as well as most of the mythical, religious and philosophical developments that have come to characterize the deep-rooted cultural and epochal aspects of nations, are archetypal in nature.[1]

Lévi-Strauss' structuralist school of anthropology also described in archetypal terms the *organic and unconscious system of relationships* that were behind the collective development of language and the creation of myths in human societies. According to Lévi-Strauss, structure was to be understood as the set of living and organized relationships that gave intrinsic cohesion and distinctive quality to any given socio-cultural phenomenon. His work was built on the seminal ideas of linguist Ferdinand de Saussure, who in the early 20th century proposed that socio-cultural phenomena such as language were the result of collective representations of human societies. Saussure maintained that, just as the understanding of societies entailed grasping the nature of the relationships between its constitutive individuals and groups, linguistics had to be conceived as *semiology,* in other words as a general science of the relationship between signs.[2] Lévi-Strauss saw this as a radical notion that applied not just to linguistics, but also to other fields of human creation such as the making of myths. He suggested that, just as the significance of language resided in the relationships between signs rather than the signs themselves, the meaning of myths stemmed from the assortment of *combinations of minimal constitutive units* of the collective mind that were both universal in character and unconscious in nature. According to Lévi-Strauss, the arrangement of these 'combinations of minimal constitutive units' followed a precise logic that led to the creation of both mythical expressions as well as cultural symbols and metaphors. Myths were therefore to be conceived as narrative expressions of the "architectural logic of the human spirit which is structured on a set of relationships, just as a language."[3]

Described by psychologists and cultural anthropologists alike as the pivotal governing factors of the collective human mind operating unconsciously, it is not surprising that archetypes have been found to wield pervasive influence in all aspects of the collective human activity. This influence transcends time and geography, and is found wherever human communities arise and develop — either in tribal, regional or national forms. This book examines one archetype in particular that might be central to understanding the way in which modern organizations — those human communities of sorts — go about attaining superior performance across cultural, geographic and organizational boundaries.

This archetype has been named: The Harmonic Fusion of the Two Great Powers. As cultural anthropologists have shown, it has inspired the oldest mythological narratives and can be traced in the mythical stories of every human society across time and space. Not less importantly, its essential constituent elements — the male and the female — have found empirical support in the modern neurological, genetical, managerial, psychological and behavioral sciences. As both sets of perspectives are vital for the understanding of this archetype, a mythical as well as a scientific account of it are provided in the following sections.

A Rather Ancient Archetype

The Harmonic Fusion of the Two Great Powers into wholeness is the oldest and most universal human archetype. We know this not only because it has inspired the earliest myths known to mankind, but also because it has been central to the development of alchemy — the world's oldest formal discipline of physical transformation — both in Eastern and in Western societies. A Taoist scholar summarizes its importance for the ancient Chinese alchemical quest:

> The primary theme in creation mythology is the emergence from the One of the Two, the creation of the primordial pair and the beginning of duality. This male-female symbolism is basic to alchemy, since the male sulphur and the female quicksilver must work on and with each other in balanced relationship. They are different but complementary, seeking out each other to bring about the resoration of original wholeness. They must continually stimulate each other.[4]

Central to the ancient myths of creation was also the original emergence of a duality, the primeval male and female pair. The story that recurs in all of these myths tells of the first male descending into suffering despair, physical mutilation or metamorphosis and — in some cases — death, as he yearns to return to the original unifying wholeness. The primordial female rescues him from his agony and death, instilling a new life into his disemboweled body or witnessing his triumphant resurrection, after which they enter into a sacred marriage that seals their harmonic reunion. These mythical themes are found — with astonishingly little variation — in the belief systems of distant ancient cultures such as the Peruvian, Egyptian, Indian, Sumerian, Chinese, Greek, Jewish and — interestingly — the early Christian communities: Mamacocha and Pachapapa, Isis and Osiris, Maya and Varuna, Ishtar and Tammuz, King Gao Xin's daughter and Pan Gu, Kore and Hades, Haveh and Adonai, Mary Magdalene and Christ.

As highlighted by anthropologists, psychologists and religion historians alike,[5] humankind's archaic myths of creation symbolize, in a narrative form, the archetypal set of relationships governing the flow of life in all its dimensions, the immutable series of principles overseeing the organic flow of life in both natural phenomena and human activities. Interestingly, I found the same archetypal principles at play in the organizations that were more successful at performing across cultural, geographic and organizational boundaries. Let us therefore examine further the archetypal elements underlying these kinds of narratives, by looking at the Peruvian creation myth in more detail. This creation myth is the oldest known to humankind, and — although it has never before rendered into the

English language comprehensively — it epitomizes in a compelling way The Harmonic Fusion of the Two Great Powers.

The Longest Word for "God"

The longest word for God is also the oldest. It was symbolized in stone 15,000 years BC at the Kalasasaya temple, a megalithic structure within the Aymara city of Tiwanaku, which lies 3,810 m (12,500 ft) above sea level in the Andean Mountains and 20 km away from the shores of the Titicaca lake — astride the border between Peru and Bolivia.[6] Within the superbly incised masonry of the temple's walls, there is a gateway made up of a single block of andesite rock that is 3 m high. At the top of this gateway, a mysterious human figure is sculpted, with a feathered-looking crown and holding one snake-like baton in each hand, one of which is two-headed. Three superimposed lines of winged humanoids converge toward this central figure. When the first Spanish Conquistadores first visited the site in the 16th century, they asked the locals who this figure was. Their answer was strange and very long:

> *Apu Kon Ti-Ti Illa Tecsi Kailla Wiracocha Pachayachachi Kuruna Camac*

The European invaders thought this was the local's name for God, and abbreviated it to "Wiracocha". They thought it was the One supreme God of the Peruvian civilization, because they had found similar figures revered in more than 100 nations and languages scattered across the territory of today's Peru. Like the Aymara people of Tiwanaku, most of these nations and cultures — including the Chimus, the Sipans, the Chavins, the Nazcas, the Paracas, the Chachas and the Waris — had built large and perfectly organized imperial states thousands of years before the Kichuas came to dominate them in the 13th century, imposing the rule of their King, the *Sapa Inka* (true Inka). Although some of these nations had remained fiercely defiant toward the Kichuas at the arrival of the Spaniards in the 16th century, all of them held in high reverence the mysterious figure with the two batons which the Spaniards thought of as their Creator.

But the Conquistadores were wrong. What they were looking at was not a representation of God, but the figure of Tunapa Wiracocha Wajinqira, one of the great Andean teachers and astronomers (in Kichua language: *amautas*). This amauta had taught the ancient Peruvians about The Harmonic Fusion of the Two Great Powers, as other great teachers such as Kon, Naylamp and Aiapaec had. His feathered-looking crown ranks him as a holy man. The two-headed snake he carries in one hand represents the Pachamama (or Pachapapa), symbolizing the Father Earth or the

Photo: www.sacredsites.com

Figure 3: The mysterious gateway of Tiwanaku.

phallic power of fertility. The single-headed snake represents the Mamacocha, the Mother Sea, the female power of fecundity. The three superimposed lines of winged humanoids that converge towards Tunapa Wiracocha Wajinqira represent three of the four "worlds" that were part of the ancient Peruvian's cosmos. The *Hanan Pacha* is the "world of above", or the visible heavens with the planets, stars and galaxies. *Kay Pacha* — "our world" — comprises the surface of the Earth and the seas with all its creatures. The *Ukhu Pacha*, the "world of below" is the subterranean realm where the chaotic energies of planet Earth concentrate. There was an additional "world" in the Andean cosmology, which was invisible and was therefore not represented in the Tiwanaku gateway. This was the *Hawa Pacha*, the first "world", comprising a set of universes — some of which are only possibilities — that occupy a different time and space and cannot be perceived by the human senses. The *Hawa Pacha* is strikingly similar to the modern notion of the *multiverse* in quantum physics: the idea that the universe we can observe is only part of the whole physical reality, a sub-set of possible universes.[7]

Thus, the long phrase that the Conquistadores heard at the Tiwanaku gateway was not the name of "God". The ancient Peruvians did not name nor conceptualized important phenomena — much less personified them — lest the mental concepts would hinder a deep understanding of the real thing. Thus, for "God" to be named, represented or personified it would have meant that the human intellect could understand its divine essence, a laughable notion for the Andean people. For them, "God" could not be intellectually understood but only slightly grasped through direct experience. And this was exactly what the Conquistadores had heard at the Tiwanaku gateway: the description of the archetypal experience of grasping the Andean paradigm of cosmic order.

Grasping the Harmonic Order of the Cosmos

Let us examine eight Kichua words that the Conquistadores heard half a millenium ago at the Tiwanaku gateway but could not understand. They will help us journey into the Andean paradigm of cosmic order. The first two words are *Apu Kon. Apus* were minor mountains, which, together with the very high mountains (in Kichua: *ruwales*) had, according to the ancient Peruvians, the power to communicate with the cosmic energy (*kallpa* in Kichua). Thus the term is also used to denote "natural environment" or "power". Apu Kon was therefore "the powerful Lord Kon", who, as mentioned, was a legendary amauta who taught in ancient Peru. *Ti-Ti* means "two Suns" or "double Sun". The Kichua word for Sun was *Ti*. Thus, *An-Ti* is the rising Sun, *In-Ti* is the Sun at its zenith, *Kon-Ti* is the Sunset, and *Wa-Ti* is the Sun when it remains invisible to the naked eye, following the Sunset. *Ti-Ti* was a primeval time when the Earth was burning and lifeless and there were two Suns in the horizon.

Illa Tecsi are two Kichua words alternatively signifying "mysterious and incomprehensible creation", "ineffable divine beginning" or "eternal light". *Wiracocha,* is a term where some scholars see Aymara roots. It is made up of two words. *Wira,* meaning "fertilizing foam" or "fertility grease" (as in 'sperm' or 'plankton') as well as "fire", "male" or "emission". And *Cocha,* signifying "sea", "water", "female" or "receptacle". *Wiracocha,* therefore denotes the harmonic fusion of the male and the female, of the sperm and the sea, of the emission and the receptacle.

Pachayachachi, is also a combination of words. *Pacha,* is made up of the word *Pa*, meaning the diversity of physical forms and species we call 'space'; and the term *Cha*, signifying the harmonic order we denote as 'time'. The *Pacha* is therefore the space-time, or the four harmonic "worlds" of the Andean Cosmos with all that they contain: the universe plus the multiverse.[7] *Ya* is the real world we experience, and *Chi* means "to act", or "to carry out". *Pachayachachi* therefore means: to carry our actions out in the real world in accordance to the principles of the cosmic harmony. Finally, *camac* is the intrinsic order and the gentle wind that generates and preserves life. Let us now go back to the sentence:

> *Apu Kon Ti-Ti Illa Tecsi Kailla Wiracocha Pachayachachi Kuruna Camac*

This is the archetypal Andean story of creation and cosmic order:[8] In the ancient time, the powerful Lord Kon (*Apu Kon*) arrived to the central coastal Kingdoms of Pirúa (Peru). He was an *amauta* and a holy man who taught the people with great wisdom. He taught that the four "worlds" of the *Pacha* (the Cosmos) — the *Hawa Pacha,* the *Hanan Pacha*, the *Kay Pacha* and the *Ukhu Pacha* — had always existed but were constantly changing. He also spoke about the *Kausay* and the *Supay*, the two primordial opposing energies that — like hot and cold, light and dark, living and lifeless — kept the *Pacha* in constant movement.

And Kon taught about an archaic time when our planet Earth (*Kay Pacha and Ukhu Pacha*) was lifeless, like a rock lost in space. This was the time when there was *Ti-Ti* (the double Sun) in the *Hanan Pacha* (the heavens). Then the Earth suddenly awoke, its belly burning with fire and looking like an anxious man — or like a sterile woman. But *Ti-Ti* noticed the Earth's apprehension with kindness. And He sent to the Earth its life-giving sperm — the *Kamaqen* — in the tail of an *Ako Chinchay* (a comet). The *Kamaqen* carried fragments of the primordial and eternal cosmic light — that mysterious One Principle which cannot be named nor comprehended (*Illa Tecsi*). And then Kon evoked the memorable time when the *Ako Chinchay* plunged into the sea and produced a fertilizing foam that floated over the surface of the waters. And cosmic life sprung out on the Earth from the foam of the sea, as the male energy of the *kamaqen* and the female essence of the water blended themselves harmonically into a unifying whole (*wiracocha*).

From that time, Kon taught, every year during the *Capac Sitwa* (the month of August), the Father Sun shining in the zenith (*Tayta Inti*) sends His live-giving sperm to the Earth, thus bestowing it with fertilizing powers *(Pachamama or Pachapapa)*. The *Pachapapa* then blends harmonically with the nurturing powers of the waters — the *Mamacocha* — in order to renovate the cycle of life. Sometimes, warned Kon, cataclysmic events — the *Pachakuteq* — will erupt like a fearsome warrior and will purify the land, spreading fire, death and destruction everywhere. But the harmonic cycle of life will ensue with renewed vigor after the *Pachakuteq* is gone. And Kon taught that acting in accordance to these great cosmic principles keeps the gentle wind of life in the *Pacha* regenerating and evolving harmoniously.[9]

Pacha-Yacha or the Art of Acting in Cosmic Harmony

When they abbreviated what they thought was the Andean name for God into 'Wiracocha', the Spanish Conquistadores inadvertently underscored The Harmonic Fusion of the Two Great Powers archetype itself. By contrast, from times immemorial, the ancient Peruvians' abbreviation for the sentence highlighted the term *Pachayachachi,* or simply *Pacha-Yacha.* With this they were emphasizing that the whole point of their creation myth was to experience the cosmic harmony through *a concrete way of acting and behaving out there in the real world*. In other words, the archetype of The Harmonic Fusion of the Two Great Powers represents for the Andean civilization a guide of behavioral principles for concrete action — rather than an effort to *understand* the principles of creation in an intellectual fashion. This is the *Pacha-Yacha:* the art of behaving and acting in harmony with the cosmic principles. As I found strikingly similar notions at play within the organizations that were more successful at performing across cultural, geographic and organizational boundaries, let us dwell in more detail into five fundamental tenets of the *Pacha-Yacha*.

First, to the ancient Peruvians, the principle of men and women behaving in accordance with the cosmic harmony (*Pacha-Yacha*) is what ensures that the maximum level of fitness (performance) is reached in any field as a result of our actions. This calls for people to be conceived not as 'individuals', but as *collective-individuals* (in Kichua: *runa-ayllu-apu*). In other words, for the Andean people Man was not the pinnacle of creation, endowed with a divine right of lordship over nature. Rather, for them the people were just one of many intrinsic parts of the interconnected cosmos. Thus, each person was seen as made up of three indivisible elements: his/her individuality (*runa*), her/his set of *social* relationships with the community (ies) she/he belongs to (*ayllu*) and his/her set of relationships with their surrounding natural environment (*apu*). These are the three constitutive parts of every person, none of which is more important than the other and all of which must be preserved and nurtured integrally. Note that, in this context, 'collective' refers not only to social relationships between individuals but also between these individuals and their surrounding natural environment. Collective-individuals wisely handle the boundaries, tensions and apparent contradictions between the individual and the collective realms and go on to creating harmonic relationships with others and with their surrounding environment.

Second, the principle of *collective-reciprocity* was the way in which this apparent paradox — collective-individuals — made its way into a paradigm of real and positive human action in ancient Peru. *Ayni*, the Kichua word that roughly translates into collective-reciprocity, means: *when everybody agrees to give first in order to receive*. This notion was the timeless and immutable principle of action in all Andean societies, one that is often misunderstood and which is behind their extraordinary achievements in every aspect of human activity. Collective-reciprocity, in the Andean world, did not mean 'equality'. There was a strong sense of leadership in ancient Peru, with the *Sapa Inka* and the local *Curacas* wielding authority over a stratified society. But every collective-individual and community in ancient Peru had an *equal right* to enjoy — and an obligation to practice — reciprocity when engaging in relationships of any kind with others. Collective-reciprocity is therefore not to be confused with 'selflessness', 'charity' or 'solidarity'. In the Andean civilization, collective-individuals gave to others *in order* to receive roughly equivalent things in return. This does not mean that for the ancient Peruvians collective-reciprocity was the same as 'calculating' or 'transactional' behavior. Rather, it was a collective mind-set and a social behavior where each and *all* collective-individuals *agreed* to give to others first and with generosity. Therefore, a positive and equivalent return from others was to be expected with the inexorability of a physical law. *Ayni* is often confused with the word 'partnership' as well. These words are not equivalent though they are connected in an important way. Collective-reciprocity did in fact involve a fundamental social partnership of sorts between the Andean peoples, who *together* agreed to follow a common principle of behavior: that of giving to others first in order to receive from them.

Third, *Pacha-Yacha* was *a way of human action to attain concrete results out in the real world.* The actions it encouraged were not only of the meditative type, and the expected results of these actions were not limited to the attainment of certain kinds of spiritual enlightenment — as pursued in elitarian disciplines such as Taoist Zen in ancient China. There was of course a series of Andean disciplines pursuing these aspects of the *Pacha-Yacha.* However, rather uniquely in the history of civilization, codes of behavior and action embodying the archetype of cosmic harmony were applied widely, pervasively *and* successfully throughout the entire fabric of Andean socio-economic and political organizations. In the Andean societies, work (*llank'ay*) and economic organizations were in fact the *main* areas of application of the principles of the *Pacha-Yacha*, involving the larger masses of the people. This was captured in one of the Kichuas central adages: "work is the great gateway to experiencing the cosmic harmony" (*llank'aymi pachay-achachiq capaq ñan*). Thus, their macro-economic institutions, their pre-industrial factories — similar to the medieval guilds of Europe — and their managerial approaches, all pursued actively the harmonic blending of their constitutive male and female characteristics in order to achieve the maximum levels of performance over the long term. This was practiced broadly and successfully within Andean organizations thousands of years before a contemporary author suggested that, in our own business milieu, "new theories of entrepreneurship that incorporate the experiences of both men and women [...] are needed."[10]

Fourth, the *Pacha-Yacha* recognizes that 'male' and 'female' are different and complementary principles at the individual, communal, planetary and cosmic levels. However, it also makes clear that these principles are not just to be passively acknowledged as complementary, but *through our concrete actions we ought to relentlessly help* them seek each other out and blend themselves harmonically into a unifying whole — at every level. Only when the harmonic wholeness between the male and the female (*wiracocha*) is restored, collective-individuals, communities, organizations and states will reach the maximum level of fitness (performance) in harmony with the interconnected cosmos (i.e. over the long term).

Finally, as the most ancient history of the Andean societies demonstrate, the *Pacha-Yacha* embodies a leadership and managerial paradigm that can be termed *harmonic reciprocity*. In other words, an approach that instills a strong and positive sense of leadership that is made legitimate by a social commitment involving *all* members to enact and embody the principles of collective-reciprocity and of the harmonic blending of the male and the female characteristics. This is different from the command-and-control paradigm, where there is a strong sense of authority — just like in *harmonic reciprocity* — but rests on a very different set of sources: those of explicit controls, rewards and punishments imposed from above. And, although it does involve the establishment of a broad social partnership of sorts between organizational members, *harmonic reciprocity* is not to be associated with the lessening or the outright elimination of hierarchical structures that typify so much of the 'partnership' paradigm of leadership. This latter point is important. The Inka empire (*Tawantinsuyu:* the realm of the four regions) was an authoritarian and centrally organized society — albeit very different degrees of hierarchical arrangements co-existed within the four major regions of the empire. Likewise, within the best-performing organizations I examined, the tenets of *harmonic reciprocity* could be found successfully at play in our own times, both within horizontally structured, 'flat' and decentralized organizational settings as well as within more hierarchically and centrally organized institutions.

In fact, as will be further described in the next chapters, the leadership cadres of the best-performing organizations I studied were able to span boundaries of gender, cultural differences as well as organizational and geographic divides because they possess what I call 'boundary-spanning character traits'. Chief among them are a giver's mentality — another term for collective-reciprocity, and wholeness, i.e. the ability to blend harmonically 'male' and 'female' leadership traits by empathizing with others in order to build co-operative relationships across boundaries, while at the same time taking tough decisions decisively whenever the situation requires it. These boundary-spanning leaders relentlessly pursue the creation of a collective good — the Common Glue — within their organizations. And the way they do this is both in harmony with — and in reinforcement of — their individual goals. This collective good — the Common Glue — is made up of social ingredients such as a common language, cross-functional business initiatives that excite and involve all organizational members, shared beliefs and one set of common performance measurements. I found that a strong Common Glue allows these organizations to consistently outperform their competitors over time and across cultural, organizational and geographic boundaries.

This should be hardly surprising. The Andean societies had achieved similar results many centuries before by applying the same kinds of leadership principles. Over the vast expanse of South American territory that is traversed by the Andean mountain chain, a great diversity of nations flourished during several millennia based on the principle of collective-reciprocity. Long before the arrival of the Europeans, these nations built on each other to form cities and imperial states that successfully applied socio-economic institutions, laws and statistics on a scale never seen before — and very seldom afterwards. The *Tawantinsuyu* — the Inka empire which the Spaniards found in the 16th century — created a precursor of our modern welfare states. Unique in history until the second half of the 20th century, the Inka state provided full employment, pleasant living standards, health care, public education and a superb infrastructure of roads, mail services, asset reserves, legal systems, law enforcement, agricultural development and scientific research over a territory that includes today's republics of Peru, Ecuador, Colombia, Bolivia, Argentina and Chile. It was the systematic violation of their ancient principles of collective-reciprocity by Inka Yupanqui (aptly called *the Pachakuteq:* the destructor) in the 15th century, and especially by Inka Waskar and his brother Atawalpa in the early 16th century, that plunged Andean societies into chaos and civil war, just as the Spanish Conquistadores — with fateful timing — were reaching for the first time the Northern coastal shores of the *Tawantinsuyu.*

Scientific Evidence for the Archetype

As previously mentioned, the central mythical and archetypal elements of the Andean *Pacha-Yacha* are common to the later creation myths of other ancient civilizations, ranging from the Sumerian, the Egyptian and the Mediterranean to the Chinese and the Indian. But The Harmonic Fusion of the Two Great Powers might not be 'just' an archetype of global presence. Evidence supporting the essential elements of this archetype has been provided over the course of the 20th century by a diverse array of scientific disciplines that have looked into the phenomenon of gender differences, including: neuroscience, genetics, psychology, behavioral science and management science. The available empirical evidence is vast and suggests that there is a real organic and physical basis underlying the archetype of The Harmonic Fusion of the Two Great Powers.

In the following sections, we will examine some of the fundamental aspects of this scientific evidence stemming from a diversity of scientific fields. We will do this by following two logical steps. First, we will examine the vast scientific evidence from a number of scientific fields suggesting that women and men *are* in fact organically different, in a way that strongly resonates with the 'female–male' elements of the archetype of The Harmonic Fusion of the Two Great Powers. This scientific evidence has been summarized in Figure 4.

Second, we will examine another set of scientific evidence — including cultural anthropology and the history of civilizations — supporting other important characteristics of the archetype. This additional data demonstrates that *both* 'female' and 'male' genetic patterns exist in every human being. Equally importantly, the scientific data also demonstrate that differences in gender roles as observed in any given human society at a particular time period *do not* always correspond to the organic and behavioral differences that have been found between the genders (nor with the associated 'female–male' archetypal elements). Rather, throughout history, gender roles have been found to be the product of *cultural norms* which evolve dynamically and in multiple directions. Thus, in any period of time, we can find societies where men play 'female' roles, while women carry out 'male' ones — and vice versa. Even more pointedly, it has been observed that *within the same societies or cultural groups* men and women often dynamically interchange 'female' and 'male' roles over time.

All of this suggests that each individual man *and* woman has the capability to play either male or female roles — or *both at the same time.* For individuals living in a society, it seems that the way to play these roles is rather an issue of context as well as a matter of choice. We must keep in mind that, from time to time, exercising these choices often requires these individuals, groups, organizations — or even entire societies — to challenge and transcend their deeply rooted cultural constraints.

Men and Women are Different Species

According to recent genetic research, men and women belong to genetically different species. The human genome project showed that while there is just a 1.6% genetic difference between a male human and a male monkey, and similarly between a female human and female monkey, the genetic difference between a male and a female human (and between a male and female monkey) is 5% ![11] Ginger therefore notes that if we discount the qualitative aspects of genetics, for example, genes that enable the development of language, art, philosophy, a man is more physiologically similar to a male monkey than to a woman.[11]

The male and the female brain exhibit a number of differences. Most neuroscientists agree that the right hemisphere of the brain tends to be more developed in men, while the left hemisphere is more developed in women. In addition, women's brains tend to have more links between its two hemispheres, allowing women to multi-task more effectively than men.[11] The cranial capacities of men and women differ as well.[12,13,14]

	Genetics & Neuroscience (Physical)	Psychology & Anthropology (Behavioral)	Management (Work-related)
Male	• Right hemisphere more developed: Mathematics, verbal, logical, facts, deduction, analysis, practical, order, linear, sees fine detail • Left hemisphere more grey matter than right • Three-dimensional spatial rotation advantage • Better spatial & mechanical aptitude • Use Euclidean information to navigate • Sight more developed • Hearing the *what* (more sensitive listening with left side of brain) • Sense of touch and smell less developed • Communication as way to convey urgent information	• Score higher on expressing aggression • Experiences represented in individualistic, objective and distant ways. • Identity based on individuation and dependence • In a position of socio-cultural superiority • Diplomatic skills less developed • Psychologically defensive & insecure • Patriarchal societies more hierarchical • Focussed on competition within a zero-sum game • Systematizing and objectivity	• Value power, competency, efficiency, achievement • Risk-averse behaviour • Transactional leaders • Entrepreneurs focus more on general economic conditions in the market • Paternalistic approach –formal relationships, chain of command, bureaucratic, rigid • Less prone to crossing boundaries
Female	• Left hemisphere more developed: Creative, artistic, visual, intuition, ideas, imagination, holistic, non-linear, sees big picture, multiprocessing • More symmetrical distribution of grey matter between hemispheres • Superior in denomination of concrete objects & time-sensitive tasks • Better perceptual speed and memory for meaning • Use landmark information to navigate • Better visual memory • Hearing the *what* and the *how* (listening with both hemispheres of the brain) • Sense of touch and smell more developed • Communication as social function	• Minimize hostility & conflict through empathy and interpersonal relationships • Define themselves through relationships and connections • Experiences represented in interpersonal, subjective, immediate ways • Position of socio-cultural subjugation • Diplomatic skills more developed • Psychological individuation and dependence less problematic • Matriarchal societies more representative • Focussed on cooperation for a win-win outcome • Nurturing & empathizing	• Value communication relationships, working together to common goal • More risk tolerant • Transformational leaders • Entrepreneurs more adaptive, engage more in long-term planning • Fraternalistic/partnership approach – informal relationships, flexible, collective decision-making • Less 'ego boundaries': more prone to crossing boundaries

Figure 4: Male and female differences according to diverse scientific disciplines.

The left hemisphere of the male brain has larger percentages of gray matter than the right hemisphere; however in female brains, the percentage of gray matter is more symmetrical.[15] Differences exist not only between the male and female brain, but also between the heterosexual male and homosexual male, as noted by Rahman et al., who in 2003, reported that the brains of homosexual men have larger neuronal populations in the suprachiasmatic nucleus, smaller interstitial nuclei of the anterior hypothalamus, larger anterior commissures and larger isthmus of the corpus callosum than heterosexual males.[16]

In addition to physical differences, the male and female brains have different abilities. With a more developed right hemisphere, the male brain tends to have an advantage in three-dimensional spatial rotation, whereas the female brain, with its more developed left hemisphere, tends to be superior in denomination of concrete objects and in time-sensitive tasks.[17] The male brain seems to demonstrate higher performance on spatial and mechanical aptitude than the female brain, whereas the female brain tends to perform better on perceptual speed and memory for meaning.[18]

In a study on navigation, Leason et al.[19] found that men tend to perform best on average when using Euclidean information (descriptors such as cardinal directions and exact distances that impart flexibility in navigation), whereas women's average performance was best when using landmark information (a spatial representation providing details about major landmarks, and where to turn left or right is relatively rigid and sequential.) These findings suggest different capacities of the female and male brains in using different types of navigational information.

Men and women have different sense of sight, smell, hearing and touch. Sight tends to be more developed in men, but women have a better visual memory.[11] On the other hand, men hear sounds that are on average 2.3 times quieter than women; while men listen mostly with the left side of their brain, women tend to use both hemispheres when listening.[11] In this way, women tend to hear not only *what* is being said, but also *how* it is being said, i.e. being sensitive to the tone of voice and the breathing rhythm.[11] The female sense of touch is more developed than the male: women typically have ten times more skin receptors than men.[11] Women's vomero nasal organ (VNO) tends to be more developed than men's, enabling into an increased perception of pheromones.[11] At certain periods of the menstrual cycle, the female sense of smell is 100 times sharper than the average male sense of smell.[11]

Another way in which men and women differ is in their approaches to communication. In a study of a 50-min kindergarten class, boys talked on average for 4 min, while girls talked for an average of 15 min.[18] As adults, men's phone calls average 6 min, while women's average 20 min.[19] Ginger attributes this to a differing perception of communication. While men tend to view conversations as a way to convey urgent information, *communication also has a social function for women.*[11]

Men and Women Behave Differently

Just as there are important differences between the male and female brain, there are equally important differences between what is gendered as male and female behavior. Whether these differences are the result of differences between the male and female brain is beyond the scope of this book. What is clear, though, is that these differences between behavior gendered as male and female crosses time, geography and civilizations.

Many psychological and behavioral studies have noted that most men score higher than most women on forms of expressing aggression. Ginger reported that kindergarten boys fight ten times more often than girls.[11] They are also more likely to engage in mock fighting and verbal insults, or to counter-attack if attacked.[20] A study of male and female preschoolers (aged 4–5 year) and adolescents (aged 12–13) showed that while the aggressive response by females was relatively stable over age, aggression by males increased rapidly.[21]

While men tend to exhibit higher levels of aggression, women tend to excel in minimizing hostility and conflict, through empathy and interpersonal relationships. Girls are more interested in social stimuli than boys,[22] *and exhibit greater interest in people.*[22] They expect to resolve psychological crises in their families, seeing their role as "to support, explain, comfort and encourage all other family members."[23]

A number of cultural anthropologists confirm these differences between male and female behavior. Owing to the patriarchal structure of the vast majority of human civilizations and societies, Rosaldo noted that "since women must work within a social system that obscures their goals and interests, they are apt to develop ways of seeing, feeling and acting that seem to be 'intuitive'[…] with a sensitivity to other people that permits them to survive."[24] Chodorow observed that women, more than men, define themselves through relationships and connections with other people, and thus come to possess *more flexible ego boundaries and less individualistic personalities.*[25] Gutmann suggested that women are less concerned with self/other distinctions and demonstrate greater subjectivity than men.[26] Testing Gutmann's claims, Carlson concluded that "males represent experiences of self, others, space, and time in individualistic, objective, and distant ways, while females represent experiences in relatively interpersonal, subjective, immediate way."[27]

Wolf observed that women are potentially better diplomats.[28] Writing about the experiences of villagers in rural China, he remarked that women learn "to assess moods and evaluate the consequences of their own and others' actions", "to be sensitive to attitude change", and "to understand and make use of the kin and emotional relations between people", from early childhood. Having perfected these skills in the domestic setting, they continue to practice them throughout life.[28] By contrast, men's diplomatic talents "are developed later in life, in a different setting, and are less crucial to the quality of their existence: [...] within the family, boys are so valued that they can simply demand, and insofar as possible their demands are met [...] Women improvise."[28]

Collier expanded upon how women's manipulative skills developed as a way to leverage their subordinate position in society:

> Many ethnographers who have noted the unhappiness of brides in a patrilocal extended household have attributed their sadness solely to their traumatic change of residence and role. But it is also true that brides have far more to gain by sulking than by playing Pollyanna.[29] The bride who works hard and strives to please can be safely ignored, but the one who cries or threatens to leave must be heeded and placated. Where women are denied a legitimate voice in family councils, they must affect decisions by causing an uproar that forces others to pay attention to their wishes [...] Women in such households may ostensibly fight over trivialities, but the real stakes are political – the capacity to determine the actions of others.[30]

Chodorow further suggested than men and women differently handle the issues of individuation and dependence.[25] While for boys and men, individuation and dependence become "tied up with the sense of masculine identity", for girls and women, female identity is "not problematic in the same way."[25] Consequently, while men find themselves in a position of socio-cultural superiority to women, they often remain "psychologically defensive and insecure."[25]

Rosaldo and Lamphere wrote that, "sexual asymmetry is presently a universal fact of human social life."[31] Vivante highlighted that "of the societies that call themselves matriarchal, many show a social system that differs considerably from hierarchal structure of patriarchal societies."[32] She contrasted vertical and "oppressive" patriarchal system with horizontal and "respecting" matriarchal ones.[32] Lai noted that demonstrations of strength, power and the need to conquer are reflective of a "masculinist" outlook, while feminine model is associated with tranquility, stillness and emphasis on all-encompassing, receptive approach.[33]

Men and Women Manage in Diverse Ways

Management scientists Colwill and Townsend suggest that men value "power, competency, efficiency and achievement." [34] On the positive side, these values lead men to strive to perform. On the negative side, they can cause men to fear being "not good enough", to avoid making mistakes and to engage in a risk-averse behavior.[34] At the same time, the authors believe that female executives value "communication, relationships", and "working together toward a common goal".[34] On the positive side women are less threatened by mistakes, which are regarded by them as something to be corrected, and not as a sign of incompetence. On the negative side, women have difficulty when they feel they are not being understood and risk placing relationship issues over business objectives.[34]

In an article that set the tone for debate on male–female leadership in the 1990s, Rosener noted that men tend to perceive themselves as having the characteristics of "transactional" leaders, while women, in their own eyes, gravitate more toward a "transformational" approach.[35] Transactional style equates management conduct with a series of transactions between a manager and his or her employees, in which the manager dispenses rewards for outstanding service or punishment for inadequate performance. A transformational style requires the manager to persuade subordinates to put their own interest below the interest of the organization by setting a common goal. Rosener calls the "transformational" style "interactive" as it encourages participation and sharing of power and information, as well as enhancing the employees' feelings of self-worth.[35] It is characterized by a dialogue between a manager and the employees and by open recognition of the employees' contributions to a task, either through a written statement or verbally, in the presence of others. Rosener adds that female leaders who practice transformational management believe that when employees feel involved, they are more likely to support management choices and less likely to develop an unexpected opposition."[35]

Bass demonstrates that "transformational" leadership has high practical value. His research indicates that women are more likely than men to be described as "charismatic leaders", "leaders with whom subordinates want to identify", and "leaders with whom they [subordinates] can form a strong emotional attachments."[36] In Bass' survey of 69 world-class leaders, (60 men and 9 women) females in the aggregate scored higher on the transformational factor than their male counterparts. Bass concluded that *in every part of the society, be it government, military, or business, transformational leadership has consistently contributed more to organizational effectiveness than transactional "contingent recognition" approach.*[36] Chirikova and Krichevskaia echo this statement by noting that the female management style, which takes human uniqueness into account and preserves employee dignity, is particularly useful under uncertain conditions.[37]

Buttner found that compared with men, female entrepreneurs are more adaptive, more socially aware, delegate more and engage more in long-term planning.[38] A survey of 459 retail owners-managers in 12 states of the United States conducted in 1996 by Gaskill et al. suggested that female retailers pay extra attention to forecasting market growth, identifying sales trends, offering broad range of products and services, servicing special customer groups, introducing new and refining existing product lines and ensuring customer satisfaction on a continuous basis. By contrast, male retailers focus more on general economic conditions in the market.[39]

According to Samartseva and Fomina, while the first women managers had to accept men's rules of the game to achieve success, the "second wave" of female executives created their own management styles. Their research shows that women prefer fraternalistic and partnership approaches to administrative organization while men gravitate to paternalism and bureaucratic approaches.[40]

The fraternalistic approach is characterized by a high degree of informality in relationships, collective decision-making, flexible institutional arrangements and considerable independence given to employees in performing their duties. A lack of institutional hierarchy and the presence of collective decision-making are also properties of the partnership approach; however, each employee is assigned precise functions, and in spite of a collective atmosphere, relationships remain formal and impersonal.

Under paternalism, institutional hierarchy is explicit and well defined, and relationships, while personal in tone, strictly follow the chain of command; the unity of the organization is maintained through the personal influence of the manager, and employees are expected to be loyal to their boss. Finally, the bureaucratic approach is characterized by institutional rigidity, explicit delineation of duties for each employee, a system of checks-and-balances and formal interaction between a manager and subordinates that does not extend beyond business matters. Samartseva and Fomina note that in a fraternalistic system managers aspire to the role of a "leader", in a partnership they act as "coordinators", under paternalistic arrangements they behave as "masters", and in a bureaucratic setup they act like "bosses". The authors also observe that female managers are known to employ mixed strategies, such as "coordinator-boss" or "master-leader", while men tend to use just one style.[40]

Transcending the Gender Differences

The scientific evidence we have so far examined demonstrates that men and women *are* significantly different from the organic, psychosomatic and genetic perspectives. However, the scientific data also show that important connections exist between both. Neuroscientists have found that a mixture of *both* 'female' and 'male' genetic patterns exist in differing proportions in every human being, to the point that around 20% of men have a feminine brain, while 10% of women have a masculine brain.[11]

Equally importantly, the organic and genetic differences between genders should not be equated to differences in gender roles. Rather, social expectations appear to supersede the underlying physical influences in the construction of gender roles. This is an important notion supported by scientific evidence. Weiss examined 97 college students (51 women and 46 men) using neuropsychological tests, which focused on verbal and visual–spatial abilities. He found that generally women performed better than men on verbal tests and men outperformed women on visual–spatial assignments. What was more interesting, however, is that when men and women were asked to rate themselves, men rated their spatial abilities superior to those of women, while women did not rate their verbal abilities superior to those of men. This, Weiss suggests, is the evidence of the influence of socio-cultural, educational and training factors on gender roles.[41]

Likewise, while archetypal notions of male and female are timeless cognitive realities that seem to be common to all human beings, their practical manifestations in human societies do not always follow a linear or a static correspondence. Even within the same society, culture or location, the male–female archetypal notions can be manifested dynamically and constructed differently, given different meanings and behavioral attributes that change over time, in some cases quite dramatically. While the association of the male–female archetypal notions to cultural meanings and behavioral norms is in itself a timeless and universal fact, the associated meanings and norms themselves can vary significantly across different societies. It follows that the archetypal notions of male and female are not to be confused with the specific cultural meanings or behavioral norms that any given society attaches to it at a particular time period. New customs and social institutions create new myths, as well as new myths create new socio-cultural patterns.[42] Kinney, for example, traced the progress of yin and yang interpretation in Chinese cosmology:

> The earliest usages of the terms *yin* and *yang* refer most generally to darkness and light, respectively. By the time of the Eastern Zhou dynasty [770–256 B.C.], yin and yang came to signify the two complementary powers of the universe, which interact, alternate, and bring all matter into being. As systematizing philosophies developed in the late Warring States period [480–221 B.C.], thinkers begun to associate yang with Heaven above and yin with Earth below. Somewhat later, because of the existing cosmic and spatial relationship between Heaven and Earth, yang and yin also assumed the gendered social meaning of superior male and inferior female.[43]

The Confucian tradition emphasized all that was masculine, hard, dominating, and aggressive.[43] It was only after this that the philosophy of Tao Te Ching re-interpreted the male versus female concepts and linked non-assertion and submissiveness associated with being female to a winning strategy.[33] For example, Chapter 61 points out, "if a small country submits to a great country, it can conquer a great country."[44] The text continues: "therefore those who would conquer must yield, and those who conquer do so because they yield."[44]

The Tao is of course one of the better known archetypal myths of the Harmonic Fusion of the Two Great Powers. In Chinese philosophy, the universe originates in the Tao, which is the indivisible unity of two polar opposites of Yin and Yang. The Tao unites the Yin (female power) with the Yang (male power) to symbolize the manifestation of divine creational power, since creation is only possible by unifying the male and female harmonically. The archetypal notion of Tao not only affected social norms and gender roles in China since antiquity, but also its scientific exploits. Similar to the Peruvian *Pacha-Yacha,* what is of particular importance to the understanding of Tao Te Ching is that it does not advocate the notion of femininity over the notion of masculinity, but instead hails the harmonic complementarity of the opposites, all of which have their place in the cosmic order of existence.[33, 45]

The Role of Culture in Transcending Gender Differences

The decisive influence of culture in the construction of gender differences that can vary dramatically between societies — as well as within the same society over time — has been well documented in disciplines such as cultural anthropology and the history of civilizations. Malinowski classified culture as an instrumental system of organized activities, the body of "implements and commodities, charters of social organization, ideas and customs, beliefs and values" that assists people in fulfilling their biological requirements.[46] While men and women create culture, culture, in turn, influences humans by modifying their "raw psychology" through teaching of skills, morals and development of tastes.[46]

Miers characterized differences in gender roles as "constructed differently in different cultures and epochs and within different classes, ethnic groups and age groups."[47] She further remarked that according to social system theory, values and behavior attributed to females corresponded to the roles women undertook in society and to their subordinate status.[47] Ungerson pointed out that gendered attributes associated with women, for example, caring, and men, for example, authority, have been culturally created and sustained.[48] Connell noted that both men and women in a modern society are constrained by "hegemonic masculinities" through expectations about the body, sexuality, and social roles.[49] Along the same lines, Oakley defined differences in gender roles as "cultural expectations" associated with the biological categories of male and female.[50]

Quigley remarked that the individual's reactions in terms of behavior, feelings, and thoughts are largely determined by the culture. Contrasting the development of a human child with that of an offspring of a sea turtle, he wrote that "where a turtle lays dozen of eggs and hopes that some turtles from those eggs can be carried to maturity by obedience to fairly rigid instincts, the human has almost no rigid instincts, and adapts his personality to his culture."[51] Quigley further observed that "not only is human personality formed by the social environment; the social environment (or culture) is largely made up of personalities it has created."[51]

Connecting human behavior to the power structure of a society, Rosaldo and Lamphere emphasized that archetypal femininities and masculinities are a product of social interaction: "where power and authority are in the hands of men, women work to influence them, and come into conflict with each other. Where authority is shared by men and women [...] women do not need to play the game of subtle influence and "behind-the-scenes" manipulation; in such societies women are able to form strong co-operative ties with their female kin and other women." [52]

Let us examine in more detail how differences in gender roles have played out with great diversity across human societies and cultures over time. Quigley split societies into parasitic and producing societies, and then into simple tribes or bands and civilizations.[51] Vasilenko defined civilizations as "types of human community that are brought to life by certain associations in the domain of religion, architecture, painting, morals, and culture."[53] In a seminal work, Toynbee described civilization as an "intelligible field of study" and "a society containing a number of communities of the species", and identified 7 unique, 14 affiliated, 3 abortive (embryo) and 5 arrested (immobilized) human civilizations. Toynbee's taxonomy of civilizations is presented in Figure 5.[54]

Danilevskii (1869) identified 12 cultural–historical civilizations: ancient Semite (Assyrian, Babylonian, Phoenician, Chaldean), Chinese, Egyptian, Greek, Hebrew, neo-Semite (Arabian), Indian, Iranian, Mexican, Peruvian, Roman and Romano-Germanic (European).[55] Huntington, who identified civilization as "the highest cultural grouping of people and the broadest level of cultural identity people have short of that which distinguishes humans from other species," counted eight major civilizations: African, Confucian, Hindu, Islamic, Japanese, Latin American, Slavic Orthodox and Western.[56]

In the *Native American Iroquois* nation, "women were the heads of the clans and villages that were organized into groups of longhouses [...] Chieftain titles were the rights and privileges of certain maternal lineages, and the clan mothers were responsible for the selection of the chief [...] Iroquois women could depose, or "dehorn," a chief if he did not do the will of the people... Women could ask for a raid or war; they often took part in the torture of captives and decided their fate."

Iroquois men were appointed to fulfill governmental duties and were primarily responsible for the external affairs of the tribe and of the Iroquois confederacy, consisting of the Mohawk, Oneida, Onondaga, Cayuga, Seneca, and, later, Tuscarora.[57] But no major decision could be made without the advice or agreement of the

Civilization	Relations	Time and Place of Origin	Universal State
Unique			
Andean	Unique	Andean coast and plateau; beginning of Christian Era	Incaic Empire
Egyptiac	Unique	Nile River valley; before 4000 B.C.	Middle Empire, New Empire
Indic	Unique	Indus and Ganges river valleys; 1500 B.C.	Mauryan Empire, Guptan Empire
Mayan	Unique	Central American tropical forest; before 500 B.C.	First Empire of the Mayas
Minoan	Unique	Aegan Islands; before 3000 B.C.	Thalassocracy of Minos
Sinic	Unique	Lower valley of Yellow River; 1500 B.C.	Ts'in and Han Empire
Sumeric	Unique	Lower Tigris-Euphrates valley; before 3500 B.C.	Empire of Sumer and Akkad
Affiliated			
Arabic (fused to produce Islamic)	Affiliated to the Minoan/Syraic	Arabia, Iraq, Syria, North Africa; before A.D. 1300	
Babylonic	Closely affiliated to the Sumeric	Iraq; before 1500 B.B.	Neo-Babylonic Empire
Far Eastern	Affiliated to the Sinic	China; before A.D. 500	Mongol Empire, Manchu Empire
Hellenic	Loosely affiliated to the Minoan	Coasts and islands of the Aegean; before 1100 B.C.	Roman Empire
Hindu	Affiliated to the Indic	North India; before A.D. 800	Mughal Raj
Hittite	Loosely affiliated to the Sumeric	Cappadocia; before 1500 B.C.	
Iranic (fused to produce Islamic)	Affiliated to the Minoan/Syraic	Anatolia, Iran, Oxus-Jaxartes; before A.D. 1300	
Japanese	Offshoot of the Sinic/Far Eastern	Japanese archipelago; after A.D. 500	Hideyoshi dictatorship and Tokugawa Shogunate
Mexic (fused into Central American)	Affiliated to the Mayan	Limestone shelf of Yucatan peninsula; after A.D. 629.	
Orthodox Christian (Kievan Rus)	Affiliated to the Minoan/Hellenic	Kievan Rus; A.D. 988	Muscovite Empire
Orthodox Christian (main body)	Affiliated to the Minoan/Hellenic	Anatolia; before A.D. 700 (final rupture with the West in 11th century)	Byzantine/Ottoman Empire
Syraic	Loosely affiliated to the Minoan	Syria; before 100 B.C.	Achaemeniean Empire Arab Caliphate
Western	Affiliated to the Minoan/Hellenic	Eastern Europe; before A.D. 700	
Yucatec (fused into Central American)	Affiliated to the Mayan	Limestone shelf of Yucatan peninsula; after A.D. 629.	

Figure 5: Toynbee's taxonomy of civilizations.

Civilization	Relations	Time and Place of Origin	Universal State
Abortive			
Far Eastern Christian	Affiliated to the Minoan/Hellenic	Oxus-Jaxartes basin; after A.D.	
Far Western Christian	Affiliated to the Minoan/Hellenic	Ireland; after A.D. 375	
Scandinavian	Affiliated to the Minoan/Hellenic	Scandinavia, after A.D. 500	
Arrested			
Eskimos	Unique	Arctic ocean	
Nomads	Unique	Eurasian steppe	
'Osmanlis	Affiliated to the Nomads, Orthodox Christian/Hellenic, and the Syraic/Iranic	Anatolia	Ottoman Empire
Polynesians	Unique	Polynesian archipelago	
Spartans	Affiliated to the Minoan/Hellenic	Aegan	

Figure 5: Continued.

women, who wielded ultimate power and authority.[57] According to Fox, "property remained separate during the marriage and was inherited by the maternal family of their clans upon death. If the marriage dissolved, the home belonged to the woman and the man was stripped of all he had but his personal property."[57]

In the *Asia-Pacific* women enjoyed a similarly elevated status. Chodorow described *Javanese* families as "formally centered upon a highly valued conjugal relationship based on equality of spouses," although financial and decision-making control often resided in the hands of the women.[25] Women's marital role and rights were greater that those of men: "children always belong to the woman in case of divorce," and "when extra members join a nuclear family to constitute an extended family household, they are much more likely to be the wife's relatives than those of the husband."[25] According to Chodorow, in *Atjehnese* families in Indonesia "women stay on the homestead of their parents after marriage and are in total control of the household. Women tolerate men in the household only as long as they provide money, and even then treat them as someone between a child and a guest."[25]

Women were treated as equal to men in *Ancient Japan*. Aoki writes that "division of labor between men and women was not always clearly defined. Hence women as well as men were among the pool of workers with special skills, such as builders, blacksmiths, potters, bow makers, saddle makers, shield makers, water engineers."[58] Aoki explains that "the notion of patrilineal family was foreign to most island residents before the introduction of Chinese institutions in the late 7th and early 8th centuries, initiated by the Great Taika Reform. For a long time, married women lived in their parents' households and received occasional visits from their husbands."[58] What is even more remarkable is that in a society where women currently hold a relatively subordinate status, between the late 6th and mid-8th centuries AD, they often ruled the state. "All together six women came to the throne as full-fledged sovereigns (*tenno*) of Japan, four during these two centuries. Of these four, two ascended the throne twice, which no male *tenno* ever did, making six governments (reigns) under female leadership in this period. Contrary to a general assumption about imperial succession in early Japan, there was no "one imperial family" or clan that successively produced the heir to the throne. Instead, the throne was given to the candidate selected from the pool of sons and daughters of former *tennos*. The higher a candidate's matrilineal pedigree, the better chance she or he had to ascend to the throne."[58]

In *Ancient Mesoamerica* males and females were, too, regarded as equals, although women did not hold identical power to men in all social spheres.[59] Stone noted that, "the head of the domestic unit was husband and wife. Men generally assumed leadership roles; however, a wife's contribution to her husband's endeavors was essential."[59] For example, "among the *Aztecs* [...] a man could acquire land only after entering into marriage [...] Property brought into a marriage by a woman remained in her possession after divorce...Girls could enter religious school called the *calmecac*, or secular schools called the *telpochcalli*, as did young boys. Indeed, in 1519, the Aztecs may have been the only people in the world with universal schooling for both sexes."[59] Stone wrote that, in fact, it has been a common practice in indigenous Mesoamerican communities even well into the 20th century that "men cannot hold high political office unless they are married and receive the active support of their wives in carrying out their ritual and political obligations."[59]

In *Ancient Peru* the principle of harmonic male–female duality presided over every aspect of life. The first Spaniards who came into contact with the Inka empire in the 16th century, were astonished by the egalitarian treatment enjoyed by the Andean women, some aspects of which they found mystifying. Thus, observing Andean sexual practices first-hand in the 16th century, one baffled Spanish chronist wrote that: "single women enter into sexual relationships quite freely with any man they fancy [...] Men do not get upset if their brides do not arrive virgins to the wedding – quite the contrary [...] Nevertheless each man had only one wife [...] and in the same way that women could marry only one man, so a man could not repudiate his wife [...] However, adulterous spouses were severely punished."[60] This puzzled chronist was referring to *servinacuy*, a widespread Andean practice with no real equivalent in European societies until the late 1960s:

> Servinacuy is a Kichua word denoting an ancient conjugal practice
> of social initiation in Peru's Andean civilizations of millennia in

age. Within certain Andean communities, whenever a young couple contemplates future marriage, they move in together for a number of months. If the experience of living together is satisfactory, they go on to marry. In any other case, the couple gives up their marriage hopes to once more become single individuals ready for servinacuy with another partner in the community [In servinacuy the] partners expect — and are expected by the community — to marry, and so they prepare mentally and emotionally as individuals beforehand […] Servinacuy thus resolves for the Andean people the timeless paradox of building solid conjugal relationships. On the one hand, a couple *does* get the chance of building their shared dreams together. On the other, they get to know, take risks and experience first-hand the practicalities and uncertainties of *cooperating* with each other as a couple *before* entering a life-long commitment. […] Servinacuy is still practiced in a number of Andean communities within Perú. Since antiquity [it] was assisted by phitotherapeutical contraceptive practices, and it was the man who had the formal prerogative of renouncing the subsequent step of marriage. However, in such cases he had to provide adequate compensation to his servinacuy partner.[61]

In the Andean communities of the Inka empire (*ayllu*), women shared the work equitative with men. Gifted women could learn and practice a professional discipline at the *acyawasi*, a public institution similar to the medieval guilds of Europe but exclusively devoted to women. There is also considerable evidence that Andean women were active in the military, not only performing supporting tasks for the male soldierly but often as soldiers themselves, occasionally reaching the ranks of generals. In the 16th century, Spaniard Francisco de Orellana was leading the first European contingent downstream an immense river in what is today Peru's rain forest region, when they were suddenly attacked by an army of fierce female warriors. This vast river was eventually named the *Amazonas,* in remembrance of Orellana's remarkable encounter with the women warriors. Women were also very active in the political institutions of the Andean world. The *Sapa Inka* was always portrayed together with his Queen (*Koya*). This was not just owing to artistic convention. Peruvian *Koyas* had a long tradition of wielding real influence over the key political decisions of the Inka empire. According to Sarmiento de Gamboa, a 16th century Spanish historian, one of these *Koyas*, Mama Wako, was one of the main leaders of the party of Kichua people that founded the city of Cuzco, which went on to become the capital of the Inka empire.[62] Leading political roles for women were also the norm in many other

Andean nations throughout the Inka empire. In the northern coastal regions of the empire, there lived a powerful sea-faring nation called the *Tayanes* — the first Peruvian people that Francisco Pizarro met in the 16th century — that was ruled by women: the *Capuyanas*.[63]

The situation was drastically different in *Ancient Mesopotamia*. Nemet-Nejat observed that, "in the ancient Near East the family was patriarchal. The father was head of the family and exercised authority over his wife and children until he died. In a hymn, the goddess Gula (the patron goddess of doctors and healing) described the stages in a woman's life: "I am a daughter, I am a bride, I am a spouse, I am a housekeeper." In other words, women were not completely independent from men in the roles they played in their lifetime."[64]

In *Ancient Greece* "women were lifelong jural minors without inheritance rights or any basis for autonomy."[65] Denich explained that "passed from father's to husband's household, they [women] were restricted to the domestic sphere and to the production of male heirs for their families and ancestral gods."[66] Vivante echoed that "all evidence from the Archaic (8th–6th centuries BC) and Classical (6th–4th centuries BC) periods suggests that women did not formally participate in the decision-making, governmental processes. In ancient Athens women were excluded from public, political activity. Athenian women were considered citizens only to legitimize the citizenship of their male offspring but not for political purposes."[66]

The status of women was only somewhat more favorable in *Ancient Egypt*. Robins argued that while on the one hand the law treated women "as separate individuals, responsible for their actions, whether married or not" and "did not need a male guardian to act on their behalf", on the other hand, "there is no evidence that women normally sat as members of the court" or performed functions of high government officials.[67] "At Deir el-Medina, where lawsuits were usually for the recovery of debt, women were more often defendants than plaintiffs, suggesting that their economic status was lower than that of men."[66] Still, women "possessed property in their own right, conducted their own business transactions, and went to court as plaintiff, defendant, and witness."[67]

In summing up this cultural overview, it is useful to borrow from Vivante, who pointed out that even though women's "chores", such as bearing and raising children and engaging in household activities, are similar across cultures, it is how the work is valued, what makes one society different from another.[65] For example, Hoffer noted that, "there is a tendency in Western culture to define women as weak and needing protection, since they bear children. In West Africa the same biological facts are given a different cultural interpretation. The bearing of children demonstrates that women are strong and active agents in a society, capable of holding political office."[68]

Transcending Gender Differences in Management

Rosaldo provided an interesting observation about *Contemporary American* society that can be applied to numerous post-industrial societies elsewhere: "American society is in fact organized in a way that creates and exploits a radical distance between private and public, domestic and social, female and male. It speaks, on one level, of conjugal family, while on another it defines women as domestic (an invisible army of unemployed) and sends its men into public, working world. This conflict between ideal and reality creates illusions and disappointments for both men and women [...] We are told that men and women should be equals and even companions, but we are also told to value men for their work."[24]

This situation is of course expected to change as an increasing amount of women join the business world — both as employees and as entrepreneurs — continually since the late 1900s. However, the argument has been raised that, rather than a 'female' leadership approach, what we often see at work in contemporary organizations are women — both individually and as a group — engaging in gender-appropriate labeling, while enthusiastically practicing the leadership approaches of their male counterparts. In an argument questioning the existence of the transformational, "female" leadership approach that Rosener had proposed[35] Epstein remarked that men and women tend to stereotype their own behavior and the behavior of other groups according to societal norms of gender-appropriate activities.[69] She cited an example of her own research on female attorneys, when a lawyer who described her own style as "caring" was characterized by an associate as a "barracuda".

It should be noted, however, that Rosener herself wrote that: "linking interactive leadership directly to being a female is a mistake."[35] Her research showed that women are entirely capable of making their way through corporations by adhering to a transactional model, while some men use transformational leadership.[35] Samartseva and Fomina also demonstrated that men actively use traditionally female techniques and sometimes adopt management models that are more feminine than those women employ.[40]

Sonnenfeld advised that "approaches to understanding differences, whether they be in gender, race, religion, ethnicity, or age should not be based on faulty stereotypes that define the "appropriate" and "natural" behavior for a given category."[70] He gave a perfect example: Athena, the goddess of war in Greek mythology, was as much a woman as was Aphrodite, the goddess of love. Campbell wrote that in universal mythology woman "represents the totality of what can be known."[71] She is a presence "nourishing and protecting" as well as "the death of everything that dies."[70] As an illustration, Campbell described the statue of the Cosmic Mother erected in a suburb of Calcutta, India:

> The temple image displayed the divinity in her two aspects simultaneously, the terrible and the benign. Her four arms exhibited the symbols of her universal power: the upper left hand brandishing a bloody saber, the lower gripping by the hair a severed human head; the upper right was lifted in the "fear not" gesture, the lower extended in bestowal of boons. As a necklace she wore a garland of human heads; her kilt was a girdle of human arms; her long tongue was out to lick blood. She was Cosmic Power, the totality of the universe, the harmonization of all the pairs of opposites, combining wonderfully the terror of absolute destruction with an impersonal yet motherly gesture.[71]

Similarly, Stone shows that among Aztecs, "women's role as supernatural patron was not limited to her nurturing, reproductive activities. Female supernaturals had affiliations with warfare and are laden with symbols of death and human sacrifice [...] The enigmatic Aztec goddess Itzpapolotl ("Obsidian Butterfly"), was a slayer of warriors, and her child, kept swaddled in her arms, was a deadly obsidian knife."[59] Stone further describes that Aztec women who died in childbirth "were likened to brave warriors and thought to inhabit a paradise in the western sky [...] The body of a woman who died in childbirth was considered so powerful that it was sought after as a protective charm by warriors."[59]

Using the Archetype to Unleash Organizational Performance

The Harmonic Fusion of the Two Great Powers is represented in Figure 6. It is an archetype of sorts, and a potent one at that. Not only the female–male archetypal differences are timeless and universal but they also seem to be aligned with the genetic and neurological make up of the two genders, on their psychosomatic attributes, and on their culture-induced roles. As we have seen in this chapter, in the archetype human characteristics are attributed as either male or female, and the harmonic fusion between these two elements are universally seen as the crux of living fitness at all levels in the cosmos. On one side there is the female set of characteristics — empathic, flexible, and good at multi-tasking. On the other, there is the male — aloof, firm and singular in its vision and its goal-orientation. The harmonic blending of the two — as both our mythical narratives as well as

FEMALE	**MALE**
❖ Developed Left Brain	❖ Developed Right Brain
❖ Subjective, synthesis	❖ Objective, analyst
❖ Multi-Task Oriented	❖ Single-Goal Oriented
❖ Greater Memorization Abilities	❖ Greater Spatial Orientation Abilities
❖ Listening with 'Both Brains'	❖ Listening with Left Brain
❖ Spontaneous, 'Out-of-the box' Creativity	❖ Gradual, 'Step-by-step' Innovations
❖ Conversation as Social Function	❖ Conversation as Information Exchange
❖ Conciliatory	❖ Aggressive
❖ Empathizing	❖ Systematizing
❖ Intuitive	❖ Logical
❖ Flexible	❖ Firm
❖ Interpersonal	❖ Individualistic
❖ Immediate	❖ Distant
❖ Diplomatic	❖ Straightforward
❖ Democratic	❖ Hierarchical
❖ Risk Acceptant	❖ Risk Averse
❖ Valuing Joint Effort	❖ Valuing Personal Success
❖ Emphasizing Interoperability	❖ Emphasizing Efficiency
❖ Organizations as Social Communities	❖ Organizations as Machines
❖ Focusing on Relationships	❖ Focusing on Competency
❖ Prioritizing Sharing	❖ Focusing on dividing up
❖ Transformational	❖ Transactional
❖ Adaptive	❖ Rigid
❖ Partnership ("Coordinator")	❖ Paternalistic ("Master")
❖ Fraternalistic ("Leader")	❖ Bureaucratic ("Boss")
❖ Nurturing	❖ Fertilizing
❖ Yielding	❖ Dominating
❖ Receptacle	❖ Emission
❖ Creative	❖ Destructive

F M	NEUROLOGICAL CHARACTERISTICS
F M	PSYCHOLOGICAL/BEHAVIORAL ATTRIBUTES
F M	MANAGERIAL ATTITUDES
F M	PHILOSOPHICAL DESCRIPTORS

Figure 6: The harmonic fusion of the two great powers.

the natural sciences suggest — might unleash the full performance potential of individuals working within social communities.

We will explore this notion further in Chapter 2. While The Harmonic Fusion of the Two Great Powers is present universally, what we are interested in here is to find out what this archetype can tell us regarding the issue of: how do organizations go about attaining superior performance within complex environments. Even though over most of the 20th century this issue has remained a central subject of enquiry within important areas of economics and in the management science, the prevailing approaches have so far led to seemingly insufficient responses:

> On the one hand […] *external* approaches to strategic management assume that companies competing within an industry are nearly homogeneous in all important aspects. On the other hand, *internal* approaches do pay attention to the internal assets and resources that underpin a company's competitive advantages. However, they are less insightful in explaining how companies evolve and adapt in the face of sudden environmental changes […] Moreover, *transactional* theories view a company as an entity that displaces market organizations. These approaches maintain that a company's contracts are efficient means of allocating property rights in ways that cannot be done in the marketplace. This is due to the transaction costs and the incentives to competition over cooperation that characterize market-like economic transactions. However, contracts alone cannot explain distinctive elements of a company's internal organization such as learning or entrepreneurial activity, which can be crucial to its competitive performance. A company knows more than what its contracts can say. Therefore, it must be conceived as considerably more than a bundle of contracts.[72]

Thus, finding more meaningful responses to the key issues behind organizational performance remains a fundamental challenge — with a relevance that goes well beyond the purely scientific or the epistemological arena:

> […] some of the business initiatives that best embody the very essence of globalization have evidenced a dismal performance track record. For example, a well documented body of literature, impressive both in the variety of approaches utilized and in the depth and scope of the underlying empirical analyses, suggests that the failure rate of all mergers, acquisitions and alliances is well over 50 percent. Strikingly similar findings have been reported in the case of other major undertakings such as large-scale re-engineering, re-structuring and outsourcing, global expatriate programs and change initiatives. In the field of management

science, traditionally fraught with contradictory approaches and seemingly opposing views around single phenomena, such empirical evidence has enjoyed a remarkable degree of consensus over most of the 20th century [...] The issue of how a company generates and sustains competitive advantages therefore seems more relevant today [in the early 2000s] than it ever was in the past.[72]

Against this background, the archetype suggesting the harmonious blending of the male and the female could provide an innovative approach to scrutinizing the issue at hand. As this archetype has been found to resonate strongly with organic and living realities that are common to all human beings, it might allow us to examine the issue of organizational performance from an organic and a holistic perspective that have been largely absent from the literature to date. Moreover, as it universally predicates the harmonious attainment of living fitness, the application of this archetype could provide not only a more suitable managerial taxonomy, but also a guide for identifying which missing pieces might still be needed to develop a more balanced and meaningful theory of organizational performance. Equally importantly, as this archetype — just as most others — has been found to operate within the realm of the *collective* human mind, it could help us address the important *social* and collective issues underlying organizational performance. In Chapter 2 we will thus use the archetype represented in Figure 6 as a taxonomy as well as a guide that might shed light on previously neglected areas, where fresh approaches could help us find more balanced and meaningful responses to the fundamental issues behind the attainment of organizational performance across cultural, organizational and geographic boundaries.

Notes and References

[1] Morosini, P. (1998) *Managing Cultural Differences*, Pergamon, Oxford, pp. 112.
[2] Saussure, F. (1993) [Pergamon Press,] *Saussure's Third Course of Lectures on General Linguistics*. Oxford, *[1910–1911.]*
[3] The quote is from: http://biografieonline.it. For an introduction to Lèvi Strauss' ideas, see: Leach, E. (1970) *Claude Lévi-Strauss*. Viking Press, New York. A good exposition of *Lévi-Strauss*; in the Chapter The Structure of Myth, Leach offers structural analysis of several Greek myths. See also: Lévi-Strauss, C. 1966[1962], *The Savage Mind*, Chicago, University of Chicago Press.
[4] Cooper, J.C. (1990) *Chinese Alchemy*. Sterling Publishing Co, Inc, New York.
[5] See for example: Campbell, J. (1991) *The Power of Myth,* Anchor Books, New York. Anesaki, M. (1930) *The History of Japanese Religion,* Kegan Paul, London; Robertson, R. (1995). *Jungian Archetypes,* Nicolas-Hays, York Beach.

[6] German archeologist Arthur Posnansky used astronomical measurements to date the Kalasasaya structure, a method developed within the scientific discipline of "archaeometry" or "archeoastronomy". Kalasasaya is an Aymara term meaning "the standing pillars" because the structure is in fact a rectangular enclosure delineated by a series of vertical stone pillars with an East–West orientation. By measuring the lines of sight along these stone pillars and the intended deviations from the cardinal points, Posnansky was able to show that the structure was aligned to the angle between the plane of the Earth's orbit and that of the celestial equator (which at the present time forms an angle of 23° and 27 min). This astronomical angle is called *the obliquity of the ecliptic*. Dating methods based on this astronomical principle are rendered possible because the obliquity of the ecliptic tilts cyclically by approximately 1 degree every 7,000 years. (This cycle is not to be confused with the precessional cycle of 25,920 years, or 1 degree of movement every 72 years.) In 1911, Posnansky estimated that at the time when the Kalasasaya structure was built, the obliquity of the ecliptic was 23° 8 min, and 48 sec, or equivalent to 15000 BC. His measurements were confirmed in 1930 by a team of four German astronomers from the University of Bonn and the Astronomical Institute in Postdam: Rolf Müller, Hanns Ludendorff, Friederich Becker and Arnold Kohlshutter. In the 1990s, Oswaldo Rivera, Director of the Bolivian National Institute of Archeology along with archeoastronomer Neil Steele made independent measurements at Kalasasaya that dated its antiquity to 12000 BC. Further evidence of the antiquity of this site is provided by the fauna sculpted in Kalasasaya, which include 'Toxodontes,' large mammals the size of horses that were extincted in South America by 10000 BC. (Tourist guides often refer to these sculptures mistakenly as 'elephants', animals which — of course — never lived in South America until brought by the Spaniards after the 16th century.) Moreover, although today is 20 km away from the shores of the Titicaca lake, Tiwanacu originally was a port city as its massive harbor structures of wharfs and piers can be clearly seen today in a city site called the "Puma Punku". Geologists suggest that the city was violently moved from its original site as a result of a cataclysmic event that took place around 12,000 BC. The remains of Tiwanacu in fact show all the signs of a catastrophic shattering and evacuation. Heavy stones from the city's buildings, some of which weighing up to 470 tons, are scattered away as if shattered by a colossal earthquake. (To give the reader an idea of the construction — let alone the scaterring around — of a building with single stones weighing 100–470 tons in a rugged and mountainous site at over 12,500 ft, consider that 470 tons is the equivalent of moving about 500 cars simultaneously. Today's highways have in fact a 40-ton weight limit and the largest earthmoving trucks available in year 2004 held a maximum weight of 350 tons working in open pit mines). See: K. J. Knudson and T. D. Price, J. E. Buikstra and D. E. Blom, "Tiwanaku migration and mortuary rituals in Bolivia and Peru, *Archaeometry* Volume 46 Issue 1 Page 5 - February 2004, Blackwell Publishers, Ltd. Posnansky, Arthur (1945), *Tiahuanacu, the Cradle of American Man,* New York, JJ Augustin Publisher. Posnansky, Arthur (1918), "El Gran Templo del Sol en los Andes. La Edad de Tihuanacu", Bulletin No. 45 of the *Geographic Society of La Paz.* Müller, Rolf and Ludendorff, Hanns, "Arthur Posnansky's Investigations on Tiahuanacu", *Baesler Archives* Vol. XIV, pp. 123–142.

[7] In: http://en.wikipedia.org we read: "The term "multiverse" was coined in December 1960, by Andy Nimmo, then vice chairman of the British Interplanetary Society, Scottish Branch, for a talk to the branch on the many-worlds interpretation of quantum physics which had been published in 1957. This was given in February 1961, and the word with its original definition, "an apparent universe, a multiplicity of which, go to make up the whole universe" was then first used. This was because, at the time, the definition of the word 'universe' was "All that there is" and etymologically one cannot have "Alls that there is". "Uni" means one, and "multi" means many, so this meaning allowed for many multiverses".

[8] My description of the Andean myth of cosmic harmony is based on the scrutiny of a vast literature of ancient as well as contemporary writings on the Andean myth of cosmic harmony. Not less importantly, I am indebted to two wise Peruvian men from Lima and Cuzco respectively, whom I met in a series of unforgettable trips to Peru in search of the oral traditions of the *Pachayacha*. These wise men would only want to be identified by their first names — Florencio and Carlos — and gave me access to the oral traditions of the *Pachayacha* — traditions which have been kept alive from immemorial times through a long and unterrupted series of wise men such as them.

Emeritus Professor Maria Luisa Rivera Tuesta, at the San Marcos University of Lima, provides one of the best guides to the ancient chronicles of the myths related to Wiracocha. I have followed her excellent article as a guide for these sources: "*Wiracocha (Dios), pacha* (mundo) y *runa* (hombre) en la cultura prehispánica (incaica)". In: *Filosofía, humanismo y realidad. María Luisa Rivara de Tuesta, Profesora Emérita UNMSM.* Actas del IV Congreso Nacional de Filosofía Arequipa, 2-6, diciembre, 1991 (Arequipa, Universidad Nacional de San Agustín), 1994, pp. 113–119.

When looking at the ancient sources, one should distinguish the ones coming from Spanish chronists from the ones written by either mestizos or authors of Kichua blood and culture.

There are three fundamental 16th century sources that shed light on the Andean civilization's thought and philosophy regarding cosmic harmony. They come from one Kichua author, Yamqui Santacruz Pachacuti, and a mestizo called Blas Valera, the son of a Spanish conquistador and a Chacha princess from the Northern rain forest regions of the Inka empire. Both of these authors grew up within a Kichua-dominated society and culture which still maintained all its integral elements in place. One of these three sources, *La primera nueva crónica y buen gobierno*, was discovered by chance in the Copenhagen Royal library in 1936. Its supposed author, Felipe Guamán Poma de Ayala, was a Kichua speaker with very little command of Spanish, no formal education and a penchant for alcohol. It is more likely that the author of this stunning work — which was written in both Kichua and Spanish — was the same Blas Valera, a mercurial personality who was trained as a Jesuit in both Peru and Spain. His 'revolutionary' ideas and knowledge on Andean civilization were looked upon as dangerous by the Spanish Crown. Looking at this work one easily understands why Blas Valera would rather hid his authorship behind somebody else's name. Besides portraying one of the most compelling and complete set of texts and figures about Andean cosmogony that we have in existence, the book contains the key to decipher the Peruvian alphabet, an alpha-numerical scripture with a sophistication that went well beyond what is normally ascribed to the mathematical kiphus (the Inka numerical accounting system based on nodes). The Spanish Crown, in its desire to justify their violent conquest and evangelization of the *Tawantinsuyu* (the Inka empire), created an 'official history' that denied the ancient Peruvians some of their most central and stunning cultural achievements. However appalling this may sound, it was only the prelude of a comprehensive work of deliberate destruction that the Spaniards carried out throughout the *Tawantinsuyu*, which ravaged the land almost uninterruptedly over the ensuing three centuries. Working from the spectacular figures in the text of: *La primera nueva crónica y buen gobierno*, English engineer Williams Burns Glynn found little difficulty deciphering the Peruvian alphabet over the decade of the 1970s. He ought to be considered the Champollion of Peruvian civilization, and *La primera nueva crónica y buen gobierno* its Roseta stone. Burns Glynn seminal work has been condensed in a small volume by: Manassess Fernandez, Lancho, *Escritura Incaica,* Universidad Nacional Federico Villareal, Lima, 2002. In the paragraphs below I list the three fundamental indigenous sources regarding Andean cosmogony:

- Santacruz Pachacuti Yamqui, Joan. *Relaciones de antigüedades deste reyno del Perú.* In: *Crónicas peruanas de interés indígena.* Madrid, Ed. Atlas, 1968. There is an insightful poem in Kichua about **Tecsi Wiracocha in:** I, pp. 287–288; II, 289; III, 292; IV, 294. (Biblioteca de Autores Españoles N° 209). The poem, which I have translated following the works of 20th century Peruvian novelist and Kichua linguist Jose Maria Arguedas, reveals the way in which "God" was perceived by the Andean civilization:

Lord of the Universes	*apo hinantima*
cosmic molder	*luttacticci*
of the heavens	*hananpachap*
of the depths	*hurinpachap*
of the endless seas	*cochamantarayacpa*
of all the rising lights	*vilca ulcaapu*
almighty maker	*hinantima pachacamac*
true lord of the heavens	*hananchiccha*
and of the shades	*hurinchiccha*
creator of humanity:	*runavallpac*
"let be man" you said	*cay caricachon*
"and let be woman"	*cay varmicachon*
The shining sun and the moon	*inticaquillaca*
the day and the night	*ppunchao catutaca*
summers and winters	*pocoyca chiraoca*
are not free	*manamyancacho*
they follow your harmony	*camachiscam purim*
they follow your commands	*vnanchascaman*
they arrive	*tupusca manmi*
to your charted destinations	*chayan*

Who are you?	*pincanque*
Where are you?	*maycanmicanque*
What do you intend?	*ymactan ñinqui*
Answer me!	*rimayñi*
Let me see you!	*mana choricayquiman*
Is in the heavens	*hananpichum*
or down in the shades	*hurimpichum*
or in the outside world	*quinraynimpichum*
that I will find you?	*capacosnoyqui*
Lord, your creatures	*apoynnayquicuna*
reach out to you.	*camman*
With weary eyes	*allcañañiyvan*
they look for you.	*riacytam munayqui*
When they will be able to see	*ricuptiy*
and understand	*yachaptiy*
and discern	*vnanchaptiy*
and reflect	*hamuttaptiy*
then you will notice	*ricucanquim*
and recognize them	*yachavanquim*
Merely whisper to me: "Hey!!"	*hayñillavay*
listen to me	*oyarillabay*
when I am still	*manaracpas*
fresh and still	*say coptiy*
alive.	*vañuptiy*
Who are you?	*pincanque*
Where are you?	*maycanmicanque*
What do you intend?	*ymactan ñinqui*
Answer me!	*Rimayñi*

- Anónima. *Relaciones de las costumbres antiguas de los naturales del Pirú.* In: *Tres relaciones de antigüedades peruanas.* Guaranía, Buenos Aires, 1950, p. 135. This work is widely attributed to Blas Valera, and includes this revealing passage : "Creyeron y dijeron que el mundo, cielo y tierra, y sol y luna, fueron criados por otro mayor que ellos: á este llamaron **Illa Tecce** [el principio], que quiere decir *Luz eterna.* Los modernos añidieron otro nombre, ques **Viracocha** ..."
- Guamán Poma de Ayala, Felipe. *La primera nueva crónica y buen gobierno.* Culltura, Lima, 1965. As explained in the early paragraphs of this reference note, this work can also be attributed to Blas Valera.

The Spanish sources provide descriptions of Wiracocha and its associated myths that are heavily tainted by their 16th century European and Iberian culture. This in itself provides a fascinating portrayal of the clash between extremely different people who nevertheless shared some important cultural notions. Not less importantly, highlights of the real

Andean thinking regarding cosmic harmony emerge quite clearly from these texts. Some of the most interesting sources are quoted in the following paragraphs, including, in most cases excerpts from the original texts in ancient Spanish where I have underscored the expressions in the Kichua and Aymara languages in bold characters:

- Acosta, J. 1954. *Historia natural y moral de las Indias*. In: *Obras del Padre José de Acosta*. Atlas, Madrid, Libro V, cap. III, p. 141. (Biblioteca de Autores Españoles N° 73). In Libro V, cap. IV, p. 144: "... atribuían principalmente el poder y mando de todo, y a los otros como dioses o señores particulares cada uno en su casa, y que eran intercesores para con el gran **Ticciviracocha**". In Libro VI, cap. XXI, p. 200 "... estando todo debajo de su poder..." In Libro V, cap. III, p. 142: "y agregando que... ningún otro Dios hay ... sino uno; y que todo lo demás no tiene propio poder, ni propio ser, ni propia operación ..."
- Cobo, B. 1964. *Historia del Nuevo Mundo*. In: *Obras del Padre Bernabé Cobo*. Madrid, Ed. Atlas, Libro XIII, cap. I, p. 146. (Biblioteca de Autores Españoles N° 92). In Libro XIII, cap. IV, p. 155: "... el poder y mando de todo... la primera causa... a quien daban títulos y nombres de gran excelencia: los más honrosos y usados eran dos, ambos translaticios y de grande énfasis: *Viracocha* el uno, y el otro, *Pachayacháchic*; al primero solían anteponer o posponer algunas palabras, diciendo unas veces *Ticciviracocha*, y otras *Viracochayacháchic*. El de *Ticciviracocha* era tenido por misterioso, el cual interpretado, significa 'fundamento divino'; el nombre de *Pachayacháchic* quiere decir 'Criador del mundo'; y la misma significación tiene el de *Viracochayacháchic*"
- Polo de Ondegardo, J. 1916. *Informaciones acerca de la religión y gobierno de los incas*. Notas biográficas y concordancia de los textos por H. Urteaga. Lima, Imprenta y Librería Sanmarti y Ca., Tom. III, p. 6.
- Cabello Valboa, M. 1951. *Miscelánea Antártica, una historia del Perú antiguo*. Lima, Universidad Nacional Mayor de San Marcos, Facultad de Letras, Instituto de Etnología, cap. 14, p. 297.
- Betanzos, J. 1968. *Suma y narración de los incas*. In: *Crónicas peruanas de interés indígena*. Atlas, Madrid, cap. I. "Que trata del **Con tici Viracocha**, que ellos tienen que fue el Hacedor, e de cómo hizo el cielo e tierra e las gentes indios destas provincias del Perú.", p. 9. (Biblioteca de Autores Españoles N° 209).
- Cieza de León, P. 1947. *El señorío de los incas*. Instituto de Estudios Peruanos, Lima. 1967. Cap. V. "De lo que dicen estos naturales de **Ticiviracocha**, y de la opinión que algunos tienen que atravesó un Apóstol por esta tierra, y del templo que hay en Cáchan y de lo que allí pasó", p. 8. In cap. V, p. 11. "... mas lo que vemos y entendemos es que el Demonio tuvo poder grandísimo sobre estas gentes, permitiéndolo Dios". Also see: Cieza de León, Pedro. *La crónica del Perú*. In: *Historiadores primitivos de Indias*. Madrid, Ed. Atlas, Tom. II, cap. CI, p. 444. (Biblioteca de Autores Españoles N° 26).
- Molina, C. 1959. *Ritos y fábulas de los incas*. Lima, Ed. Futuro, I. "Los orígenes y el diluvio". In p. 16: Cap. I, "... el Hacedor, a quien en lengua de éstos le llaman **Pacha yachachi**, y por otro nombre **Tecsi Viracocha**, que quiere decir incomprensible dios,

a quien ellos decían que era el padre de **Ymai mama** y de **Tocapo Viracocha**, mandó que desde allí [Pucara, ciudad a cuarenta leguas del Cuzco] se partiese el mayor de sus hijos, llamado **Ymai mama Viracocha**, en cuyo poder y mando estaban todas las cosas, y que fuese por el camino de los Andes y montañas de toda la tierra; y que fuese dando y poniendo nombres a todos los árboles, grandes y pequeños, y a las flores y frutas que habían de tener, y mostrando a las gentes las que eran para comer y las que no, y las que eran buenas para medicina; y asimismo puso nombres a todas las yerbas y flores, y que éste mostró a las gentes las yerbas que tenían virtud para curar y las flores que podían matar. Y al hijo llamado **Tocapo Viracocha**, que quiere decir en su lengua Hacedor en que se incluyen todas las cosas, le mandó [que] fuese por el camino de los llanos visitando las gentes y poniendo nombres a los ríos y árboles que en ellos hubiese, y dándoles sus frutos y flores por la orden dicha …Dicen también … que en **Tiahuanaco**, donde dicen hizo todas las gentes, hizo todas las diferencias de aves, macho y hembra de cada uno, y dándoles cantos que habían de cantar cada uno, y a los que habían de residir en las montañas que se fuesen a ellas, y a los que en la tierra, cada uno a las partes y lugares que habían de residir; y que asimismo hizo todas las diferencias de animales de cada uno, macho y hembra, y todas las demás diferencias de culebras y demás sabandijas que en la tierra hay, mandando a cada una que los que habían de ir a las montañas fuesen a ellas y los demás fuesen por la tierra; y que allí manifestó a las gentes los nombres y propiedades que las aves y animales y demás sabandijas tenían"

- López de Gómara, F. 1946. *Historia general de las Indias.* In: *Historiadores primitivos de Indias,* Atlas, Madrid, Tom. I, p. 233. (Biblioteca de Autores Españoles N° 22).
- Sarmiento de Gamboa, 1965. *Historia índica.* "Fábulas del origen de estos bárbaros indios del Perú según sus opiniones ciegas". In: *Obras del Inca Garcilaso de la Vega,* Atlas, Madrid, Apéndice, Tom. IV, [6], p. 206. (Biblioteca de Autores Españoles N° 135), p. 206. In p. 207 : "… y por esta creación le llamaron **Viracocha Pachayachachi**, que quiere decir Criador de todas las cosas".
- Murúa, M. *Historia del origen y genealogía real de los reyes incas del Perú,* Madrid, Consejo Superior de Investigaciones Científicas, Instituto Santo Toribio de Mogrovejo, MCMXLVI, Libro II, pp. 108-109.

An excellent introduction to contemporary works about Wiracocha and the ancient Andean cosmogony can be found in:

- Garcia, F. and P. Roca. (2004) *Pachakuteq, una Aproximación a la Cosmovisión Andina,* Lumbreras Editores, Lima, Perú.
- Valcárcel, L. E. (1959) *Etnohistoria del Perú Antiguo. Historia del Perú (Incas).* Universidad Nacional Mayor de San Marcos, Patronato del Libro Universitario, Lima, 7. Religión, p. 139.
- "El pensamiento incaico". (1992) In: *Filosofía iberoamericana en la época del Encuentro,* Trotta, Madrid, Tom. I, pp. 127-153. (Enciclopedia Iberoamericana de Filosofía Vol. I).

Equally importantly, the more technically oriented readers will find an extraordinarily rich literature on Peruvian civilization in general and Andean cosmogony in particular, in the works of outstanding American archeologist John Howland Rowe. His vast research output for the 1940–1967 period has been compiled comprehensively by Robert E. Pfeiffer, the Librarian at the Anthropology Library of the University of California, Rowe's *alma mater*: Robert E. Pfeiffer; "John Howland Rowe, Bibliography, 1940-1967, Berkeley *Kroeber Anthropological Society Papers,* no. 40, Spring, 1969, pp. 112-132. Berkeley. This bibliography was revised from 1963 and extended to 1992 by Rowe (http://sunsite.berkeley.edu/Anthro/rowe).

[9] Even within contemporary Peru, the *Pachamama* is often mistakenly translated as "The Mother Earth" by authors who are operating under an excessively Western cultural mindset. "The Mother Earth" was an ancient cult and a cosmogony that flourished all around the Mediterranean basin since the Neolithic times. It was associated with female fertility rites that were widespread in this area, and has been seen as a precursor of the "sacred feminine" philosophies that flourished during the early Middle Ages in Europe. These ideas have no connection at all with the *Pachamama.* The *Pachamama* is the phallic archetypal element of the Andean cosmogony. This was clearly engraved in the golden gates of the *Koricancha* — the Golden Temple — the most sacred shrine at the heart of Cuzco, the capital of the *Tawantinsuyu* (the Inka empire). These gates represented one of the supreme works of art of the Inka civilization and constituted a true altar of Andean cosmogony. Their effect on the visitors was perhaps comparable to that felt by those glancing at the bronze gates of the Baptistery of Florence, marvelously sculpted by Renaissance Italian artist Lorenzo Ghiberti — roughly at the same time period when the *Koricancha* gates were being fashioned in gold by the Andeans. However, as a work of art, today it can only be imagined what these gates looked like to the observer. This is because the Spanish Conquistadores robbed these sacred golden gates in order to melt the gold – just as they did with nearly every other golden artifact they could set their eyes on within the Inka empire.

Fortunately for us, the engravings of the *Koricancha* golden gates were copied in paper before the Spaniards melted them. This was the work of Yamqui Santacruz Pachacuti, a Kichua wise man thanks to whom we can still glance at this fundamental image of the Andean cosmogony in close resemblance to its original form. Santacruz Pachacuti's drawing is now engraved in a golden-looking surface that meets the tourists who visit the *Koricancha* in Cuzco. The drawing is also reproduced below, with an explanation of its archetypal elements in Spanish language besides the figure.

Santacruz Pachacuti's drawing is clear and leaves no room for doubt: the *Pachamama* is a solar attribute, representing the masculine archetype of 'emission', 'fertilizer' and 'phallus', which is associated with summer, the lightning (fire) as well as with Venus in the rising morning. On the other hand, the *Mama Cocha* epitomizes the lunar attributes of the female, with its nurturing and receptacle qualities represented by the waters of the seas as well as by the feline figure (who sees in the darkness of the night), the hail of winter and Venus in the setting afternoon. An important part of this image is the grid-like representation at its bottom. It represented the 'sacred proportions', the mathematical

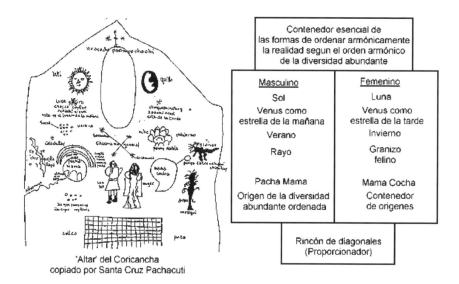

paradigm that the ancient Andeans developed in association with their cosmogony and which was behind all of their scientific and technological exploits.

In order to avoid the fastidious and mistaken confusion of the Andean *Pachamama* with the Mediterranean "Mother Earth", I have also used its synonymous *Pachapapa*. This is another — more folkloric — name for the same archetype that is widespread in today's Peruvian Andes. Although the word means exactly the same as *Pachamama*, I use it in the hope that the suffix 'papa' might evoke masculine notions in the reader as it is similar to the Latin root for the word "Father" (though this was not what the Andeans had in mind when they coined the word: their use of the suffix *papa* really is in connection with the 'potato', the basic crop of the Andes which of course relates to the fertilizing nature of the attribute).

[10] Stevenson, L. (1990) "Some methodological problems associated with researching women entrepreneurs," *Journal of Business Ethics* 9(4–5): 439.

[11] Ginger, S. (2003) "Female brains vs. male brains," *International Journal of Psychotherapy* 8(2): 139–145.

[12] Akgün, A, M. Okuyan, S. H. Baytan and M. Topba? (2003) "Relationships between non-verbal IQ and brain size in right and left-handed men and women," *International Journal of Neuroscience* 113: 893–902.

[13] Ankney, C.D. (1992) "Sex differences in relative brain size: The mismeasure of woman, too?" *Intelligence* 16: 329–336.

[14] Peters, M., L. Jancke, J.F. Straiger, G. Schlaug, Y. Huang and H. Steinmetz (1998) "Unsolved problems in comparing brain sizes in homo sapiens," *Brain and Cognition* 37: 254–285.

40   The Common Glue

[15] Gur, R. C., B. I. Turetsky, M. Matsui1, M. Yan, W. Bilker, P. Hughett and R. E. Gur (1999) "Sex differences in brain gray and white matter in healthy young adults: correlations with cognitive performance," *The Journal of Neuroscience* 19(10): 4065–4072.

[16] Rahman, Q. V. Kumari and G. D. Wilson (2003) "Sexual orientation-related differences in prepulse inhibition of the human startle response," *Behavioral Neuroscience* 117(5): 1096–1102.

[17] Kimura, D. (1999) *Sex and Cognition*, Cambridge, MA, MIT Press.

[18] Owen, K. and R. Lynn. (1993) "Sex differences in primary cognitive abilities of blacks, Indians, and whites in South Africa," *Journal of Bio Science* 25(4): 557–560, as quoted in Akgün, A, O. Mukkader, S. H. Baytan and M. Topba? (2003).

[19] Leason, J., A. MacFadden, S. Bell and L.J. Elias (2002) "Are sex differences in navigation caused by sexually dimorphic strategies or by differences in the ability to use the strategies?" *Behavioral Neuroscience* 116(3): 403–410.

[20] Whiting, B. and C. Pope Edwards (1973), "A cross-cultural analysis of sex differences in the behavior of children aged three to eleven," *Journal of Social Psychology* 91: 171–188.

[21] Poorman, P., E. Donnerstein and M. Donnerstein (1976) "Aggressive behavior as a function of age and sex," *The Journal of Genetic Psychology* 128: 123–127.

[22] Garai, V. E. and A. Scheinfeld (1968) "Sex differences in mental and behavioral traits," *Genetic Psychology Monographs* 77: 169–299.

[23] Ås, B. (1975) "On female culture: An attempt to formulate a theory of women's solidarity and action," *Acta Sociologica* 18(2/3): 142–161.

[24] Rosaldo, M. Z. (1974) "Woman, culture and society: A theoretical overview", In: *Woman, Culture and Society*, M.Z. Rosaldo and L. Lamphere (Eds.), Stanford University Press, Stanford, CA, p. 30.

[25] Chodorow, N. (1974) "Family structure and feminine personality", In: M. Z. Rosaldo and L. Lamphere (Eds.), *Woman, Culture and Society, Stanford University Press*, [Stanford, CA.]

[26] Gutmann, D. (1965) "Woman and the conception of ego strength," *Merrill-Palmer Quarterly of Behavior and Development* 2: 229–240.

[27] Carlson, R. (1971) "Sex differences in ego functioning: Exploratory studies of agency and communion," *Journal of Consulting and Clinical Psychology* 37: 270.

[28] Wolf, M. (1974) "Chinese women: Old skills in a new context", In: *Woman, Culture, and Society* M.Z. Rosaldo and L. Lamphere (Eds.), Stanford University Press, Stanford, CA, 164–166.

[29] Polyanna is a consistently cheerful title character of the 1912 novel written by Eleanor H. Porter.

[30] Collier, J. F. (1974) "Women in politics". In: *Woman, Culture, and Society*, M. Z. Rosaldo and L. Lamphere (Eds.), Stanford University Press, Stanford, CA, p. 94.

[31] Rosaldo M. Z. and L. Lamphere, "Introduction". In: *Woman, Culture, and Society*, M. Z. Rosaldo and L. Lamphere, (Eds.), Stanford University Press, Stanford, CA, p. 3.

[32] Vivante, B. (1999) "Introduction". In: *Women's Roles in Ancient Civilizations: A Reference Guide*, B. Vivante (Ed.), Greenwood Press, Westport, CT, pp. xiv-xv.

[33] Lai, K. (2000) "The daodejing: Resources for contemporary feminist thinking," *Journal of Chinese Philosophy* 27(2): p. 131.

[34] Colwill, J. and J. Townsend (1999) "Women, leadership, and information technology: The impact of women leaders in organizations and their role in integrating information technology with corporate strategy," *The Journal of Management Development* 18(3): 209.

[35] Rosener, J. B. (1990) "Ways women lead," *Harvard Business Review* 68(6):119- 125.

[36] Bass, B. 1991. "Debate: Ways men and women Lead," *Harvard Business Review* 69(1): 151–152.

[37] Chrikova, A. and O. Krichevskaia (2002) "The woman manager: Business style and self-image," *Sociological Research* 41(1): 38–54.

[38] Buttner, H. E. (1993) "Female Entrepreneurs: How Far Have They Come? Women in Business," *Business Horizons* 36(2): 59–74.

[39] Gaskill, L., C. Jasper, H. Bastow-Shoop, L. Jolly, R. Kean, L. Leistritz and B. Sternquist (1996) "Operational planning and competitive strategies of male and female retailers," *The International Review of Retail Distribution, and Consumer Research* 6(1): 76–96.

[40] Samartseva, O. and T. Fomina (2002) "Men and women: Management in the business sphere," *Sociological Research* 41(1): 69–77.

[41] Editorial. (2003) "Major factors explain cognitive differences between the genders," *Women's Health Weekly*, October 23:83.

[42] Patai, R. (1972) *Myth and Modern Man*, Englewood Cliffs, NJ, Prentice-Hall, p. 3.

[43] Kinney, A. B. (1999) "Women in ancient china," In :*Women's Roles in Ancient Civilizations: A Reference Guide*, B. Vivante (Ed.), Greenwood Press, Westport, CT, pp. 3, 31.

[44] Lao Tsu Lao Tsu, *Tao Te Ching*, Translated by Gia-Fu Feng and J. English, 1989. Vintage Books, New York, NY, p. 63.

[45] Lai. 2000. Op cit: 132, 134. Also, an insightful poetic rendering of the *Tao* can be found in: Lao Tsu, *Tao Te Ching*, Translated by Gia-Fu Feng and Jane English. 1989. Vintage Books, New York, NY, pp. 24, 28. The poem reads as follows:

Yield and overcome;
Bend and be straight;
Empty and be full;
Wear out and be new;
Have little and gain;
Have much and be confused.

This is called perception
of the nature of things.
Soft and weak overcome
hard and strong.

[46] Malinowski. B. (1962) *Sex, Culture, and Myth*, Harcourt, Brace & World, Inc., New York, NY, pp. 199, 229–230.

[47] Miers, M. (2002) "Developing an understanding of gender sensitive care: Exploring concepts and knowledge," *Journal of Advanced Nursing* 40(1): 69–77.

[48] Ungerson, C. (1987) *Policy Is Personal: Sex, Gender and Informal Care,* Tavistock, London.

[49] Connell, R.W. (1995) *Masculinities,* Polity Press, Cambridge.

[50] Oakley, A. (1998) "Science, gender and women's liberation: An argument against postmodernism," *Women's Studies International Forum,* 21: 133–146.

[51] Quigley, C. (1961) *The Evolution of Civilizations, An Introduction to Historical Analysis,* The Macmillan Company, New York, NY, p.15.

[52] Rosaldo, M. and L. Lamphere (Eds) (1974) *Woman, Culture and Society,* Stanford University Press, Stanford.

[53] Vasilenko, I.A. (2000) "Dialog of culture, dialog of civilizations," *Russian Social Science Review* 41(2): 6.

[54] Toynbee, A. J. (1946) *A Study of History, Abridgement of Volumes I-VI by C.C. Somervell,* Oxford University Press, New York and London, 3, 566.

[55] Danilevskii N. (2000) "Rossiia i evropa. Vzgliad na kul'turnye i politicheskie otnosheniia slavianskogo mira k romano-germanskomu," *Zaria,* No. 5–9, as quoted in Vasilenko, op.cit.

[56] Huntington, S. P. (1993) "The clash of civilizations?" *Foreign Affairs* 72(3): 24–25.

[57] Fox, M.J.T. (1999) "Native Women in Ancient North America: Ojibway and Iroquois". In: *Women's Roles in Ancient Civilizations: A Reference Guide,* B. Vivante (Ed.), Greenwood Press, Westport, CT, 356–357.

[58] Aoki, M.Y. (1999) "Women in ancient japan". In: *Women's Roles in Ancient Civilizations: A Reference Guide,*B. Vivante, (Ed.), Greenwood Press, Westport, CT, p. 75, 70, 77.

[59] Stone, A.J. (1999) "Women in Ancient Mesoamerica". In: *Women's Roles in Ancient Civilizations: A Reference Guide,*B. Vivante (Ed.) Greenwood Press, Westport, CT, p. 298–300.

[60] Acosta, J.d. *De procuranda indorum salute.* Libro VI, cap. XX, pp. 585–587, who wrote in the 16th century. The original and complete text in (ancient) Spanish from which these remarkable excerpts come from, read as follows:

"Había, pues, verdaderos matrimonios entre nuestros indios, aunque, lo que muchas veces me ha admirado, no conociesen el nombre, y españoles e indios usan ahora el nuestro. Tenía, sin embargo, cada uno su mujer, y los bárbaros, naturalmente, odiaban la república que soñó Sócrates y la condenaban. Como a la mujer no era lícito casarse con otro, así el marido tampoco podía repudiar a la que una vez había tomado. Si se descubría algún adulterio, era castigado con atrocísimos suplicios; porque aunque entre los célibes [solteros] usan de mayor licencia que nosotros y la fornicación queda impune, sin embargo los adulterios de los casados son castigados con mucha mayor severidad. Y el estupro contra las vírgenes consagradas al sol o al Pachayachachi o al mismo Inca ... era tenido por sacrilegio tan horrendo, que los dos eran sepultados vivos en tierra. Y al vulgo sólo era lícito tener una sola mujer con la que vivía de por vida. Todas estas cosas conforme a la ley natural profesaban estos bárbaros. [Hay otra] cosa monstruosa, pero que está tan arraigada en el corazón de los bárbaros, que raro es el cristiano en quien no perdura. La virginidad, que entre todos los hombres es mirada con estima y honor, la desprecian estos bárbaros como vil y afrentosa. Excepto las vírgenes consagradas al Sol o al Inga, que están guardadas en cercos sagrados, todas las demás mientras son vírgenes se consideran despreciadas, y así, en cuanto pueden, se entregan al primero que encuentran. Los mismos maridos cuando hallan corrompidas a sus esposas no lo llevan a mal, tanto que si algunas llegan vírgenes al matrimonio lo toman a afrenta, como si de nadie hubiesen sido amadas . De este error nace el abuso abominable de que nadie toma mujer sin haberla conocido y probado antes por muchos días y meses, y, vergüenza da decirlo, ninguna es buena esposa si no a sido antes concubina"

[61] Morosini, P. (2005) "Nurturing successful alliance across boundaries". In: *The Handbook of Strategic Alliances,* O. Shenkar (Ed.), Sage, Thousand Oaks, CA.

[62] Sarmiento de Gamboa, P. (1965) *Historia índica.* "Fábulas del origen de estos bárbaros indios del Perú según sus opiniones ciegas". In: *Obras del Inca Garcilaso de la Vega.* Atlas, Madrid.

[63] See: *Los Incas, Economia, sociedad y estado en la era del tahuantinsuyo,* Waldemar Espinoza Soriano, 1997, Amaru Editores, Lima, Perú.

[64] Nemet-Nejat, K. R. (1999) "Woman in ancient mesopotamia," In: *Women's Roles in Ancient Civilizations: A Reference Guide*, B. Vivante (Ed.), Greenwood Press, Westport, CT, p. 87–88.

[65] Vivante, B. Z. (1999) "Women in ancient greece" In: *Women's Roles in Ancient Civilizations: A Reference Guide*, B. Vivante (Ed.) Greenwood Press, Westport, CT, pp. 219–220, 243.

[66] Denich, B.S. (1974) "Sex and power in the balkans". In: *Woman, Culture, and Society,* M. Z. Rosaldo and L. Lamphere (Eds.), Stanford University Press, Stanford, CA, 1974, p. 244.

[67] Robins, G. (1999) "Women in ancient egypt". In: *Women's Roles in Ancient Civilizations: A Reference Guide*, B. Vivante (Ed.), Greenwood Press, Westport, CT, p. 181.

[68] Hoffer, C. P. (1974) "Madam yoko: Ruler of kpa mende confederacy." In: *Woman, Culture, and Society*, M. Z. Rosaldo and L. Lamphere (Eds.), Stanford University Press, Stanford, CA, p. 173.

[69] Epstein, C. F. (1991) "Debate: ways men and women lead," *Harvard Business Review* 69(1): 150.

[70] J. Sonnenfeld. (1991). "Debate: Ways men and women lead," *Harvard Business Review*, 69(1): 160.

[71] Campbell, J. (1968) *The Hero With A Thousand Faces*, 2nd Edition, Princeton University Press, Princeton, NJ, p. 113–116.

[72] Morosini, P. (2004) "Competing on social capabilities." In: *Next Generation Business Handbook,* S.Chowdhury (Ed.), Wiley, New York, pp. 251–252.

Chapter 2

Male and Female Theories of Organizational Performance

> When an evolving and enhanced understanding is translated into action, organizational learning is like the fountain of youth
> Mary M. Crossan and Andrew C. Inkpen[1]

Classical economists addressing the issue of organizational performance in the 19th century provided it with an archetypal male start. Their ideas on the pursuit of maximum personal utility as a key to individual happiness as well as efficiency-for-profit-maximization as the chief economic driver of firms, laid an intellectual framework that was to reveal its decisive imprint over the ensuing 200 years. However, by 1979 some of the key drawbacks of the industrial economies that were built upon these principles had become all too clear:

> The possibility of unemployment is closely related to the profit-making motive, and, in particular, to decentralization which in many respects we regard as one of the virtues of the system [...] The price system is not, in fact, [...] causing the user to understand the costs he is imposing on society [...] The legitimacy of profits when they are derived from social bads rather than social goods is surely questionable [...] The managers receive a relatively small fraction of profits; as stockholders they characteristically have a half of one percent or one percent of the total stock outstanding. Therefore, it is not clear why should they want to maximize profits. Many decisions are being made not by the top management, but by the middle management [...] They are interested in technique for its own sake. The motives of the firm become essentially its self-preservation, its growth, its ability to innovate, rather than its maximization of profit [In] a complicated organization it is impossible to maximize profits. It is just too hard to know what is going on.[2]

Regarding the assumption that individuals behaved in ways that pursued the maximization of personal utility, already in 1956 economists Cyert and March observed that: "The theory of the firm as it exists in present economic literature is a deductive system based on assumptions of human motivation that appear doubtful in the light of present day psychology, and on assumptions of organizational behavior that are implausible."[3] Classical economists' convictions of an "invisible hand" underlying the efficiency of free markets were also criticized in 1996 by Kogut and Zander, who observed that: "In the contemporary and industrialized settings, norms of equity tend to prevail [...] The importance of fairness as a consideration has persistently surprised game theoretical predictions. Studies on ultimatum bargaining (i.e. one shot offers to take it or leave it) show that individuals are highly sensitive to fairness [...] In a study conducted in the United States, Kahneman and his colleagues (1986) find that people object to the use of the market, that is to prices, as a way to ration goods during the crisis."[4]

Other pundits underscored that the classical explanation was also at a loss to describe the processes taking place within enterprises where market forces had little relevance, such as non-profit and governmental institutions.[5] It was also highlighted in 1984, that classical economics paid insufficient attention to important factors behind organizational performance such as know-how, whereas it focused excessively on volume and price dimensions, disregarded entrepreneurship by assuming cost-free and equal access to information by all parties involved, and heavily simplified markets by "assuming away" reputational effects and institutional supports such as trust, laws and reciprocity.[6]

Some Missing 'Female' Elements in the Classical Theory

A number of theorists set out to address some of the main disadvantages of classical economics to explain organizational performance. During the decade of 1975–1985, Williamson wrote a series of works that built on earlier ideas by economist Ronald Coase,[7] proposing that firms and markets represent the alternative models for managing transactions. In their view, it is organizational structure – rather than technological functions – that determines performance. This line of reasoning became known as transaction cost economics – a comparative institutional approach to economic organization that regards firm as an incomplete contracting arrangement. The hypothesis on which transaction cost economics is based is that different transactions gravitate toward different governance structures, which affects the costs of the outcome. For example, if a supplier is faced with a choice of using customer-specific or generic equipment to manufacture the parts, he would need to be provided with price incentives, contract safeguards, and institutional dispute resolution mechanisms to induce him to select the assets that cannot be easily redeployed if a contract is unexpectedly terminated.

Thus, under transaction cost theory the performance goal of the firm is to economize transaction costs instead of maximizing profits. In turn, the performance results are presumed efficient when there is no superior alternative with net gains that can be both described and implemented.[8] The underlying perspective does include important firm-specific aspects as determinant of organizational performance. However, its one-sided — "male" — transactional focus on contracts is at odds to explain other important elements of a firm's internal organization such as learning or entrepreneurial activity, which can also be critical to performance. As previously observed: "A company knows more than what its contracts can say. Therefore, it must be conceived as considerably more than a bundle of contracts."[9]

Classical economists' ideas of organizational performance typically include the assessment of a firm's physical capacities in relation to its flow of output. The limited applicablity of some of their notions in today's economic environment have been attributed to the fact that the milieu of the classical economists was the capital-intensive industrial world of the 19th century. However, in 1992 Chandler observed that: "[even within] the capital-intensive industries [...] the actual economies of scale and scope, as measured by throughput [or the amount actually processed within a specified time period], are organizational [depending upon] knowledge, skill, experience, and teamwork [In other words,] on the organized human capabilities essential to exploit the potential of technological processes."[10]

This type of perspective identifies the archetypally "female" elements of coordination and interoperability as critical to organizational performance. Already in 1945, Von Hayek had suggested that the application of these kinds of ideas were not to be thought of as restricted to the realm of firms: "The economic problem of society is [...] not merely a problem of how to allocate "given" resources [...] It is rather a problem of how to secure the best use of resources known to any of the members of society, for ends whose relative importance only these individuals know."[11] In 2000, Teece, Pisano and Shuen built on these notions by observing that, while price mechanisms synchronize the functioning of the market economy, managers coordinate activities within the firm; and how effectively internal coordination is achieved will depend on the nature of the organization.[12] For example, a study of air-conditioning product manufacturers revealed that the quality of performance was related to special organizational routines, such as information gathering and processing, linking customer experiences with engineering design, and coordinating factory and component suppliers, and not to capital investment or the degree of automation.[13] Supporting these findings, studies examining project development in the automobile industry showed that the degree of variation in organizational structure and coordination of business processes had a significant impact on development costs, development lead times and quality.[14]

The 'Female' Challenge of Turning Labor into Capital

Classical economists identified capital as one of the key financial drivers of organizational performance. Their primary focus of attention was "male" and mechanistic, looking at capital investments as a crucial ingredient to provide the underlying machinery of firms with efficient production facilities. This emphasis was to shift dramatically over the second half of the 20th century to favor investment in human resources by firms competing within the new economic realities of fast-paced and continuous environmental changes. In 2002, Drucker pointed out that workers on whose productivity and performance the company relies for its success and survival should be regarded as capital and not as labor.[15] These workers required special management approaches: while in a traditional workforce employees serve the system, in a knowledge-driven environment the system must serve employees. This called for "female" organizational characteristics of the interpersonal kind into play. In other words, company management had to: "spend time with the promising knowledge professionals: to get to know them and to be known by them; to mentor them and to listen to them; to challenge them and to encourage them."[16]

Adapting to this radical shift of mindset proved to be no easy task for organizations, but a rather major challenge of far-reaching implications. In 2002, the same year of publication of Drucker's article on knowledge professionals, management pundits Bartlett and Ghoshal summarized the prevailing challenges:

> The hardest mind-set to alter [within organizations] is the long-standing, deeply embedded belief that capital is the critical strategic resource to be managed and that senior managers' key responsibilities should center around its acquisition, allocation and effective use [But in today's economy there is] a surplus of capital chasing a scarcity of talented people and the knowledge they possess [That] is the constraining — and therefore strategic — resource. The implications for top management are profound. First, human-resources issues must move up near the top of the agenda in discussions of the company's strategic priorities. That means that a first-class human-resources executive must be at the CEO's right hand. Eventually, traditional strategic-planning processes will need to be overhauled and the financially calibrated measurement and reward systems will have to be redesigned to recognize the strategic importance of human as well as financial resources.[17]

The idea that talented people, knowledge workers and the like, are to be considered a key strategic driver of organizational performance within complex environments had been raised before in the business literature. In 1987, Andrews highlighted that the operational power of a company inheres in the strengths and weaknesses of its employees, the effectiveness with which individual capability is applied to the common task, and the quality of coordination of individual and group effort. [18] Andrews' attention to human resources is revealing. There is no shortage of buzz-words in the business literature, and expressions abound such as: "competitive revi-talization," "corporate genetics," "simultaneous engineering," "right-sizing," etcetera, that often make readers forget that people *and* the relationships between them are to be considered as key driving forces of organizational performance. It is people who make decisions about strategy, technology, and processes, and people whose aspirations, actions, accomplishments or mistakes boost or diminish an organization's success.

The notion of people as strategic drivers of organizational performance super-sedes to a certain extent the classical economists' traditional division between capital and labor. However, as previously mentioned, the same notion has brought about a different kind of dilemma. While knowledge workers can be regarded as capital and as strategic resources by 21st century organizations, the latter might not always be capable of identifying, attracting, developing and retaining them. As previously mentioned, addressing these challenges success-fully might call for female-like organizational abilities such as: listening with 'both brains', nurturing and interpersonal bonding — more centrally into play within today's corporations.

> In the late 1980s, the search for more dynamic, adaptive and sus-tainable advantage led many [organizations] to supplement their analysis of external competition with an internal-competency assessment [and many] companies recognized that their people were not equal to the new knowledge-intensive tasks [Moreover,] few [organizations had] built the human-resources systems, processes or cultures that can even offset, let alone challenge, [their] deeply embedded bias toward financial assets [...] Converting recruitment into a strategic task means making an ongoing commit-ment to locating and attracting the best of the best at every level and from every source [...] After a company has acquired top talent, the building challenge also requires the human-resources function to lead company efforts in constantly developing those talented indi-viduals. That requires more than traditional training programs pro-vide. Today development must be embedded in the company's bloodstream, with all managers responsible for giving their team members ongoing feedback and coaching. [19]

'Male' and 'Female' Conceptions of Economic Firms

Distinctive 'male' and 'female' features can be recognized in economists' and management theorists' conceptions of what economic organizations are — or should be. These differing characteristics have in turn led to diverse ideas of what is important to consider as organizational performance. On the one hand, the primary focus of classical and neoclassical economic approaches is the marketplace. Its central paradigm is 'male': a firm that takes the form of a production function which ought to transform inputs such as labor and capital into outputs, with the maximum levels of profitability, efficiency and competency. On the other hand, another school of thought is distinctively 'female' in that it is constructed around the notion of organizations as *social* settings, emphasizing social identity, coordination, the social function of conversations and the transformational power of knowledge through social learning and relationships between members as the central constitutive elements of firms.

Although the *social* paradigm of firms is relatively recent, it has suffered no shortage of proponents since the mid-1990s. In 1994, North had argued that: "institutions are the humanly devised constraints that structure human interaction. They are made up of formal constraints (e.g., rules, laws, constitutions), informal constraints (e.g., norms of behavior, conventions, self-imposed codes of conduct), and their enforcement characteristics."[20] However, it was not until 1996 that management theorists Kogut and Zander articulated the fundamental tenets of the *social* paradigm of firms in a seminal article, where it was argued that:

> A firm [is] a social community specializing in the speed and efficiency in the creation and transfer of knowledge. [Firms] provide the normative territory to which members identify. This identification […] defines the conventions and rules by which individuals coordinate their behavior and decision-making […] Second, the identification sets out the process by which learning is developed socially through the formation of values and converging expectations.[21]

These ideas resonate strongly with some of the central principles of systems theory that see organizations as living entities, intrinsically integrated with a diversity of elements that go well beyond those that form part of a production function. As Barnard wrote:

> Every formal organization is a social system, something much broader than a bare economic or political instrumentality or the

functional legal entity implicit in corporation law. As social systems organizations give expression to or reflect mores, patterns of culture, implicit assumptions as to the world, deep convictions, unconscious beliefs that make them largely autonomous moral institutions on which instrumental political, economic, religious, or other functions are superimposed or from which they evolve.[22]

Barnard highlighted the crucial role of formal organizations in creating common moral grounds for cooperation amongst its members. In 2002, management pundits Bartlett and Ghoshal highlighted the interplay between the establishment of a strong sense of social bonding, identity and moral commitments among a firm's members, and the attainment of superior organizational performance:

> Companies must reject the notion that loyalty among today's employees is dead and accept the challenge of creating an environment that will attract and energize people so that they commit to the organization. Higher employee turnover, the use of temporary help and the expansion of outsourcing are all part of the envisioned future. But if a company can outsource services or hire temporary expertise, so can its competitors. Such actions, therefore, are unlikely to lead to any competitive advantage [...] But the bonding process involves more than creating a sense of identity and belonging. It also must lead to an engaging and energizing feeling of commitment to the organization and its goals.[23]

Notwithstanding these notions, most of the theories of the firm developed over the second half of the 20th century are deeply inflenced by the 19th century 'male' paradigm of the firm that sees it as akin to a profitable and efficient production function. In 1992, Chandler described some of the prevailing theories of the firm, where its social aspects are seemingly reduced to co-ordination and monitoring activities of a rather administrative kind:

> At least four attributes of the firm have [...] appeared in the theoretical literature: [First] the firm is a legal entity — one that signs contracts with its suppliers, distributors, employees and often customers. It is also an administrative entity, for teams of managers must coordinate and monitor its different activities. Once established, a firm becomes a pool of physical facilities, learned skills and liquid capital. Finally, although this is rarely mentioned in the literature, "for profit" firms have been and still are the primary

instruments in capitalist economies for the production and distribution of current goods and services and for the planning and allocation for future production and distribution.[24]

Williamson's taxonomy of corporate organizations illustrates some of the
"administrative" aspects that Chandler probably had in mind. First, Williamson
defined the *integrated (unitary) corporation* as a centralized, functionally depart-
mentalized company that possesses a formal administrative center manned by
salaried managers. Second, the *multi-division corporation* consisted of semi-
autonomous operating units (profit centers) organized along product, brand, or
geographic lines. Third, the *conglomerate* rose to prominence following World
War II and had a diversified character that evolved as a technique for managing
diverse assets and coping with anti-trust legislation that targeted horizontally and
vertically integrated companies. Finally, while the conglomerate extended asset
management from specialized to diversified lines of business, the *multinational
enterprise* extended asset management from a domestic to an international base.[25]

   Other economic and management theorists have advanced their own classifications of modern corporations, where the view of the firm as primarily a production function seems to remain paramount. In 1985, Teece defined the
multinational enterprise as a firm that controls and manages production in more
than one country. It can generate similar kinds of output in different locations (a
horizontally integrated multinational enterprise) or use outputs from one location
as inputs for another (a vertically integrated multinational enterprise). The two
categories are not mutually exclusive and can (and often do) overlap.[26] Earlier on,
in 1973, Lorange had defined three types of multinational enterprise: a geographically oriented company, a product-oriented company, and an evolving
global company.[27] In the *geographically oriented company,* national units manufacture and market goods or services to address local preferences and demands.
The *product-oriented company* arranges its activities along product lines. The
evolving global company is the one in which management can "structurally,
behaviorally, and legally" allocate resources on an international basis.[28] In 1988,
Dunning defined the multinational enterprise as a multi-activity firm that engages
in foreign direct investment.[29] He noted that these kinds of enterprises undertake
cross border-transactions akin to international trading companies and operate two
or more production units similar to multi-plant domestic firms. Unlike the domestic firms or international trading companies, Teece saw multinational enterprises
owning and controlling foreign production facilities as well as internalizing
global markets for their intra-unit transactions.

   Already in 1986, the production-function and transactional metaphors underlying numerous theories of the firm were seen as insufficient to explain organizational

performance within the new economic and business realities that were emerging in a more global and inter-connected world. Thus, in 1986, Contractor wrote that:

> Our stereotype of the multinational corporation may need to be changed for at least some industries. A decade ago it was seen as a monopolistic entity, controlling or owning its inputs and outputs, and expanding alone into a foreign market, based on its technological, managerial, and marketing dominance [...] Alternatively, it was seen as a transnational chain of control "internalized" within the firm [...] In this view, the corporation appropriates unto itself the gains from global vertical or horizontal integration. Today we are in a more negotiated, circumscribed, and competitive world. In many situations, the international firm is better seen as a coalition of interlocked, quasi-arms length relationships. Its strategic degrees of freedom are at once increased by the globalization of markets [...] and decreased by the need to negotiate with other firms and governments. [30]

Against this background, additional taxonomies of firms arose where — interestingly — the new 'female' issues of co-operation underlying much of Contractor's view of a 'more negotiated, circumscribed world' seem to be missing. Instead, these new classifications continued to one-sidedly reflect the view of a fiercely competitive environment, where firms within industries address each other as rivals. Thus, in 1998 Hout, Porter and Rudden separated multinational enterprises into "multidomestic" and "global" categories. A *multidomestic company* is one that "pursues separate strategies in each of its foreign markets while viewing the competitive challenge independently."[31] Overseas subsidiaries of a multidomestic company are essentially self-governed, with strategically distinct operations. By contrast, a *global company* competes with its rivals worldwide and has centralized operations and strategy. While its subsidiaries may enjoy some degree of autonomy, their activities are driven by the demands of the enterprise as a whole. Subsidiary performance is judged vis-à-vis the effects it has on the company's global position.

The application of these taxonomies left outside not only important — female-like — aspects of the firms under study but also entire groups of new organizational forms that emerged throughout the 1990s in the eve of the information technology revolution, the increasing globalization and the end of the Cold War. During the first years of the 21st century, management theorists were able to describe these new organizations unveiling a surprising number of female-like characteristics intrinsic to them such as: adaptability and flexibility, an emphasis on co-ordination and interoperability, a preference for partnering together with other firms, the valuing of joint-efforts between partner firms, and a focus on sharing and co-operation.

One of these new types of organizational forms was the so-called *virtual enterprise*. In 2002, Chesbrough and Teece described it as an arrangement under which individual firms outsource part of their business activities to partner institutions. Virtual enterprises base their competitive advantage on flexibility and responsiveness. In environments characterized by rapid technological change they can use market forces and mechanisms to procure the latest technology and human skills, and design, assemble, promote, sell, and support their products faster and better than traditional corporations. Chesbrough and Teece pointed out that the real challenges of virtual corporations were their ability to co-ordinate and to create co-operative bondings between partner firms, especially whenever tensions might arise between the common good and the self-interest of the individual partners.[32] In 2003, Bartlett's and Ghoshal's definition of *transnational enterprise*, highlighted the integration of diverse people, joint responsibility and decision making, co-ordination among operating units, and cross-functional teams among its central characteristics.[33] In 2001, Winter and Szulanski, proposed *replicators* as separate institutional forms pursuing the "creation and operation of a large number of similar outlets that deliver a product or perform a service."[34] A fast-food hotel or banking chain as well as tax advisory outlets, test preparatory centers, and the like are typical examples of organizations that grow and adapt through *replicators*. Replicators achieve competitive advantage by creating and refining a business model, identifying its value-adding components, developing capabilities to understand and codify the processes involved in the utilization and commercialization of these features, discovering new environments in which the business model can be successfully grafted, and reproducing the operation with different human resources each time.

The impact of the new economic and business realities of the 1990s in the emergence of new organizational forms with female-like characteristics, also had an effect in the way in which management theorists thought about sources of company performance and competitive advantages. Cross-functional integration, inter-unit co-operation and the importance of the bondings between people in order to create valuable organizational knowledge, acquired a new relevance in these theorists' writings. In 2001, for example, pundits Martin and Eisenhardt coined the term 'cross-business synergies' as the total sum of the value created by a multi-business corporation's business lines minus the sum of the value that each business line could have generated on a stand-alone basis.[35] The resulting 'cross-business synergies' were an estimate of the organizational advantages that these corporations can achieve in excess of the traditional economies of scale, scope and market power. Positive cross-business synergies might arise whenever the sharing of resources (such as knowledge and the organizational skills of key managers) takes place among different business lines, leading to reconfiguring the organization in response to environmental changes and in a way that fosters greater internal co-operation as well as lower unit costs of production.

'Male' and 'Female' Approaches to Organizational Growth

It should be of little surprise that 'male' and female-like notions underlying how theorists think about economic firms have left its clear imprints in the way in which organizational performance is both defined and measured. Not only this has led to different groups of authors emphasizing fairly diverse aspects of organizational performance but also it is possible to recognize fundamentally different approaches to articulating *the same* performance dimensions within the relevant literature. The divide examined in the previous section between traditional economies of scale vis-à-vis the notion of cross-business synergies provides a good illustration of the former. An example that epitomizes how substantially different approaches to the same performance dimension can co-exist, is provided by the issue of organizational growth.

Growth is one aspect of organizational performance that is universally regarded as paramount within any reasonably market-oriented and capitalist economy. Notwithstanding this, fundamental differences in approach can be recognized at play once one looks slightly beyond the labels. On the one hand, one set of authors look at organizational growth as akin to physical enlargement, material increase or mechanistic expansion. This is usually expressed not only from the perspective of an organization's enlargement within the marketplace (i.e. revenue and market share growth) but also in terms of its manufacturing expansion (i.e. increase in production output, capacity or investments), the increase in the number of business-lines within the organization, the development of its geographic reach, its material size and so on. Thus, in 1979, Chandler pointed out that modern industrial enterprise grew not by merely expanding existing production, but by acquiring new manufacturing and distribution capabilities, sales and purchasing offices, transportation components, and research and development labs.[36]

On the other hand, a number of authors see organizational performance from a rather female-like perspective, as assessing the progress of the firm's shared understanding of — and ways of relating with — both its constitutive elements and the surrounding environment. These types of approaches regard learning and the firm's ability to overcome its organizational and cultural boundaries for continuous renewal, as critical aspects of organizational growth. As Inkpen and Crossan observed in 1995:

> Organizations can grow in the traditional sense of increased capital or revenues. From a learning perspective, organizations grow when there is an increase in shared understanding involving the organization, its environment and the relationship between the two [...] When an evolving and enhanced understanding is translated into action, organizational learning is like the fountain of youth: it represents the organization's ability to undergo continual renewal, thereby prolonging the organization's life indefinitely.[37]

In 1986, Bartlett and Ghoshal applied these notions within the context of multinational companies growing out of their organizational boundaries. They noted two structural problems they believed could hold multinational organizations back — overcentralization and "headquarters hierarchy syndrome."[38] The problem of overcentralization occurs if multinationals treat their foreign subsidiaries homogeneously, expressing subsidiaries' roles and responsibilities in the same general terms, applying uniform control systems worldwide, and evaluating country managers against standardized criteria. The headquarters hierarchy issue grows out of the overcentralization problem and represents a strong tendency by headquarters managers to try to co-ordinate all key decisions and control global resources. This type of tendency makes subsidiaries act purely as implementers and adapters of the global strategy in their localities. Bartlett and Ghoshal pointed out that the effects of these two problems impede the effectiveness of a multinational enterprise in three ways. First, symmetrical treatment results in overcompensation for the needs of smaller and less crucial markets and under representation of the requirements of strategically important ones. Second, relegation of subsidiaries to the role of implementers leads to the underutilization of a company's worldwide assets and organizational capabilities. Finally, over expanding control of headquarters deprives country managers from their creative energies making them feel disenfranchised.

Overcoming cultural boundaries has also been recognized as crucial for organizations determined to release themselves from some of their main constraints to growth. A classical example of this is given by the interplay between an organization's national culture vis-à-vis the cultures of the countries it operates in. For instance, Dunning and Bansal remarked that culture impacts the activities of a multinational enterprise in two ways. First, culture influences key national institutions such as government, the legal system, property rights and so on, by supporting certain kinds of behavior and then compensating those who comply and by penalizing those who do not. For example, the keiretsu and government–business relationships in Japan would be considered inappropriate in the United States with its system of checks and balances and separation of power between legislative, executive, and judicial. Dunning and Bansal noted that culture affects multinational enterprises insofar as it creates competitive advantages or poses disadvantages to corporations competing on a global scale. Second, as an enterprise looks to operate beyond national borders, its choices will be impacted by the culture it grew in. The home culture of a multinational enterprise will determine its propensity to engage in foreign direct investment, make locational and modal choices, relying on specific organizational techniques, and be able or incapable of adapting to local capabilities and tastes. As Dunning and Bansal explained, a multinational enterprise will also have an effect on the host country culture based on the level of host country's ethnocentricity, multinational's length of stay, and embeddedness.[39] In 1985, Kogut echoed these notions by proposing that institutional and cultural differences could pose powerful barriers to the transfer of critical elements of the value-added that drive the competitive advantage of multinational enterprises, such as marketing programs, distributional networks and after-sale services.[40]

From the perspective of how organizations address the issue of top-line growth, they can essentially look either internally or externally for growth opportunities. A rapid way to grow is often to look externally to the surrounding marketplace for companies to acquire, merge or ally with. Alternatively, firms can look internally to their own strengths and resources for strategic growth options. Internal growth might be slower but often result in enhanced sustainability and durability, and indeed in improved performance, over the long term. Nurturing internal growth is achieved by focusing on a firm's internal strengths and capabilities, and on maximizing the benefits resulting from these strengths. This may include growing the portfolio of products, services and markets, through existing clients, as well as winning new clients. This approach prioritizes delighting the customer, which can be defined as engendering customer loyalty by exceeding expectations, delivering a clearly differentiated product or service and superior customer service. It uses continuous innovation to create new business opportunities. Because an internally oriented approach focuses on nurturing a firm's capabilities to achieve sustainable and organic growth, and it places a premium on strengthening relationships with existing customers, it can be regarded as a 'female' approach to top-line growth.[41]

Companies that proactively pursue an external strategic approach to growth strive to achieve their business goals through mergers & acquisitions(M&A), alliances, joint ventures, and the like. Benefits of external growth approaches include an increased portfolio of products and services, diversity of their offering, as well as access to new clients and (in the case of cross-border activities) geographic markets.M&A, takeovers and leveraged buyouts are all ways of growing by buying other companies that have been identified as strategically important, and incorporating them into the existing business. Strategic alliances are usually intended to enable a company to exploit the strategic advantage of another company in a way that is mutually beneficial. The aim of joint ventures is often to allow companies to reduce risk in an unknown market, with local partners being compensated for their knowledge, experience and contacts.

There are a number of immediate benefits of this type of external growth, such as access to markets, earnings, employees and other corporate assets. Additionally, there are synergistic benefits resulting from technical economies (such as scale economies for a more efficient use of resources), pecuniary economics (resulting from the market power due to firm size), and diversification economies (due to greater leverage for improved loan conditions) and lessened costs (due to the reduced probability of bankruptcy). Aiello and Watkins describe the core challenge in assessing potential acquisitions as the need to balance strategic thinking with opportunistic action. As such, savvy acquirers assess a large volume of opportunities, while maintaining a strategic focus. They stress the need to remain analytical; to avoid getting caught up in the excitement of the deal as this can mask fundamental flaws in the operating assumptions.[42]

The disadvantages of external approaches to growth are mainly centered on the risks involved with any type of partnership: mistrust, lack of strategic or corporate cultural fit, and an inability to integrate. External approaches to growth usually are 'male' and predatory in nature, focused on hunting down competitors and creating alliances with companies aimed at gaining an advantage. Although occasionally 'mergers of equals' are approached as intrinsically co-operative forms of external growth, it is doubtful whether such a thing as an egalitarian merger has been ever implemented in practice. Regarding strategic alliances, although in many cases they are considered as co-operative forms of external growth, the mainstream literature paradoxically regards the chronic instability of alliances as stemming from primarily transactional, positional and conflict-related sources:

> [Six major groups of] theories have been advanced to explain the instabilities [of] alliances. A first group of theories regard alliances as relational contracts, where instability stems from a lack of historical, trusting involvement between the allies. The second set of theories maintains that alliances allow the joining firms to achieve lower transaction costs vis-à-vis the marketplace, with instability arising as a result of the opportunistic behavior of the allies.

	Economic Factors		Growth		Nature of Firms		
	Capital	Labor	Organizational	Top-Line	Classical	Transactional	Interactional
Male	The acquisition as well as the efficient allocation and utilization of capital is one of the key drivers of profit maximization and the economic performance of firms (Penrose, 1959).	The acquisition as well as the efficient allocation and utilization of labor is one of the key drivers of profit maximization and the economic performance of firms. Employees must serve the needs of the system (Penrose, 1959).	Organizations grow by increased capital and revenues, by expanding production and by acquiring new manufacturing and distribution capabilities, sales and purchasing offices, transportation components, research and development labs, etc. (Chandler, 1979).	External top-line growth via acquisitions, mergers, strategic alliances, joint ventures, and the like. (Aiello & Watkins, 2000; Das & Bing-Sheng Teng, 2000)	The firm is a legal, administrative, and physical entity involved in producing and distributing goods and services efficiently in order to maximize profits. Firm's profits depend on its possession of resources important to production and distribution (Penrose, 1959; Conner, 1991).	Firms and markets are alternative models for managing transactions (Coase, 1937). The performance goal of the firm is to economize transaction costs instead of maximizing profits (Williamson, 1975).	
Female	Workers on whose productivity and performance the firm relies for its success should be regarded as capital and not as labor, and ought to be nurtured as knowledge professionals within the firm (Drucker, 2002).	In the knowledge driven environment, the system must nurture the needs of the employees in order to foster firm's productivity and performance. (Drucker, 2002; Bartlett & Ghoshal, 2002).	Growth as a firm's ability to transcend its organizational and cultural boundaries for continuous renewal that prolongs the organization's life indefinitely (Inkpen & Crossan, 1995; Dunning & Bansal, 1997).	Internal top-line growth via the nurturing of organic revenue enhancing efforts within the organization (Kim & Mauborgne, 2004)			A firm is a social community specialized in the transformation of knowledge and learning into economically valuable products and services (Kogut & Zander, 96). Virtual enterprises obtain performance advantages based on flexibility (Chesbrough & Teece, 2002).

Note. Examples of authoritative references are provided between parentheses and described fully in the references section of this chapter.

Figure 7: Some economic approaches to explaining organizational performance.

A third category of theories views alliances as bargaining negotiations and business games that the allies play for market advantage, where instability arises whenever cheating an ally or acting based on self-interest provides greater payoffs than cooperative behavior. The strategic management school of thought regards alliances as a company's means to achieve superior strategic positioning vis-à-vis its rivals, with instability stemming from setting unrealistic strategic goals. The resource dependence and transitional theories maintain that the instability of alliances is to be expected after the allies achieve the kind of resources they wanted from each other, or as a result of alliances naturally evolving into different organizational forms. Lastly, the internal tensions perspective suggests that the instability of alliances stems from the development of pairs of competing forces, i.e. cooperation versus competition, rigidity versus flexibility and short-term versus long-term orientation.[43]

However, in many cases, firms give little thought to post-deal implementation, and as a result mergers and similar deals fail in implementation as often (or indeed more often) as they succeed. The difficulty of managing cultural and organizational boundaries during the post-deal integration stages is often cited as a major cause of failure in M&As, joint ventures and strategic alliances alike.[44]

'Male' is Knowledge 'Female' is Understanding

Most theories of the firm exhibit – in a more or less articulated fashion — the notion that properly managing knowledge within a firm is fundamental to organizational performance. Their ideas have led to a vast output, part of which is grouped within the so-called 'knowledge management' field whereas other important aspects can be found in attempts to formalize a 'knowledge-based' theory of the firm. Both these areas are relevant to examining how different management authors have addressed the issue of 'organizational knowledge'[45] in connection to organizational performance. Most authors looking at this connection have proposed knowledge management models that subscribe to either of the two main schools of thought. One set of approaches look at knowledge as akin to a tangible asset that can be clearly identified, categorized and transferred in support of organizational tasks, through explicit, logical and efficient knowledge management processes. Not surprisingly, the use of information technology (IT) for efficient codification and storage of knowledge as well as to render such explicit knowledge available throughout the organization in an efficient way, are central issues to these kinds of approaches. Because the organizational knowledge stemming from the application of these models closely resembles a firm's stock of *codifiable* intellectual capital at any given point of time, one could refer to them as 'intellectual capital' models of knowledge management.

Nevertheless, in 2002, Birkinshaw and Sheehan pointed out that although knowledge is not static, these types of models frequently treat it as if it were.[46] An alternative school of thought in fact sees knowledge as dynamic and inseparable from an individual's organic and cognitive functions — body and mind. From this perspective, organizational knowledge is seen as firmly rooted in the organization's social and learning processes. These models thus emphasize social structures and processes within which knowledge is created and shared. Since knowledge is transferred between people, the social element of knowledge management is critical. Central to this approach are, for example, communities of practice, or groups whose members regularly engage in knowledge sharing and learning based on common interests. Organizational knowledge cannot be separated from the relationship between action, understanding and communication, which is a key component of knowledge creation and dissemination. As such, the notion of organizational conversation is key. The use of storytelling to communicate explicit and tacit knowledge, as well as to nurture community, is one way to facilitate organizational conversation. These social models also emphasize the complexity of organizational knowledge. The latter is neither entirely explicit nor tangible and central to knowledge management is the social component in which interactivity plays a key role. Therefore, important parts of organizational knowledge are bound to resist codification, as they rely heavily on social interactions that are, to a great extent, of a subjective, *tacit,* subconscious and spontaneous nature. These social models also highlight the transformational capability that organizational knowlege has to synthesize the subjective cognition of individuals, and turn it into products and services that customers demand — or into new organizational configurations that allow a firm to adapt within a constantly changing marketplace.

Intellectual capital models of knowledge management appear as largely 'male' in that they conceive knowledge as tantamount to an objective and tangible resource that ought to be handled competently and efficiently in support of organizational tasks. On the other hand, social models of knowledge management, with their emphasis on social interactions, transformational relationships and their view of organizational knowledge as a synthesis of individuals' subjective cognititon through joint and shared efforts, appear as rather 'female' in nature. Interestingly, whereas the social interpretations of organizational knowledge closely follow the original meaning of the term *knowledge*, the intellectual capital models of knowledge management treat it in ways that recall the ancient meaning of the words 'data' and 'information'. This point is revealing of the more subtle differences and complementarity between what has been termed the 'social' and the 'intellectual capital' approaches to knowledge management.

Greek philosophers such as Plato and Aristotle distinguished between *theoretical knowledge* and *knowledge through direct observation and experience*. In *either* case, they used the word *gnosis* to denote the "intuitive process of gaining a deep insight of oneself and nature, attained through an intimate and personal *relationship* between self and object, and implying a direct acquaintance, acceptance and equality between both. This is equivalent to the ancient philosophical interpretation of *gnosis* as 'understanding intuition', or the modern psychological one as 'perception by the way of the unconscious'."[47] Gnosis thus refers to a cognitive psychological process of subjective learning and deep understanding through a flow of both spontaneous and reflective thoughts inside an individual's mind and body, the central parts of which are of an intuitive, subconscious and *tacit* nature. In turn, the word 'knowledge' comes from the Latin *verb cognoscere*. In its original form, this very important word was made up of the Latin prefix *co*, meaning 'experiencing something together with somebody else' (i.e. as in 'co-llaborate' — to labor together with others —, or 'co-operate' — to operate jointly with others, 'compassion' and so on), and the Greek word *gnosis*. Therefore, *co-gnoscere* — the Latin *verb* from where our word 'knowledge' derives — simply means: *to experience gnosis together with others*. In other words, it means for a group of people to get together and carry out social interactions in order to gain a first-hand insight and a deep understanding of any specific subject matter. *Cognoscere* thus refers to the enactment of a living and social process involving groups of individuals cooperating together around a common purpose, a process that is at the same time conscious and subconscious, spontaneous and reflective, aware and intuitive.

By contrast, *indicium,* the Latin equivalent of our term 'data', also means 'evidence' or 'an indication'. It is therefore something empirical, factual, manifest, which can be recognized objectively and gathered as evidence. And *informationem* — the root of our modern word for information — comes from the Latin words *in* and *forma,* meaning: to put the empirical elements of a phenomenon *in* a concrete *form*, shape or representation. In other words, *informationem* is data subjectively modified (or mediated) by the individual(s) giving it a concrete form or representation.

Thus, if an ancient Roman philosopher could materialize inside our modern corporations through some sort of magical 'time-channel', he or she would refer to all of an organization's objective, codifiable and codified data, information and knowledge (including *all* of its IT software and hardware tools) simply as *indicium et informationem*, and would refer to the social dialogues and living interactions between managers (either face-to-face or through telephone, video-conferencing and the like) as *cognoscere*. Our ancient Roman friend will no doubt surprise us by her initial difficulty to use the term 'knowledge' as a noun — like we do — but her dynamic use of it as an *action verb* instead. 'Knowledging' or 'to knowledge' — he would "mistakenly" remark — whenever she would notice managers in face-to-face meetings or engaged in telephone and video conferencing. This is in revealing contrast to our more static rendering of the term 'knowledge' in modern times.

Indicium and *informationem* are the original terms that describe more closely the 'intellectual capital' models' treatment of organizational knowledge whereas the verb *cognoscere* captures with stunning precision the 'social' models' definition of organizational knowledge. But this tells only part of the story. There are of course inherent complementarities between these two approaches to organizational knowledge, and it is the way in which these are recognized and blended inside organizations what seems to drive performance results in the end:

One key reason why knowledge management initiatives fail so often is that companies misunderstand what drives knowledge advantages in the first place. Knowledge exists in the minds of *knowers*, that is people - individuals, groups and teams - communicating meanings and interpretations of reality. Outside people's minds, knowledge does not exist – only information [Therefore the] centre-piece of any knowledge management strategy, system or structure should refer to the particular ways in which individuals and groups of people learn and communicate, ably supported by the right information resources and technology. Instead, however, companies often start in exactly the opposite direction. They first choose to buy or design a 'knowledge management system', often relying on outside IT specialists, and subsequently move on to train the employees who will use the system by gathering existing company 'knowledge', or by creating, codifying and distributing new information. Companies that think about knowledge management primarily in terms of IT or automation implicitly believe that *real* knowledge is akin to the possession of critical information, which can be stored, codified or somehow *freezed* internally. Indeed, it is common to hear management executives, academics or practitioners talk about *explicit* or *tacit* knowledge, unaware that this might represent a fundamental contradiction in terms. Indeed, by its very definition, all knowledge is tacit: an individual or group-based psychological experience of learning.[48]

'Male' and 'Female' Knowledge-Drivers of Performance

Most authors looking at the connection between knowledge management and organizational performance have advanced perspectives that reflect their underlying 'male' or 'female' views of organizational knowledge. A typical illustration of this is provided by the debate around where should we look for the sources of knowledge-based performance advantages within organizations. On the one hand, some authors take a rather 'male' response to this issue, highlighting the critical importance of making knowledge available in a compact, explicit, coherent and *efficient* way throughout the organization. This line of thought is been around for some time. Already in 1945, for example, Von Hayek argued that: "the knowledge of the circumstances of which we must make use never exists in concentrated or integrated form, but solely as the dispersed of incomplete and often contradictory knowledge which all the separate individuals possess."[49] On the other hand, a series of authors have stressed an organization's leadership qualities, in particular its leaders' ability to shape a shared purpose, social values and key organizational structure, processes, routines and procedures, as critical drivers of knowledge-based performance advantages. Supporting these notions, in 1998, Sanderson pointed out that unlike structural capital — which is not specific to an organization — human capital needs to be placed within an organization's unique web of procedures and systems. He defined knowledge management as a key part of these organizational procedures that help a firm transform human intellectual capital into organizational capital, and to codify the procedure for repeated use.[50] In 2002, Bartlett and Ghoshal echoed this type of perspective and placed it in a far broader organizational context:

> At the heart of the problem is a widespread failure to recognize that although knowledge management can be supported by an efficient technical infrastructure, it is operated through a social network. [...] Senior managers [...] main contribution has shifted from deciding the strategic content to framing the organizational context. That means creating a sense of purpose that not only provides an integrating framework for bottom-up strategic initiatives, but also injects meaning into individual effort. It means articulating company values that not only align organizational effort with the overall enterprise objectives, but also define a community to which individuals want to belong. And it means developing organizational processes that not only get work done effectively, but also ensure the empowerment, development and commitment of all members of the organization. The philosophical shift requires executives to

expand beyond strategy, structure and systems to a simultaneous focus on the company's purpose, process and people.[51]

Bartlett's and Ghoshal's views of what drive knowledge-based organizational advantages, reflect the notion that, within organizations, human beings often need to make decisions within highly fluid, complex and constantly changing organizational environments. In this context, Von Hayek's vision of a fully integrated, efficient and coherent informational environment is to be largely regarded as an elusive dream. In fact, in a series of seminal works published over the second half of the 20th century, Simon highlighted that human beings have a limited ability to grasp complex situations and to adapt to their external environment. He called this phenomenon *bounded rationality* and suggested that when a new challenge arises, a person's natural response is to focus on the aspects of the situation she or he considers as key, and to form a model of the challenge based on the chosen characteristics and trends. A rational assessment of the external reality then takes place within the context of the model instead of the actual challenge. Within organization theory, this type of explanation is referred to as subgoal determination. Whenever an organizational objective cannot be directly and explicitly linked to known actions, decisions will be based on subordinate goals that possess the required links. The formulation of subordinate goals is neither universal nor consistent; their selection depends on knowledge, experience, and the organizational role of the decision-maker.[52] By contrast to classical economic theory, which assumes rational choice, constant utility, and complete knowledge of characteristics, probabilities, and consequences of all alternatives available, the model of bounded rationality suggests that organizational decisions are made under imperfect information, and that a decision-maker rarely possesses a consistent utility function for comparing heterogeneous alternatives. These kinds of views were clearly illustrated in 1964 by Arrow, who defined organizations as groups of individuals embarking upon achieving some common goals.[53] These groups are cohesive but not uniform: every member of an organization has his or her own objectives, which are often different from the objectives of the organization itself. Within an organization, each individual can make a range of decisions that are bounded in part by the external environment and in part by the decisions of other members. Members of the organization communicate to each other some but not all of their observations about the functioning of an organization and about the outside world. In 1992, Chandler further illustrated the critical role played by unique organizational characteristics such as a firm's leadership approaches as well as its key processes, routines and procedures, in driving knowledge-based organizational performance:

> Such learned knowledge manifested itself in the firms' facilities for production and distribution. It was even more evident in the firms'

product- and process-specific human skills. Of these skills the most critical were those of the senior executives – the top managers who recruited and motivated the middle and lower level managers, defined and allocated their responsibilities, monitored and coordinated their performance, and who, in addition, planned and allocated resources for these enterprises as a whole. Such knowledge and skills were developed by learning through trial and error, feedback and evaluation; thus, the skills of individuals depended on the organizational setting in which they were developed and used. Such learned skills and knowledge were company-specific and industry-specific. They were not, of course, patentable. They were difficult to transfer from one industry to another, or even from one company to another, precisely because they had been learned within a very specific organizational context.[54]

Moreover, in 1996 Kogut and Zander suggested that an organization's behavior is embedded in the unique way in which it develops know-how (or *procedural knowledge*) over time: "Firm behavior reflects the enactment of learned skills and routines grounded in the acquisition of procedural knowledge."[55] These views echo Simon's earlier notions that human learning within organizations is very much influenced by the internal environment. By occupying a formal position within a company, for example, each employee takes on a role, defined by Simon as "a system of prescribed decision premises."[56] Roles tell employees where to look for information and what techniques they ought to use in order to process it. The learned experiences associated with their roles determine the body of knowledge of each employee. This body of knowledge is known in psychology as a "production system", and the collection of the production systems of a firm's employees collectively represents the memory of the organization. The organizational structure influences this memory in two ways. First, laterally, that is by assigning roles and prescribing the paths of organizational learning. Second, dynamically, in other words by facilitating the speed of organizational turnover. Simon noted that high organizational turnover could be a double-edged sword. On one hand, it allows an institution to import new skills and knowledge both quickly and cheaply, and get rid of organizational rut. On the other, it increases the costs of training and socializing and can undermine organizational memory by inhibiting the creation of a common culture. Organizational structure is also conducive to organizational problem solving and decision-making — choosing issues, setting goals, developing suitable courses of action, and evaluating and deciding among alternatives.[57] When employees assume organizational positions, their roles dictate what types of decisions to make, based on which information and how to enforce them. These decisions are in turn influenced by the organizational hierarchy and its associated flow of information among the various organizational units.[58]

Another set of views linking knowledge management to organizational performance highlight a firm's female-like ability to make knowledge a fully *interactive* and *social* dimension within the organization. One way in which firms do this is by developing *ad-hoc* capabilities to transferring and sharing prior knowledge that individual members have, for future use. These knowledge sharing and knowledge transferring activities not only refer to the internal organization but also to the interfaces between the organization and the external world. This is the essential idea behind Cohen and Levinthal's concept of 'absorptive capacities':

> The premise of the notion of absorptive capacity is that the organization needs prior related knowledge to assimilate and use new knowledge [...] An organization's absorptive capacity will depend on the absorptive capacities of its individual members [...] A firm's absorptive capacity is not, however, simply the sum of the absorptive capacities of its employees [It] refers not only to the acquisition or assimilation of information by an organization but also to the organization's ability to exploit it. Therefore, an organization's absorptive capacity does not simply depend on the organization's direct interface with the external environment. It also depends on transfers of knowledge across and within subunits that may be quite removed from the original point of entry. Thus, to understand the sources of a firm's absorptive capacity, we focus on the structure of communication between the external environment and the organization, as well as among the subunits of the organization, and also on the character and distribution of expertise within the organization.[59]

In 1998, Inkpen echoed these notions within a more general framework by arguing that: "While organizations cannot create knowledge without individuals, unless individual knowledge is shared with other individuals and groups, the knowledge will have a limited impact on organizational effectiveness. Thus, organizational knowledge creation should be viewed as a process whereby the knowledge held by individuals is amplified and internalized as part of an organization's knowledge base."[60] In the same year, Kusunoki and Nonaka proposed an interactive model of knowledge-based organizational advantages that looked at corporate performance as a function of strategy and structure, which, in turn, were nothing more than the stable patterns of interaction between the components of the organization's knowledge base. Their model thus divided organizational knowledge into three layers: knowledge base, knowledge frame and knowledge dynamics.[61]

Knowledge base is the layer that includes distinctive units of knowledge capable of generating organizational competencies. It can be functional knowledge held by a specific group of employees, product or process patents, information technologies, databases and the like. Knowledge base represents a registry of knowledge capabilities an organization possesses, similar to a company's balance sheet. Knowledge frame is a layer that captures direct and indirect linkages between individual units of knowledge, their hierarchy and shape. According to the two authors, knowledge frame details configuration of organizational knowledge and the effects of the knowledge structure on knowledge acquisition, creation and application. While knowledge frame takes a snapshot of knowledge linkages, knowledge dynamics evaluates knowledge interactions over time. For example, knowledge dynamics include the processes of communication and co-ordination across different units, leadership or strategy continuity, and so on. Knowledge dynamics describe how knowledge is combined and transformed, and how the change in an organization's knowledge base or knowledge frame can have a non-linear impact on organizational performance. Nonaka and Konno thus suggested that organizational knowledge leads to organizational performance through a four-stage knowledge management process they called SECI: socialization, externalization, combination and internalization. The first stage of the knowledge management within a company, socialization, implies the sharing of tacit knowledge between individuals. This sharing leads to externalization — the articulation of tacit knowledge and translation of knowledge into explicit in order to be understood by others. After externalization comes combination — the communication, diffusion and systematization of explicit knowledge into a more complex set of ideas. Finally, the higher-order explicit knowledge is internalized and becomes tacit again, but this time at an organizational level.

In 2002, Holsapple and Joshin proposed an alternative framework to SECI that takes the outside world into account. They divided firm-wide knowledge activities into four categories: acquiring knowledge, selecting knowledge, internalizing knowledge and using knowledge.[62] Acquiring knowledge is to accept a unit of knowledge from the external environment and to transform it into a concept or a process that can be used internally by the organization. Selecting knowledge refers to extracting a unit of knowledge from the organization's internal knowledge base and giving it an appropriate form to be used in a specified activity. Internalizing knowledge means altering the existing organizational knowledge that could be either internally generated or acquired. Finally, using knowledge means applying current organizational knowledge to generate new knowledge or to externalize the existing one.

During the same year of 2002, Hansen added another important element to these kinds of *interactive* knowledge management approaches in the form of: inter-unit knowledge sharing.[63] Hansen's inter-unit knowledge sharing is slightly different from Nonaka and Konno's idea of socialization, in that it deals with knowledge that has already been made explicit but cannot be yet considered as knowledge combination. Rather, inter-unit knowledge sharing stands for assessing related knowledge content by using lateral organizational networks across business-unit boundaries. Such sharing can be direct — that is, provide immediate access to knowledge — or indirect, in other words providing information about opportunities. Hansen's study of inter-unit sharing in new product development showed that business units with short (direct) path lengths in a knowledge network obtained more existing knowledge from other units and completed their projects faster than those with long (indirect) path lengths. A primary reason for this is that long path lengths lead to information distortion, making the search for useful knowledge more difficult. For example, people who exchange information are prone to misunderstand each other, forget details, and inadvertently or deliberately filter information, failing to mention all that they know or withholding specific aspects. Yet, direct knowledge pathways can be a double-edged sword: while they provide immediate cross border access to knowledge and are helpful when such knowledge is non-codified or tacit, they are costly to maintain and are no different from indirect pathways when the knowledge to be transferred is explicit or codified.

The female-like views of organizational knowledge as adaptive and transformational emphasize these *dynamic* aspects of knowledge as critical to organizational performance. In 1992, Chandler illustrated these notions by arguing that:

> If […] company-specific and industry-specific capabilities continued to be enhanced by constant learning about products, processes, customers, suppliers and other relationships between workers and managers within the firm, enterprises in capital-intensive industries were usually able to remain competitive and profitable. If not, they normally lost market share in domestic and international markets to those firms that did.[64]

The idea that the dynamic aspects of knowledge are critical to organizational performance was also acknowledged in Birkinshaw and Sheehan's theory of knowledge lifecycle. In their view, organizational knowledge follows a traditional S-curve that has four stages: knowledge creation, knowledge mobilization, knowledge diffusion, and knowledge commoditization. Knowledge creation is the emergence of a new idea in someone's head. At this stage the idea is tacit and knowledge creation follows ad hoc procedures. It cannot be described well using formal statistics or statements. The first stage of knowledge life cycle is heavily dependent on creativity and experimentation, but also requires accountability and discipline. Knowledge mobilization is the stage at which the idea becomes more concrete and its value is established through testing and validation. Knowledge moves from tacit to explicit and becomes codified so that the information about a discovery can be shared. At this stage the company stimulates the refinement of the new knowledge internally but tries to keep it concealed from an outside world. It becomes a source of a company's competitive advantage. Knowledge diffusion is the stage when the idea transcends company boundaries and becomes widely accepted in the marketplace. The idea stops being a source of competitive advantage and becomes available to anyone who wants to use it. Company extracts value from the idea by selling it to customers, licensing it to cooperators, and attempting to position it as an industry standard. The last stage, knowledge commoditization is a period when the idea moves from restricted to unrestricted domain, and becomes a public good. It permits companies and academics to study best practices and keep abreast of the latest developments, contributing to the general knowledge. For the company that supplied the idea, the commoditization stage provides an opportunity to promote its name. Birkinshaw and Sheehan also noted that while all organizational knowledge follows the lifecycle, the speed of the movement varies from case to case. They described three factors that can accelerate the movement, and two factors that can slow it down. The accelerating factors are the ability of competitors to acquire private organizational knowledge through reverse engineering, personnel pouching and the like, the natural leakage of knowledge through interaction with suppliers and customers, and the intentional codification and diffusion by a company. The decelerating factors are the extent through which an idea can be protected by product or process patent, and the tacit nature of some knowledge, which defies codification.

A distinction between SECI and the knowledge lifecycle model must be drawn. At a first glance the two models look very similar: both have four stages, both use comparable names. However, the two frameworks describe entirely different processes. The knowledge lifecycle addresses the growth of a competitive idea. By the end of the knowledge lifecycle, the new knowledge moves from the private to the public domain and becomes explicit. The focus of the SECI model is on organizational interaction. By the last stage of the SECI, knowledge has once again become tacit and remains restricted to only the company employees. The SECI approach describes a repeating cycle of knowledge formation within a firm, while the knowledge lifecycle portrays the interaction between the knowledge created within a company and the outside world.

The female-like views of interactive and dynamic aspects of organizational knowledge driving performance advantages raise critical issues of leadership and human resources as central to achieving these types of results within organizations. Bartlett and Ghoshal articulated some of these issues: "Unlike capital, scarce knowledge and expertise [...] resides in the heads of individuals at all levels and is embedded in the relationships of work groups [...] Therefore, rather than allocate capital to competing projects (the zero-sum game), senior managers must nurture individual expertise and initiative, then leverage it through cross-unit sharing (the positive-sum game)."[65] The issue of crossing boundaries (i.e. organizational, cultural, geographic and mindset boundaries) is also very obvious in the knowledge sharing and transferring activities that are so central to *all* the interactive and dynamic approaches to attaining knowledge-based advantages we have previously examined. Thus, some authors have highlighted that attracting, nurturing and retaining a cadre of managers with the *execution skills* to co-ordinate smoothly across these types of boundaries is critical to obtaining knowledge-based advantages within organizations.[66]

From a similar perspective, in 2002 Holsapple and Joshi defined leadership, co-ordination, and measurement as "mission-critical knowledge management activities."[67] According to them, capable leadership in the knowledge-based economy means creating conditions that encourage employees to contribute to the organization's pool of knowledge, allow easy access to knowledge resources, and promote the development of knowledge management skills. Successful co-ordination harmonizes activities by making certain that the correct knowledge resources are employed by a company at every point of time and that these resources can make connections whenever required. Measurement means installing systems and tools that are able to evaluate knowledge resources, knowledge co-ordination, and knowledge leadership, and indicate when or whether adjustments may be needed. Not less importantly, in 2003 Kim and Mauborgne identified process fairness as one of the critical elements of successful knowledge management approaches within organizations.[68] They argued that people not only care about outcomes and results but also about the processes leading to them. For example, employees want to know that their point of view was considered even if it was rejected during the application of a knowledge management process. Kim and Mauborgne suggested that process fairness can be achieved in this area by using three mutually reinforcing principles: engagement, explanation and clarity of expectations.

'Male' and 'Female' Strategies Driving Performance

The first systematic use of the word 'strategy' in modern times took place within the archetypal 'male' activity of war. In 1779, the Conde de Guibert published a volume in Neuchatel under the title: *Defense of the System of Modern War*. In this book, the Conde de Guibert coined the term 'military strategy' to describe a new discipline that concerned itself with the art of moving very large contingents of troops in a co-ordinated fashion in order to attain a given political objective.[69] This seemingly simple notion was to have a profound and lasting influence in fields well beyond the military. Strategy as a management discipline is in fact deeply rooted in military thinking. Before the advent of business schools, a military career was seen as the requisite for entering the business realm. But there also emerged epistemological connections from the outset. Within the field of strategic management it became commonplace to conceptualize the marketplace as a battlefield where companies need to design *competitive strategies* in order to aggressively gain positional advantages to take market share and undercut their competitors, and as a result obtain market dominance. Firms need to use capital and assets efficiently in production and distribution in order to gain cost advantages or to differentiate their position from their competitors. The entirety of a company's strategic actions seemed to occur in response to an external threat or opportunity — either in the long or short term. Not surprisingly, by the early 1980s, competitive strategy was largely seen as a zero-sum game.

Michael E. Porter, for example, saw the company surrounded by its suppliers, customers, competitors and substitutes, engaged in a battle with them to capture the maximum possible economic value.[70] He pointed out that the interplay of all fundamental economic and technical characteristics of an industry can be summarized using the framework of "five forces": the bargaining power of buyers, the bargaining power of suppliers, the threat of new entry, the threat of substitutes and the intensity of rivalry. Porter also suggested that a company is more competitive than its peers only if it can consistently provide a superior value to its customers at the same cost as its rivals, an equal value at a lower cost, or both. He described two channels of competitive dominance: operational effectiveness, or achievement of best practices that allow a company to efficiently utilize its inputs, and strategic positioning; or capture of larger market share based on product leadership, customer loyalty or geographic access. Unlike the behavioral economists who argue that operational effectiveness is a primary driver for the entire competitiveness paradigm, Porter associated best practices largely with cost minimization and strategic positioning largely with revenue maximization in a very classical way.

In 1994, Hamel and Prahalad added a dynamic dimension to Porter's approach to industry structure analysis.[71] They stressed that, as the competitive landscape changes over time, a skills-set that made a company the leader of today might become obsolete tomorrow, and a market that was rapidly growing might suddenly slow down or altogether disappear. Therefore within the industry rivals jockey for future positioning by attempting to create and dominate new market segments and by constantly searching for new applications of existing capabilities. Hamel and Prahalad called capabilities that are crucial for company's success the "core competencies" and defined them as skills and technologies possessed by business units that are competitively unique, contribute disproportionally to customer-perceived value, and establish the basis for entry into new markets. They argued that a company's competitiveness is a function of how well it is able to leverage its existing core competencies in the current environment, extend existing core competencies into new fields, develop new core competencies to ensure continuity of market leadership and pursue new core competencies and new markets simultaneously. The subsequent interest in building and leveraging unique internal capabilities caused a gradual shift in emphasis from value appropriation to value creation. As information and knowledge came to provide competitive advantage, the game shifted to more female-like territory. Unlike capital, knowledge actually increases when shared, thus eliminating the need for a one-sided focus on zero-sum games. Clearly, an emphasis on value creation demands a different strategic management approach than a focus on value appropriation. In 2002, Bartlett and Ghoshal captured the sign of the times by highlighting that: "Recognizing that the company's scarce resource is knowledgeable people means a shift in the whole concept of value management within the corporation."[72]

Parallel to this, Porter's system of "five forces" was being amended by Brandenburger and Nalebuff, who conceived strategy and tactics not only from the perspective of competitive zero-sum games but also in the more female-like terms of co-operation and positive-sum games. In 1997, they in fact proposed that in addition to buyers, suppliers, substitutes, new entrants and industry rivals there exists a sixth market force, which they called "complementors."[73] Brandenburger and Nalebuff defined complementors as players whose products or services create an extra profit for a company either by increasing demand for its products and services or by reducing its costs. For example, a producer whose merchandise makes customers interested in purchasing the company's products, or a business whose use of the company's supplier allows the latter to cut prices across the board, are typical examples of a company's complementors. Although similar to the microeconomic concept of complements — goods for which an increase in the price of one leads to a decrease in the quantity demanded of the other — complementors call for a wider game theory view. In order to determine whether a business is a competitor or a complementor, the company must employ allocentric (centered on others, as compare to egocentric — centered on yourself) approach and attempt to gauge objectives and interests of other players and how they relate to those of the company, not just to check the cross-price elasticity of demand.

In 1980, Porter published one of the most influential works linking strategic management to organizational performance.[74] The central idea behind this connection was the notion of *generic strategies,* in other words, a general taxonomy that categorized all possible choices of *competitive* strategies that are available to a company in order for it to attain sustainable competitive advantages over its rivals. Although Porter's specific selection of generic strategies has been later amended and completed by other authors, the notion itself that general categories of strategic choices exist that drive superior organizational performance through competitive advantages has never been seriously challenged. Porter suggested two major sets of generic strategies that focused on the cost side and on the customer dimension, respectively. A focus on innovation was later suggested as an additional generic strategy.

A Strategic Focus on Costs Driving Organizational Performance

The idea that sustainable cost advantages over competitors can be achieved by designing a strategy of *overall cost leadership* is grounded in the rather 'male' classical economists' notions of firms as production functions to be managed efficiently for profit maximization. A firm seeking to implement a strategy of cost leadership strives to be the lowest cost producer in an industry for a certain quality level, leading to positional advantages within that industry. A firm can capitalize on these advantages either by selling its products at average industry prices to earn higher profits than its rivals, or alternatively by selling its products below the industry average prices in order to increase market share. This generic strategy often requires access to capital for significant investments in production assets, skills required to enhance efficiency and a high level of expertise as well as efficient distribution channels.

Companies pursuing strategic cost advantages in the rather static way envisioned by Porter usually develop capabilities to re-engineer, restructure and downsize the organization. Michael Hammer first put forward the notion of Business Process Re-engineering (BPR), described as a "fundamental rethinking and radical redesign of business processes to achieve dramatic improvements in critical measures of performance such as cost, quality, service and speed."[75] The notion entailed identifying a firm's key processes, analyzing them, maximizing their efficiency and then putting them back together across functional divides, in a new streamlined way. In this way, the inefficient parts of functional silos were exposed and hacked away, and a lean, mean, highly efficient organization emerged.

A number of authors had earlier described the performance advantages deriving from an organizational focus on cost leadership within a broader and more dynamic context. In 1960, Hymer proposed that firms operating in foreign countries must possess some kinds of cost or marketing advantages compared to the indigenous firms. He called these advantages "monopolistic" in as much as they conferred proprietary rights on controlling firms.[76] In 1966, Vernon approached the theory of multinational enterprise from a resource allocation angle.[77] He noted that at a later stage of a product cycle, when competitive advantage shifts from innovators to imitators, it is the product cost structure — in particular labor costs — that becomes the competitive driver. If at this stage a firm's foreign markets expand, there could be an incentive to move production to a foreign location in order to drive down expenses. Vernon's argument appears to be unidirectional: while it makes sense for a firm from a developed country to move production to a developing one, the theory predicates it as impractical to do it the other way around. In 1985, Kogut placed these issues in a broader context. He argued that the decision by a multinational corporation to enter a foreign market follows two conditions: comparative advantages of a country and competitive advantages of a firm.[78] Comparative (location-specific advantage) provides an answer of where the entry will be made. Competitive (firm-specific) advantage tells what type of activities the firm is interested in carrying out in a selected location. An actual entry decision takes place within the value-added chain of a multinational enterprise itself, characterized by Kogut as "the process by which technology is combined with material and labor inputs, and then processed inputs are assembled, marketed, and distributed."[79]

Focusing on the Customer to Gain Performance Advantages

Porter argued that companies could gain competitive advantage by offering a product or service with unique attributes that are valued by customers, and perceived by them as superior or different from competing products. He called this type of generic strategy: *differentiation*. It relies on the firm's internal resources (i.e. scientific research, creative individuals and the communication ability of sales forces) to deliver products or services that are perceived as unique by the customer. By defining and measuring it in relation to competitors — i.e. to take market share away from them, or in terms of positional advantages — Porter certainly highlighted the 'male' aspects of differentiation. As such, while it is a customer-focused strategy insofar as the offering *is* for customers, Porter underscores the unique features and attributes of the offering in relation to their potential *to fight* competitors — or, in the analogy of strategy as warfare, the enemy.

But gaining market share might not be a profitable strategy when the overall market is shrinking. Some authors have instead developed all the key elements in Porter's definition of a differentiation strategy, but shifting the emphasis from undercutting competitors to *delighting the customer*. As previously mentioned, delighting the customer is about making sure the customer is happy through nurturing a collaborative, winning relationship with the customer, clearly a very 'female' approach. Companies undertaking to delight the customer strive to increase the loyalty of existing customers and gain new ones. Actively differentiating products and services, exceeding customers' expectations and offering superior customer service are all ways of achieving this. Companies pursuing strategies to delighting the customers often develop capabilities to listening to the customer, understanding his or her requirements, and then surpassing these requirements, rather than merely satisfying them. The notion of customer delight therefore includes differentiation but it is broader than it, embracing areas such as: customer relationship management, relationship marketing, one-to-one marketing, customer value models, etc.[80]

A Focus on Innovation to Drive Organizational Advantages

Another approach to strategy design focuses primarily on innovation, which is reliant on the internal resources of a firm. This innovation can relate to products, distribution systems, markets or entire value propositions. There are different views on what it takes for companies to successfully harness the creative energy of individuals within their organizations. While Christensen espouses the need to create special environments which can inspire creativity,[81] others such as Drucker write that companies can encourage innovation systematically, by changing its management systems and processes: "Innovation can be systematically managed — if one knows where to look."[82] He goes on to say that "purposeful, systematic innovation begins with the analysis of the sources of new opportunities,"[83] namely unexpected occurrences, incongruities, process needs, industry and market changes, as well as demographic changes, and changes in perception and new knowledge. Nonaka noted that in uncertain markets characterized by the proliferation of new technologies, intense competition and rapid product obsolescence, success is achieved by the consistent creation of new knowledge, the wide dissemination of existing knowledge throughout the organization, and its quick embodiment in new technologies and products. To reach this type of success, a company must build an organizational structure that is conducive to knowledge management and the utilization of its human assets.[84]

In 2000, Hamel raised the need for radical innovation to reconceptualize business models in order to deliver better value to the customer.[85] According to Hamel, it's not enough to have a strategy, resources and a value network; bridges between these elements need to be in place. A company's core strategy and its strategic resources are bridged by configuration efforts. Customer benefits bridge the core strategy with the customer interface. Finally, company boundaries link strategic resources and the value network of a company. By focusing on these elements, firms can reconceptualize business models in a non-linear manner to deliver radical innovation. This clearly 'female' approach prioritizes creativity, complementarity, connectivity and flexibility in business models as long as they deliver the end result: customer value.

Co-Opetition: Playing the Right Strategies at the Right Time

Does a strategic model exists that combines 'male' and 'female' generic options within a unifying framework? It is difficult to tell, but Brandenburger and Nalebuff's tactical notions of "co-opetition" come certainly close to it.[73] The title of their 1997 article: *Co-opetition: Competitive and Cooperative Business Strategies for the Digital Economy*, encapsulated their view of the strategic landscape of firms as including *both* competitive *and* co-operative choices, bargaining power and win-win partnerships, and where not only competitors appear to be the primary focus of the strategist but also complementors and customers can be seen as providing the organization with its main strategic impetus. Brandenburger and Nalebuff thus laid out a framework where the 'male' and 'female' strategic options of competition and cooperation could co-exist and be effective to the organization, provided that each option operated within a proper context. Hence, companies could be conceived as balancing the dynamics of competition and co-operation with different players — or even with the same player in different contexts. These views are important because they moved the strategic and tactical debate within organizations from pursuing *one* generic (and most of the time: *competitive*) strategic option, to the issue of: wisely *balancing* and continuously alternating both cooperative and competitive strategic and tactical options within a complex and constantly changing business landscape.

'Male' and 'Female' Resources Driving Strategic Advantages

Generic strategies — and the underlying competitive analyses — are strategic approaches that tend to focus *externally* on the marketplace. Resource-based views (RBV) of the firm address in a diverse way the question of why firms in the same industry perform differently. They maintain that it is the firm's attributes (or resources such as physical, human and organizational capital) that enable it to achieve a sustainable competitive advantage or above-average returns. Resources can be defined as those advantages specific to a firm that enable it to drive organizational performance and competitive advantage. There are a number of different approaches to a resource-based view of the firm which can be categorized into two broad schools of thought.

Capabilities to Run the Organizational Machine Seamlessly

On the one hand, there is a set of approaches suggesting that the firm's focus is on optimizing internal resources in order to generate operational and/or market advantages over competitors. These types of approaches are rooted in transaction cost economics, which posits that the reason for firms' existence is to avoid the costs of conducting the same exchange between autonomous contractors. In her seminal work in the field of RBV, Penrose maintained that a firm is a collection of resources and differences between firms in the same industry are due to the way they access different resources. Superior performance requires resources with certain characteristics: (1) heterogeneity: the resource must differ from resources owned by other firms (2) *ex post* limits to competition (imperfect imitability such as information asymmetries, property rights, etc.) (3) imperfect mobility: high switching costs make the resource non-tradable (transaction costs); and, (4) limited *ex ante* competition: limited competition for a resource before its acquisition led to a lower price than its value, resulting in a benefit for the firm.[86]

The types of resources with these characteristics can be grouped into three categories. Tangible *assets* include financial and physical items such as land, equipment, property and capital. *Intangible assets* include reputation, brands, patents and technology and account for the differences between balance sheet valuation and stock market evaluation. *Capabilities* are often described as invisible assets, and include items such as communication and motivation. Capabilities are often the result of either the skills of groups or individuals or processes embedded in a firm's routines. Capabilities range in complexity from organizational routines to dynamic capabilities, combinative capabilities, absorptive capacities and architectural knowledge. Organizational routines in turn range from the execution of known procedures to more complex learning or search routines. Combinative capabilities enable a firm to generate new applications from existing knowledge, through "an intersection of the capability of the firm to exploit its knowledge and the unexplored potential of the technology." [87]

A dynamic capability is defined by Zollo and Winter as "a learned pattern of collective activity through which the organization systematically generates and modifies its operational routines in pursuit of improved effectiveness."[88] Winter described a knowledge evolution cycle, in which organizational routines interact with external stimuli, leading to ideas which are then evaluated, replicated and retained; through this process knowledge becomes embedded in individuals.[89] Teece, Pisano and Shuen define dynamic capabilities as "the firm's ability to integrate, build, and reconfigure internal and external competences to address rapidly changing environments. Dynamic capabilities thus reflect an organization's ability to achieve new and innovative forms of competitive advantage given path dependencies and market positions."[90]

The RBV approach is summed up by Conner's statement: "A firm's ability to attain and keep profitable market positions depends on its ability to gain and defend advantageous positions in underlying resources important to production and distribution."[91] If the tangible and intangible assets are seen as the raw materials and energy then must be fed to the machine in order to make it run, capabilities can be seen as the cogs in wheel that enable the machine processes to run seamlessly. They are vital to the process, as indeed are cogs to the manufacturing process, but ultimately they remain a part of the production process — just another part of the machinery, which can easily be replicated. With its emphasis on efficiency, competency and power, this type of approach is clearly 'male'. The role of capabilities in this approach is defined in terms of collective learning to co-ordinate production skills and integrate multiple streams of technology. As such, they are restricted to the sphere of organizational routines and processes, and largely omit the social dimension:

> These approaches have been fruitful in highlighting a company's *internal* characteristics as determinant to performance in the marketplace. However, they have also been criticized as emphasizing on what companies require for past, rather than future competitive advantages. Hence, they are seen as inadequate in addressing competitive issues associated with rapidly changing environments [...] A series of concepts has been advanced to address the issue of fast-paced environmental changes, such as dynamic capabilities, combinative capabilities, absorptive capacities or architectural knowledge. [...] However, dynamic capabilities and the like have often been described as vague and tautological, i.e. defining capabilities as abilities. Therefore, even if one were to assume that dynamic capabilities are valuable for a company, these approaches fall short of addressing how company managers should go about developing them.[92]

Social Capabilities that Drive Performance Across Boundaries

On the other hand, the organizational capability to transcend boundaries has already been identified as one important way in which firms grow. The capabilities literature has in fact raised attention to organizational needs to blend resources by transferring knowledge, technology or organizational learning across functional boundaries, when differences in professional codes and cultures can serve as obstacles to such transfers. In addition, there are many other boundaries at play that organizations must handle in order to unleash the performance potential of its internal resources fully:

> A voluminous literature has documented the obtrusive detrimental effects of national cultural distance [...on...] international technology transfers, corporate account management processes, supply chain management, new product development and the implementation of cross-border mergers, acquisitions, joint ventures and strategic alliances. Particularly in the latter cases, the problems derived from national cultural differences are of course compounded by the different corporate cultures of the merging, target or alliance and joint-venture partner companies involved [...] Professional and cultural boundaries have therefore been regarded in strategic management as major inhibiting and risk factors to the smooth functioning of vertical and horizontal transfers. This is especially the case as the scale and scope of a company's operations increase in size, complexity and international coverage. [Moreover, the] combination and the replication of technologies, as well as the development of organizational and technological platforms for future use, offer additional grounds for the interplay of professional and cultural boundaries.[93]

The blending and smooth transfers of knowledge, technology and other key resources, across the cultural, organizational and professional boundaries of a firm are fundamental to its long-term ability to survive, grow and prosper. So how can firms address the challenge of transcending its boundaries? Firms that successfully blend key resources across cultural and organizational divides have developed the capability to create common organizing principles via the interactions of individuals. For this reason, these capabilities have been termed social. The notion of *social capabilities* thus addresses a gap in the existing capabilities literature: how organizational knowledge is actually created, integrated and transformed into useful products and services across cultural, organizational and professional boundaries. In 2004, these social capabilities were defined as:

> A company capability to create common organizing principles has been shown to facilitate communication and the transfer of technology across cultural and professional divides. This capability is termed *social* as it creates common organizing principles through the *interactions* of individuals, that facilitate the integration of the entire

organization across professional and cultural boundaries. My use of the term *social* thus avoids the potential limitation that "by defining [more generic notions such as routines,] rules, procedures, conventions or norms as knowledge [a manager or a researcher alike] fails to direct attention to [how] "organizational knowledge" is [actually] created through the *interactions* of individuals, and offers little guidance as to *how* managers can influence these processes.[94]

By developing and applying certain social capabilities, an organization's leadership cadre creates a collective asset that drives superior organizational performance across boundaries. This collective asset has been called the Common Glue. It represents the social capabilities that build cohesiveness among an organization's pivotal executive cadres and the unique way in which co-operative relationships between key members are created, blended, nurtured and transformed into valuable products and services in the marketplace. The Common Glue drives superior organizational performance by fostering a strong degree of internal cohesivesness, co-operative exchanges and transformational learning across boundaries. It has been defined as a set of five social capabilities operating in a *holistic* way within the organization:

1. *Boundary-spanning Leadership:* the extent to which a company's key leadership cadre — typically numbering a few hundred executives from many nationalities — possesses "boundary-spanning" character traits such as tolerance, patience, [wholeness,] walk-the-talk and a giver's mentality. It also includes the extent to which this key leadership cadre is managed as a truly global, cohesive and trusting group.
2. *[Company-wide] Building Blocks:* a company's capability to develop a common stock of social and organizational knowledge among its boundary-spanning leaders. This common stock of knowledge includes things such as a common language, a set of shared business values, global career development paths, and a common company-wide approach to internal reporting and performance measurement.
3. *Communication Rituals:* a company's capability to carry out a set of frank, compelling, regular and company-wide communication interactions that instill common leadership behavior in the company's boundary-spanning leadership group.
4. *Knowledge Interactions:* a company's capability to put in place cross-boundary teams, dialogues, processes, projects and communities of practice — to exchange know-how — in support of compelling, "company-wide business cases."

5. *Cross-boundary Rotations:* a company's capability to develop and implement expatriate and repatriate programs, as well as global career and reward policies fostering the smooth and continual rotation of its key executives across boundaries. [95]

The Common Glue posits that competitive advantage is achieved by transforming social knowledge and learning across cultural and organizational boundaries, into superior products and services. This approach builds upon Kogut and Zander's view of firms as "social communities in which individual and social expertise is transformed into economically-useful products and services by the application of a set of higher-order organizing principles."[96] From this perspective, the firm's reason for existence is to create conditions in which its employees can integrate their specialist knowledge and foster a sense of identity and social belonging via a shared language, conventions and rules, as well as through the joint realization of challenging company-wide business initiatives they all feel passionate about.

On the one hand, social capabilities enable activities such as vertical and horizontal transfers as well as technology replications and combinations to take place effectively and efficiently across all the professional and cultural boundaries that span the entire organization. On the other hand, by enacting these social capabilities, key company managers can create a cohesive and transformational sense of belonging across the whole company, spanning all of its professional and cultural boundaries. In this way, social capabilities allow the firm to transform socially constructed knowledge into superior goods and services across boundaries. This is an archetypally female approach emphasizing the social aspects of applying a firm's resources holistically, viewing the organization as an integrated whole requiring cross-fertilization rather than a group of autonomous business units, and relying on transformational and co-operative skills, the use of language as a social tool for integrating diverse people, the value of joint and collective efforts, and the flexibility to adapt continuously by transcending boundaries through the fostering of internal cohesiveness.

The Common Glue echoes a number of earlier approaches that have emphasized female-like and socially-grounded sources of organizational advantages. During the late 1970s until the early 1980s, Buckley and Casson, Swedenborg and Hennart emphasized on a firm's co-ordinative advantages by suggesting that multinational companies represent a mechanism for coordinating related economic activities and transactions alternative to that of the market.[97] According to this "internalization" theory international production takes place when the costs of in-house operations are less (or benefits are more) than those incurred using the market structures. In 1993, Kogut and Zander maintained that multinational enterprise is a superior organizational vehicle for transferring knowledge across borders.[98] After testing the decision by a number of multinationals to relocate technological capabilities to either a wholly owned foreign subsidiary or to other parties, Kogut and Zander concluded that the less codifiable and the harder to learn the technology was, the more likely the relocation was directed toward the wholly owned operation. In Kogut and Zander's view, the primary lesson from their study was that the boundaries of a firm could not be explained simply by governance structures. Instead, a firm acts as a "repository of social knowledge" that influences co-operative activities and creates capabilities, which are easier to transfer within the firm than across organizations. These capabilities constitute the ownership advantage of a multinational enterprise. Kogut and Zander further argued that the comparative advantages of a multinational enterprise came in two forms. First, such firms were able to transfer the tacit capabilities at a lower cost to subsidiaries than to the third parties. In this sense, the advantage could be called "the relative efficiency." Second, tacit technologies provided platforms for opening out future markets and thus embodied a multinational company's ability to grow and expand. Kogut and Zander saw a firm's foreign expansion as an evolutionary process, where initial entry integrates firm's knowledge acquired in its home market with the gradual understanding of the foreign market, and a final stage transfers knowledge learned from the foreign market internationally and impacts the accumulation and recombination of knowledge throughout the entire firm.

In 2003, Bartlett and Ghoshal emphasized on organizational flexibility and learning — the two critical aspects that are behind the link between social capabilities and organizational performance. According to them, in order to be successful, multinational enterprises have to build three strategic capabilities: global efficiency and competitiveness, national responsiveness and flexibility and worldwide learning.[99] Unlike a domestic entity, each multinational operates in diverse corporate and national environments, making it difficult to design a one-size-fits-all algorithm. In 1984, Dymsza explained that although many aspects of strategic planning for multinational enterprises are similar to those of domestic companies there are also important distinctions. The latter include decisions about: foreign country entry strategy and tactics, what product adaptations should be made for new national markets, to what extent marketing and product mixes should be adjusted, and what can a company do about exchange rate risks, political uncertainties and government regulation and controls.[100] Jacque and Lorange noted that when a firm is involved in foreign operations, an already inexact science of performance evaluation becomes even more difficult due to changes in exchange rates and rates of inflation, capital controls, different taxation codes, and so on. They argued that performance evaluation systems of multinational companies must account for the heterogeneity of the different national environments in which each subsidiary operates.[101] Bartlett and Ghoshal added another important constraint to flexibility for a multinational enterprise — its administrative heritage.[102] By administrative heritage they meant the company's existing configuration of assets, its traditional distribution of responsibility, its historic norms and values and its management style. Bartlett and Ghoshal believed that administrative heritage cannot be changed overnight, and proposed that instead of searching for the "ideal" organizational culture the company should look for ways to build and leverage its existing capabilities to address ever-changing external demands.

A crucial step in developing the Common Glue within organizations consists of identifying certain individuals that play pivotal roles as "boundary spanning leaders" both within the organization as well as between institutions. These "boundary spanning leaders" have the character traits, skills and understanding that allow them to bridge differences and ensure that a common language is developed and codified and — together with other similar organizational commonalities — it is made accessible to a wider circle of individuals. This idea of differential leadership driving organizational performance across boundaries was echoed in 2003 by Bartlett and Ghoshal, who argued that the performance of a multinational enterprise depends on the right mix of managers. They suggested that to compete successfully, such an enterprise should employ business managers, country managers, functional managers, and global executives, all of whom need to possess distinctly different sets of skills.[103] The task of a business or product-division manager is to further the company's global-scale efficiency and competitiveness and to capture the full benefit of integrated worldwide operations. To be effective, business managers must serve as strategists for entire organization, architects of worldwide asset and resource configuration and coordinators of transactions across national borders. Country managers must meet local customer needs as well as satisfy the host government's requirements and defend the company's market positions against local and external competitors. A skillful country manager would play three roles — that of a sensor and interpreter of local opportunities and threats, that of a builder of local resources and capabilities, and that of a contributor to and active participant in global strategy. Functional managers have to scan for specialized information worldwide and promote innovations that may offer transnational opportunities and applications. Finally, the global executives must understand the strategic importance of each specialist, nurture them and co-ordinate their efforts.

From a similar perspective, in 1984 Edström and Lorange argued that human resources play a critical role in developing and implementing strategies for the multinational enterprise.[104] Human capital is scarce and should be allocated and handled carefully. It is particularly important to align managers' motivation with corporate objectives: if managers do not see what is in there for them, an organization's strategic intent becomes very hard to achieve. In 1996, Lorange added three important human resources issues: manager selection and assignment process, "transferability" of key personnel, and management trade-offs between spending time on operational and strategic applications.[105] Managers must be able to understand each other, communicate key aspects of their value-added activities, and be aware of the activities of other divisions. They should also possess solid cross-cultural skills to develop a deep understanding of the operational environment. Within organization a resource is considered strategic only if it can be relocated from one area of operations to another without the loss of integrity or quality of output. Therefore, the transfer of human capital among different divisions and across national boundaries is a key task of human resources management.

Addressing Organizational Performance Holistically

Figure 8 summarizes our archetypal landscape portraying some of the main responses in the management field to the issue of: how organizations go about attaining superior organizational performance across cultural, organizational and geographic boundaries. The strategic management responses to this issue can be divided into two broad categories. *External* strategic approaches provide an array of competitive ('male') and co-operative ('female') responses suggesting that firms can drive organizational performance by the strategic pursuit of either cost advantages, a focus on customers or organizational innovation. Choices of *generic* strategies can — and should — be grounded in a formal understanding of the business milieu, which in itself can follow either a certain 'male' approach — scanning the marketplace as a competitive battlefield — or a more female-like perspective emphasizing co-operation, 'win-win' and positive-sum tactics, and the important role of complementors. Both of these views can be integrated within *co-opetitive* frameworks suggesting a balanced application of positional ('male') and co-ordinative ('female') strategies and tactics depending on context. Similar appreciations can be made of the issue of an organization's top-line growth, which might be seen as a strategic balance of *external* (i.e. mergers & acquisitions, alliances and joint ventures) and *internal* (i.e. organic growth) initiatives, of 'male' and predatorial undertakings as well as more female-like approaches to nurturing customer delight and relationships.

However, these approaches do not address the issue of organizational learning, nor look at an organization's cultural, professional and functional boundaries, both of which can have a major impact on its capability to implement strategy and attain the associated performance advantages. *Internal* strategic approaches do look at an organization's capabilities, human capital, physical assets and other such strategic resources which can underpin competitive advantages. On the one

	STRATEGY (External focus)				STRATEGY (Internal focus)	LEADERSHIP	KNOWLEDGE MANAGEMENT
	Focus on Understanding the Marketplace	Focus on Cost Leadership	Focus on Customer	Focus on Innovation	Focus on Internal Resources	Focus on People	Focus on Organizational Knowledge

MALE	• Competitive analysis
	• Aggressive, zero-sum tactics
	• Positioning advantages
		• Cost-efficiency
		• Cost-efficiency tactics, i.e.:
		  - cost-cutting
		  - re-engine-ering,
		  - restructu-ring
		  - delayering
					Firm as a Resource-Optimizing Machine:
					• Resources: tangible/ intangible; physical assets/ human assets; capabilities/ core competencies/ routines/ repertoires/ processes
					• Organizational performance as a result of the *efficient use of resources* (minimizing transaction costs)
						• Leadership approaches fostering organizational efficiency and competency:
						  - Valuing personal success
						  - Paternalistic
						  - Transactional
						  - Bureaucratic
						  - Hierarchical controls, rewards and punishments
							Intellectual Capital Models –
							Organizational performance resulting from the efficient generation, processing, application and protection of codifiable knowledge

FEMALE	• Analysis of complementors
	• Co-operative, positive sum tactics
	• Co-operative and co-ordinative advantages
			• Delighting the customer via excellent and differentiated product and service offering as well as relationship building	• Configuring the organization for continuous product, service and managerial innovations vis-à-vis *customers, suppliers and allies*	**Firm as a Social Community:**
					• Social capabilities and socially constructed knowledge
					• Organizational performance as a result of *the social transformation of knowledge* into economically useful products and services
						• Leadership approaches fostering organizational co-ordination and change:
						  - Valuing joint-effort
						  - Fraternalistic
						  - Transformational
						  - Partnership
						  - Decentralized relationships, sharing and flexible adaptation
							Social Models -
							Organizational performance resulting from the creation and transformation of knowledge through purposeful social interactions amongst members

Figure 8: Some managerial responses to explaining organizational performance.

hand, these capabilities can be looked at outside the social context of the organization, leading to useful approaches that nevertheless fall short of explaining organizational learning within changing and complex environments. On the other hand, *social* capabilities do look explicity at the issue of: how organizational knowledge is actually created, blended and transformed into useful products and services across boundaries. Looking at firms as social communities and focusing on a firm's social interactions as a transformational source of organizational knowledge certainly are 'female' types of approaches. They also underlie the social models of knowledge management vis-à-vis a more static conception that sees codifiable intellectual capital *as* organizational knowledge.

Social approaches to addressing the issue of organizational performance across boundaries rely strongly on leadership. At their core is the ability of firms to attract, develop, deploy and retain a cadre of *boundary spanning leaders* whose specific character traits allow them to bridge differences as well as to create a common language in order to synthesize knowledge and communicate across boundaries. Boundary spanning leaders blend their 'male' and 'female' aspects harmonically, being able to, at the same time, compete and co-operate, implement and inspire, exhibit rigor and adaptation, be cool-headed and show compassion, monitor goals and reach out to others across boundaries. The centrality of a certain kind of differential leadership to obtain organizational performance across boundaries builds upon and echoes notions from economics, knowledge management, human resource and strategic management, all of which have been examined in this as well as in the previous chapter.

As we saw in the previous chapter, the archetype of the Harmonic Fusion of the Two Great Powers suggests that harmonically blending the 'male' and the 'female' constitutive elements of any cosmic phenomenon unleashes its full power. When applied to the way in which management scientists and economists have thought about organizational performance across boundaries (refer to Figures 7 and 8), such a conception elucidates two clear paths going forward. First, the *co-opetitive* notion that organizations might gain performance advantages by alternating — or sometimes by exercising simultaneously — an array of both co-operative and competitive strategic choices, needs to be put to the test.

Second, *social* capabilities and related notions need to be developed further and tested vis-à-vis organizational performance, as these social approaches are relatively recent *and* can address explicitly the issue of: how do organizations go about blending their diverse characteristics in order to attain superior organizational performance across cultural, organizational and geographic boundaries. In Chapter 3 we will take important steps into these paths. In particular, we will start a discovery journey into social capabilities and the Common Glue led by managers of international organizations — the main actors in this play. This will be the prelude for a quantitative test of the link between strategies, social capabilities and organizational performance that will be presented in the following chapters.

Notes and References

[1] Crossan, M. M. and A. C. Inkpen (1995) "Believing is seeing: Joint ventures and organization learning," *Journal of Management Studies* 32(5): 595–619 (electronic version).

[2] Arrow, K. J. (1979) "The limitations of the profit motive," *Challenge* 22(4): 24–25.

[3] Cyert, R.M. and J. G. March (1956) "Organizational factors in the theory of oligopoly," *Quarterly Journal of Economics* 70(1): 44.

[4] Kogut, B. and U. Zander (1996) "What firms do? Coordination, identity, and learning," *Organization Science* 7(5): 511.

[5] Simon, H. S. (1991) "Organizations and markets," *Journal of Economic Perspectives* 5(2): 20–44.

[6] Teece, D. J. and S. G. Winter (1984) "The limits of neoclassical theory in management education," *AEA Papers and Proceedings* 74(2): 116–121.

7 Coase, R. (1937) "The nature of the firm," *Economica* 4: 386–405; O. E. Williamson (1975). *Markets and Hierarchies: Analysis and Antitrust Implications*, Free Press, New York: O. E. Williamson (1985) *The Economic Institutions of Capitalism*, Free Press, New York.

[8] Williamson, O. E. (1996) "Economics and organization: A Primer," *California Management Review* 38(2): 136–139.

[9] Morosini, P. (2004) "Competing on social capabilities". In: *Next Generation Business Handbook*, S. Chowdhury (Ed.) Wiley, New York, p. 248.

[10] Chandler, A. D. (1992) "Organizational capabilities and the economic history of the industrial enterprise," *Journal of Economic Perspectives* 6(3): 79–100.

[11] Hayek, F. A. (1945) "The use of knowledge in society," *The American Economic Review* 15(4): 519–520.

[12] Teece, D. J., G. Pisano and A. Shuen (2001) "Dynamic capabilities and strategic management," *Nature and Dynamics of Organizational Capabilities* 1(9): 334–363.

[13] Garvin, D. (1988) *Managing Quality*, Free Press, New York, cited in Teece, Pisano, and Shuen 2000 (op cit.)

[14] Clark, K. and T. Fujimoto (1991) *Product Development Performance: Strategy, Organization and Management in the World Auto Industries*, Harvard Business School Press, MA, Cambridge, cited in Teece, Pisano, and Shuen 2000 (op cit.)

[15] Drucker, P. (2002) "Knowledge work," *Executive Excellence* 19(10): 12–14.

[16] Drucker, P. (2002) Op cit.

[17] Bartlett, C. and S. Ghoshal (2002) "Building competitive advantage through people," *MIT Sloan Management Review* 43(2): 34–41.

[18] Andrews, K. R. (1987) *The Concept of Corporate Strategy*, 3 Edition, Richard D. Irwin, Inc, Homewood, IL, p. 46–47.

[19] Bartlett, C. and S. Ghoshal (2002) op cit.

[20] North, D. C. (1994) "Economic performance through time," *American Economic Review* 84(3): 359–369 (electronic version).

[21] Kogut, B. and U. Zander (1996) "What firms do? Coordination, identity, and learning." *Organization Science* 7(5): 506.

[22] Barnard, C. I. (1958) "Elementary conditions of business morals," *California Management Review* 1(1): 2.

[23] Bartlett, C. and S. Ghoshal (2002) Op cit.

[24] Chandler, A. D. (1992) op cit. (electronic version).

[25] Williamson, O. E. (1981) "The modern corporation: Origin, evolution, attributes," *Journal of Economic Literature* 19(4): 1537–1568.

[26] Teece, D. J. (1985) "Multinational enterprise, internal governance, and industrial organization," *AEA Papers and Proceedings* 75(2): 233–238.

[27] Lorange, P. (1973) "Formal planning in multinational corporations," *Columbia Journal of World Business* 8(2): 83–88.

[28] Lorange, P. (1973) Op cit, p. 84.

[29] Dunning, J. H. (1988) "The theory of international production," *The International Trade Journal* 3(1): 21–66.

[30] Contractor, F. (1986). "Strategic considerations behind international joint ventures," *International Marketing Review* 3: 75.

[31] Hout, T, M. Porter, E. Michael and E. Rudden (1982) "How global companies win out,"*Harvard Business Review* 60(5): 98–108.

[32] Henry W. Chesbrough and David J. Teece (2002) "Organizing for innovation: When is virtual virtuous?" *Harvard Business Review* 80 (8):127–136.

[33] Christopher A. Bartlett and Sumantra Ghoshal (2003) "What is a global manager?" *Harvard Business Review* 81 (8): 101–108.

[34] Winter and Szulanski (2001) p. 730.

[35] Martin, Jeffrey A. and Eisenhardt Kathleen M. (2001) "Exploring cross-business synergies." *The Academy of Management 2001 Best Paper Proceedings, Business Policy and Strategy Division.*

[36] A. D. Chandler (1979) "The Growth of the transnational industrial firm in the united States and the United Kingdom: A comparative analysis," *The Tawney Memorial Lecture*, Harvard University Press, Harvard.

[37] Crossan, M. M and A. C. Inkpen (1955) "Believing is seeing: Joint ventures and organization learning," *Journal of Management Studies* 32 (5): pp. 595–619 (electronic version).

[38] Bartlett, C. A and S. Ghoshal, (1986) "Tap your subsidiaries for global reach," *Harvard Business Review*, 64(6): 87–94.

[39] Dunning J. H and S. Bansal (1997) "The cultural sensitivity of the eclectic paradigm," *Multinational Business Review* 5 (1): 1–16.

[40] Kogut, B. (1985) "Designing global strategies: Comparative and competitive value-added chains," *Sloan Management Review* 27(1): 15–28.

[41] Chan K. W and R. Mauborgne (2004) "Value innovation," *Harvard Business Review* 82 (7/8): 172–180; T.K. Das and Bing-Sheng Teng (2000) "Instabilities of strategic alliances: an internal tensions perspective," *Organization Science* 11 (1): 77–101.

[42] Aiello, R.J and M.D. Watkins (2000) "The art of friendly acquisition," *Harvard Business Review* 78 (6): 101–107.

[43] Morosini, P. (2005)"Nurturing successful alliances across boundaries". In: *The Handbook of Strategic Alliances,* Oded Shenkar (Ed.), Sage, New York.

[44] Morosini, P. *Managing Cultural Differences,* (1998) Pergamon Press, Oxford, UK.

[45] Theories looking at 'organizational knowledge' have classified it through a broad diversity of taxonomies which differ according to the particular epistemological perspectives of their authors. Although providing a comprehensive view of these taxonomies is way beyond the subject matter of this book, it is important to offer some introductory references and a view of some of the main classificatory definitions to the reader. Some introductory references to the issue of how organizational knowledge has been classified in the relevant literature, ought to include: Alton Chua, "Taxonomy of organizational knowledge," *Singapore Management Review* 24, (2) 2002 (electronic version); Ikujiro Nonaka and Noboru Konno, The Concept of "Ba": Building a Foundation for knowledge creation, *California Management Review,* 40 (3) (Spring) 1998, pp. 40–54; Julian Birkinshaw, Robert Nobel, and Jonas Ridderstrale, "Knowledge as a contingency Variable: Do the characteristics of knowledge predict organization structure?" *Organization Science* 13 (3) May-June 2002, pp. 274–289; Andrew Hargadon and Angelo Fanelli, "Action and Possibility: Reconciling dual perspectives of knowledge in organizations," *Organization Science* 13 (3) May-June 2002, pp. 290–302; J. C. Spender, "Organizational Knowledge, learning and memory: Three concepts in search of a theory," *Journal of Organizational Change Management,* 9 (1) 1996, pp. 63–78; C.W. Holsapple and K.D. Joshi, "Knowledge management: A Threefold Framework," *The Information Society* 18, 2002, pp. 47–64. Let us now examine some of the main taxonomies that have been proposed in the relevant literature. A suitable starting point is provided by the *tacit–explicit* taxonomy of knowledge, which has achieved very broad recognition in the academic as well as in the managerial arena. *Tacit knowledge* is the knowledge, which is highly personal, situational and subjective. It is difficult to formalize and therefore to communicate and share with others. It has two dimensions: intangible "know-how" (or "knowledge") that represents skills and crafts acquired through individual experiences, and beliefs, ideas, values and mental models. Nonaka and Konno (1998) call the first dimension of tacit knowledge the technical aspect, and the second dimension the cognitive aspect. *Explicit knowledge* is the knowledge, which is tangible, objective, can be expressed unambiguously in numbers and words, and shared in the form of data, statements and specifications. It can be transferred without the loss of integrity through media and networks, and is often referred to as "information". Chua (2002) proposes that from an organizational perspective, knowledge can also be classified as public or private. *Public knowledge* is the knowledge residing in an unrestricted domain and accessible to anyone, while *private knowledge* refers to proprietary knowledge possessed by an organization. In turn, private knowledge can be divided into architectural and component, and component knowledge further segregated into individual and collective. *Architectural knowledge* is the knowledge required by an organization to perform enterprise-wide routines and co-ordinate numerous activities. *Component knowledge* is the knowledge, which refers to execution of a specific task or

encompasses a discrete aspect of organizational operation. *Individual knowledge* is the knowledge harbored by a particular employee, and, finally, *collective knowledge* is the knowledge shared by a group of organization members. Chua's separation of component knowledge on individual and collective is reminiscent of Hargadon and Fanelli's (2002) division of knowledge into latent and empirical, although Hargadon and Fanelli apply their framework to the total universe of knowledge held by a firm. *Latent knowledge* represents persistent knowledge elements and relationships situated in a particular context that are possessed by individual workers. *Empirical knowledge* is physical and social knowledge artifacts that surround individuals working for an enterprise. Hargadon and Fanelli's taxonomy is also close to that of Spender (1996), although Spender combines individual (latent) and social (empirical) framework with tacit–explicit concepts to create a four-cell matrix. Spender's individual knowledge is the knowledge that presupposes autonomous operation. It can be automatic (tacit) or conscious (explicit). Spender's social knowledge is the knowledge created through the use of institutional standards. It can be collective (tacit) or objectified (explicit). Spender and Chua's collective knowledge concepts are, therefore, different in spite of having the same nametag. Given that Chua defines his collective knowledge as capable of being shared by a group of people, Spender's equivalent is, in fact, the objectified (explicit), and not the collective (tacit) knowledge. In addition to providing a better understanding of knowledge taxonomy, this example serves to highlight that there is still no agreement among knowledge management researches about the exact use of the terms. Finally, Holsapple and Joshi (2002) separate knowledge into descriptive, procedural and reasoning. *Descriptive knowledge* is equivalent to information and portrays the state of the world. *Procedural knowledge* is the knowledge of "how-to" execution mechanisms. *Reasoning knowledge* is the knowledge, which allows for a conclusion of whether a particular line of reasoning is true or false.

[46] Birkinshaw, J and Tony Sheehan (2002) "Managing the knowledge life cycle," *MIT Sloan Management Review* 44 (1): 75–83.

[47] Morosini, P. *Managing Cultural Differences* (1998) Pergamon Press, Oxford, U.K., p. 95.

[48] Morosini, P. (2000) "Open company values: Transforming information into knowledge based Advantages". In: Don Marchand (Ed.) *Competing with Information: A Manager's Guide to Creating Business Value with Information Content*, J Wiley Chichester, pp. 243–262.

[49] Hayek, F. A. (1945), Op cit, p. 519.

[50] Sanderson, S. M. (1998) "New approaches to strategy: New ways of thinking for the millennium," *Management Decision* 36 (1): 1998, pp. 9–14 (electronic version).

[51] Bartlett and Ghoshal 2002.

[52] Simon, H. A. (1951) "A formal theory of the employment relationship," *Econometrica*, Reprinted in Herbert A. Simon, *Models of Bounded Rationality*, Vol. II (MIT Press, MA, Cambridge, (1982), Herbert A. Simon, (1979) "Rational decision making in business Organizations," *American Economic Review* 69: 493–513, Simon Spring 1991.

[53] Arrow, K. J. (1964) "Control in large organizations," *Management Science* 10 (3): 397–408.

[54] Chandler (1992) Op cit.

[55] Kogut and Zander (1996): p. 507.

[56] Simon, H. A. (1991) "Bounded rationality and organizational learning," *Organizational Science*, 2, (1): 125–134.

[57] Simon, H. A. G. B. Dantzig, R. Hogarth, C. R. Plott, H. Raiffa, T. C. Schelling, Kenneth A. Shepsle, R. Thaler, Amos Tversky, and S. Winter (1987) "Decision making and problem solving," *Interfaces* 17 (5): 11–31.

[58] Simon et al, Simon Spring (1991).

[59] Cohen W. M. and D. A. Levinthal (1990) "Absorptive capacity: A new perspective on learning and innovation," *Administrative Science Quarterly* 35 (1): pp. 128–153 (electronic version).

[60] Inkpen A. C. (1998) "Learning and knowledge acquisition through international strategic alliances," *Academy of Management Executive* 12 (4): 69–81 (electronic version).

[61] Kusunoki K. and I. Nonaka (1998) "Organizational capabilities in product development of japanese firms: A conceptual framework and empirical findings," *Organization Science* 9 (6): 699–718.

[62] Holsapple C.W. and K.D. Joshi (2002). "Knowledge management: A threefold framework," *The Information Society* 18: 47–64.

[63] Hansen, M. T. (2002) "Knowledge networks: Explaining effective knowledge sharing in multiunit companies," *Organization Science* 13 (3): pp. 232–248.

[64] Chandler (1992), Op cit.

[65] Bartlett and Ghoshal (2002) Op Cit.

[66] Morosini, P. (2000) "Open company values: Transforming information into knowledge based advantages". In: Marchand (Ed.) *Competing with Information: A Manager's Guide to Creating Business Value with Information Content*, D. Chichester: Wiley, New York, pp. 243–262.

[67] Holsapple and Joshi (2002), Op cit.

[68] Kim C. W. and Renée Mauborgne (2003) "Fair process: managing in the knowledge economy", *Harvard Business Review* 81 (1): 127–136.

[69] It is possible to identify precedents to the Conde de Guibert's idea of military strategy. Sun Tzu's *Art of War* (published in China around 2,500 years ago) is often regarded as the oldest military treatise. It discusses military strategy, tactics and maneuvers and stresses the importance of rational analysis and planning: "The general who wins a battle makes many calculations in his temple before the battle is fought. The general who loses a battle makes but few calculations beforehand. Thus do many calculations lead to victory, and few calculations to defeat; how much more no calculation at all! It is by attention to this point that I can foresee who is likely to win or lose." Carl von Clausewitz's military treatise *On War* talks about "the use of engagements for the object of the war," or deploying military resources for political purposes. The scope of Clausewitz's military theories covers how to address uncertainty, rule-breaking, strategic endgames, and competition, using observation, exploration of the opportunity, flexibility and judgment. Both the *Art of War* and *On War* are frequently referred to and drawn from in strategic thinking, and touted as classics in the field.

[70] Porter, M. E. (1998) "How competitive forces shape strategy" in Michael E. Porter, *On Competition* A Harvard Business Review Book, Boston, MA, (1979) Originally published in *Harvard Business Review* (March-April).

[71] Hamel G. and C.K. Prahalad (1994) *Competing for the Future* Harvard Business School Press, Boston, MA.

[72] Bartlett and Ghoshal (2002), Op cit.

[73] Brandenburger A. M. and Barry J. Nalebuff (1997) "Co-opetition: Competitive and cooperative business strategies for the digital economy, *Strategy and Leadership* 25, (6): 28–33

[74] Michael, P. (1980) *Competitive Strategy:Techniques for Analyzing Industries and Competitors,* The Free Press, New York.

[75] Michael, H. (1995) *The re-engineering revolution,* HarperCollins, New York.

[76] Hymer, S. The International Operation of National Firms: A Study of Direct Investment, Ph.D. Dissertation, MIT, 1960, published by MIT Press under the same title in 1976.

[77] Vernon, R. (1966) "International investment and international trade in the product cycle," *Quarterly Journal of Economics* 80: pp. 90–207.

[78] Kogut, B. (1985) "Designing global strategies: Comparative and competitive value-added chains," *Sloan Management Review* 27(1): 15–28.

[79] Kogut (1985), p. 15.

[80] Oliver, R. L. (1997) *Satisfaction: A Behavioral Perspective on the Consumer.* Irwin/McGraw-Hill; Boston, Chandler, Colby H. (1989), "Quality: Beyond Customer Satisfaction," *Quality Progress,* 22 (February), 30–32; Roland T. Rust, Anthony J. Zahorik, and Timothy Keiningham (1995), "Return on quality (ROQ): Making service quality financially accountable," *Journal of Marketing,* 59 (April), 58–70.

[81] Christensen, C. (1997) *The Innovator's Dilemma,* Harvard Business School Press, Cambridge.

[82] Drucker, P. (1998) "The discipline of innovation," *Harvard Business Review* 63(3): 149.

[83] Drucker, P. (1998) Op cit 156.

[84] Nonaka, I. (1991). "The knowledge-creating company," *Harvard Business Review* 69(1): 96–104.

[85] Hamel, G. (2002) *Leading the Revolution,* Penguin, New York.

[86] Penrose, E. (1959). *The Theory of the Growth of the Firm,* Oxford University Press, Oxford.

[87] Kogut, B. and U. Zander (1992). "Knowledge of the firm, combinative capabilities, and the replication of technology." *Organization Science* 3: p.391.

[88] Zollo, M and S. Winter (1998) *From Organizational Routines to Dynamic Capabilities,* A Working Paper of the Reginald H. Jones Cente, The Wharton School, University of Pennsylvania.

[89] Winter, S. (1987) "Knowledge and competence as strategic assets," In: *The Competitive Challenge: Strategies for Industrial Innovation and Renewal,* D.J. Teece (Ed.), Ballinger, Cambridge, MA, p. 159–184.

[90] Teece D.J., G. Pisano and A. Schuen (1997). "Dynamic capabilities of and strategic management," *Strategic Management Journal* 18(7): 516.

[91] Conner, K. R. (1991) "A historical comparison of resource-based theory and five schools of thought within industrial organisation economics: Do we have a new theory of the firm," *Journal of Management* 17: 122.

[92] Morosini, P. (2004) "Competing on social capabilities". In: *Next Generation Business Handbook,* S. Chowdhury (Ed.), Wiley, New York, p. 250.

[93] Morosini, P. (2004) "Competing on social capabilities". In: *Next Generation Business Handbook,* S. Chowdhury (Ed.), Wiley, New York, p. 256.

[94] Morosini, P. (2004) "Competing on social capabilities". In: *Next Generation Business Handbook,* S. Chowdhury (Ed.), Wiley, 2004, pp. 248–271. The quote inside this quotation can be found in page 113 of: Grant, R.M. (1996) "Toward a knowledge-based theory of the firm," *Strategic Management Journal* 17 (10): 109–122.

[95] Morosini, P. (2004) "Competing on social capabilities". In: *Next Generation Business Handbook,* S. Chowdhury (Ed.), Wiley, New York, pp. 259–260.

[96] Kogut, B. and U. Zander (1992) "Knowledge of the firm, combinative capabilities, and the replication of technology," *Organization Science* 3(3): 384.

[97] P.J. Buckley and M.C. Casson (1976) *The Future of the Multinational Enterprise,* Mc Millan, London J.F. Hennart, (1982) *A Theory of Multinational Enterprises,* University of Michigan Press, Ann Arbor, MI, B. Swedenborg (1979) *The Multinational Operations of Swedish Firms: An Analysis of Determinants and Effects,* Almquist and Wiksell, Stockholm.

[98] Kogut B. and U. Zander (1993) "Knowledge of the firm and evolutionary theory of the multinational corporation," *Journal of International Business Studies* 24: (4) 625–645.

[99] C. A. Bartlett and S. Ghoshal (2003) "What is a global manager?" *Harvard Business Review* 81 (8): 101–108.

[100] W. A. Dymsza (1984) "Global strategic planning: A model and recent developments," *Journal of International Business Studies* 15(3): 169–183.

[101] Jacque L. L. and P. Lorange (1984)" The international control conundrum: The case of Hyperinflationary subsidiaries," *Journal of Business Studies* 15(2): 185–201.

[102] C. A. Bartlett and S. Ghoshal (1988) "Organizing for worldwide effectiveness: The transnational solution," *California Management Review* 31(1): 54–74.

[103] Bartlett C. A. and S. Ghoshal (2003) "What is a global manager?" *Harvard business review* 81 (8): 101–108

[104] Edström A. and P. Lorange (1984) "Matching strategy and human resources in multinational corporations," *Journal of International Business Studies* 15(2): 125–137.

[105] Lorange, P. (1996)"A strategic human resource perspective applied to multinational cooperative ventures," *International Studies of Management and Organization* 26 (1): 87–103.

Chapter 3

The Common Glue that Blends
Organizations Together

We confer with our own eyes and make our ascent from lesser
things to higher
William Harvey (1578–1657),
discoverer of the circulation of the blood[1]

William Harvey's way of proceeding was unheard of within the scientific circles
of 17th century Europe. As one medical historian puts it: "It was seventeenth-cen-
tury thinking at a time when the great mass of philosophical men were doing just
the opposite, namely, expounding overarching theories to explain their experiences and observations."[1] Harvey's boldness in applying this new method of
inquiry amounted to a scientific revolution. One which would lead to quantum
leaps in progress not only within the medical field but also in every other natural
science where this powerful approach was applied. But the true precursor of this
method was Leonardo da Vinci (1452–1519), who represents most people's
archetypal idea of a universal genius — and possibly was a discoverer of the circulation of the blood two generations before Harvey. In a memorable paragraph,
Leonardo described succinctly this new method:

> First I shall make some experiments before I proceed further,
> because my intention is to consult experience first and then by
> means of reasoning show why such experiment is bound to work
> in such a way. And this is the true rule by which those who ana-
> lyze natural effects must proceed; and although nature begins with
> the cause and ends with the experience, we must follow the oppo-
> site course, namely (as I said before), begin with the experience
> and by means of it investigate the cause.[1]

Well into the 20th century, vast areas of the social sciences still refrained from
following Leonardo's advice. Across the various disciplines of social sciences too
often one could notice researchers, academics and pundits alike "expounding
overarching theories to explain their experiences and observations". Economics

and management were no exceptions to this. In 2004, the issue of organizational performance was seen as a case in point:

> How a company generates and sustains competitive advantages in the marketplace is a central question to business executives, academics and practitioners alike. Not surprisingly, over the past three decades of the 20th century academics, consultants and practitioners in pursuit of answers to this quest have turned it into a major area of research in the strategic management field. Quite surprisingly though, most of this research has led to unsatisfactory, incomplete or ambiguous answers with remarkably little empirical evidence to strongly support either of the many schools of thought, theories or frameworks that have emerged in order to improve our understanding of how companies generate sustainable competitive advantages.[2]

Thus, although this crucial subject had attracted considerable academic and practitioning attention for several decades, in the eve of the 21st century the numerous theories explaining what is behind the superior competitive performance of organizations were still perceived as somewhat ineffective. Already in 1967, sociologists Barney Glaser and Anselm Strauss had proposed a potential way out of this conundrum that essentially echoed Harvey's and Leonardo's approaches to scientific inquiry of nearly half a millennium earlier. In a series of seminal publications, Glaser and Strauss had proposed that social scientists use what they called a "grounded theory" approach to empirical research.[3] As its name suggests, this is a qualitative methodology that generates theory from research which is "grounded" in data. Within the social sciences, grounded theory emerged as an alternative strategy to more conventional research approaches that relied heavily on hypothesis testing, verification techniques and quantitative analysis.

Instead, grounded theory proposed a flexible, direct approach to research where both the subject under inquiry *and* the hypotheses emerge naturally and without much interference from a pre-established investigative framework on the part of the researcher. Once the basic observations and data have been gathered with unconstrained eyes, the researcher will look at it and glance emerging patterns and initial connections; a set of hypothetical relationships between categories and sub-categories of data will then follow, and these hypotheses will be tested by putting the data back together in new ways or by gathering new data and quantitatively analyzing it. The researcher thus builds theory in ways that paraphrase William Harvey's approach, in other words, by *"conferring with his own eyes and making her ascent from lesser things to higher."* Because they rely on collecting data and observations without a pre-established investigative framework, grounded theory methods are particularly well-suited to the task of looking at any subject matter in social sciences with new and fresh eyes.

In carrying out a 5-year journey to discover what is behind a firm's superior competitive performance across cultural, organizational and geographic boundaries, I followed methodological tenets that are akin to those of grounded theory. I started off by setting my mind into a vacuum, emptying it of over a decade of mental models I had accumulated within me on the subject matter. Then I went out and engaged in open conversations with employees in a variety of organizations. I talked to top leaders, managers and lower-ranked employees. I visited Northern European as well as Southern European, U.S.-based, Japanese, Latin American and Korean multinationals. These organizations represented a variety of sectors as well, ranging from: automotive, consumer electronics, clothing and electrodomestic appliances, to financial services, communications, advertisement, quality certification and professional services. Altogether, I spoke to over 200 managers in more than 20 organizations, such as Medtronic, Novartis, Daimler-Chrysler, Renault-Nissan, Diesel, Electrolux-Zanussi, Sony, NEC, DNV, Deutsche Bank, Givaudan, Euro RSCG, Embraco and Daewoo. The people I spoke to also included members of not-for-profit organizations, such as Italy's San Patrignano community for drug rehabilitation and the Delancey Street Foundation, in San Francisco, U.S. for the re-education of convicted immates. The conversations were informal and very open, with me triggering the subject matter with the same open-ended question: "within a challenging environment like yours, how does an organization go about achieving superior competitive performance results?" The conversation would then ensue, with the respondent choosing the context of his/her answers freely as well as expanding on the areas he/she wanted. Following the first question, my role was one of facilitating and engaging the conversation, rather than directing it with a pre-set questionnaire. These conversations took place in a variety of places and locations, and lasted from a few minutes to over four hours in one case.

Armed with the data from these conversations, I would go back to my office and physically place my interview notes against the wall, one besides another. I also included post-its with archival research on some of the companies whenever it served to support or expand on the responses I had been given from the managers. A couple of large walls were soon covered with these hand-written interview notes and post-its. And soon some patterns began to emerge very clearly from the data. It was stunning to see how managers from such diverse industries, organizations, nationalities and personal backgrounds, *all* pointed to the same, recurring topics in such a clear way. Albeit the responses were different in content from case to case, they could be neatly clustered in a few and very compelling categories and sub-categories. This chapter summarizes what these managers told me. Whenever relevant, arguments from the management literature that support the managers' statements will also be highlighted.

As a next step, I looked at the data I had categorized and started to elicit some hypothesized relationships between those categories. It was soon very clear which hypotheses could provide real insights into the issue of organizational performance. But it was also obvious that I would need additional data if I wanted to test these hypotheses in a rigorous way. So this time I set out a quantitative journey of discovery, which was to complete the qualitative inputs stemming from the first stage of my research. I prepared a large survey following the managerial categories and sub-categories that the conversations with managers had unveiled. With the help of a team, we then gathered sizeable amounts of data by surveying 847 managers in eleven multinational companies representing a variety of countries, industry sectors and organizational characteristics. Some of these companies, i.e. DaimlerChrysler, Euro RSCG, GateGourmet and DNV, had also been part of the qualitative discovery phase in my research. We then analyzed the data by applying quantitative statistical methods to test our hypothesized relationships rigorously. Both the hypotheses and the statistical findings are reported in the following two chapters.

Just as Leonardo had adviced, throughout this long discovery journey we had "begun with the experience and by means of it, investigated the cause". And the 'cause' we had unveiled and investigated in the end was one that hardly fit previous managerial taxonomies. It suggested that the key for organizations to obtain superior competitive performance was to blend harmonically its diversity of resources across cultural, organizational and geographic boundaries. And that crucial *blending* power of organizations — the Common Glue — was social in scope, transformational in character and strikingly 'female' in nature. This is the story that has been told in all its essential elements in the previous two chapters. This story — brought together by "ascending from lesser things to higher" — is now described in more detail in the following sections.

Strongly Bonding Diverse People Unleashes Performance

By 2001, Medtronic had embodied the very definition of superior competitive performance for one decade. This leading medical instruments multinational that gave us the cardiac pacemaker was facing a critical situation in the late 1980s. Its once highly lucrative margins in its core pacemaker business were being eroded by determined, cost-efficient competitors. A leading management consultancy gave Medtronic the strategic advice to restructure its severely deteriorating core business and significantly reduce prices on pacemakers, thereby constraining the company's future ability to invest in R&D. But in 1990, Bill George, the newly appointed CEO, took the surprising decision to reinvent Medtronic's core business and maintain prices. And in 2001, when George departed from Medtronic, he left a much larger, more global and more diverse company. Most astonishingly, its market value had soared from US$1.1 billion to over US$60 billion during that 10-year time span. By the mid-1990s, 70% of Medtronic's annual revenues were made up of new products launched within the previous 2 years. These results clearly outperformed some of the previous global "best practices" in this area — such as 3M or Hewlett-Packard — which had 25–30% of their annual revenues stemming from products launched within the preceding 5 years. George explains:

> [At Medtronic] we built very strong relationships between the people around our mission of 'restoring people to full health.' We had to focus on R&D to radically increase our new product release frequency — otherwise people would die! Strong relationships were the key for us to work across all kinds of company boundaries, so that we managed to reduce our new product release frequency from 48 months to only 16. Achieving this company-wide business initiative was the key to the whole transformation. Market share growth and shareholder value creation were just the results of it.[4]

George's statement highlights the "relationships" dimension of people — in other words their inherent capacity to nurture strong bondings across boundaries — as key to achieving organizational performance of transformational dimensions. This brings to mind the Andean notion of *collective individuals*, where a whole person is seen not only as an individual (*runa*), but also in his/her *social* dimension of relationships with the community she/he belongs to (*ayllu*), as well as her/his relationships with the surrounding natural environment (*apu*). In this case, George is stressing the *ayllu* dimension of organizational members as being critical to performance. He makes it clear that this builds upon — but is very different from — the notion of individual loyalty or personal commitment:

> What I found in the management of Medtronic when I arrived [in 1990] was that everyone was totally committed to the [company] mission. There was a unanimous, uniform commitment to building on the Medtronic mission. So there wasn't a problem getting

agreement on that. [But] a lot of the managers were not broad enough, they were functional managers, they weren't broad enough to take on greater responsibilities. So this represented a real problem.

Therefore, what was missing in Medtronic's leaders in 1990, was neither a sense of personal commitment to the company's mission nor functional competencies. Rather, what was perceived as lacking was their ability to reach out to others beyond functional boundaries. This called for what I later on termed "boundary-spanning" qualities amongst an organization's leadership cadre. Rather than technical competencies of any kind, these qualities were portrayed by the managers I spoke to as character traits that make people reach out and establish strong bondings with others across all sorts of cultural and organizational boundaries. This was the first theme that emerged from the outset: the importance for an organization to set a leadership cadre in place with the character traits to nurture a strong 'glue' of relationships amongst them. But soon there appeared to be much more than what meets the eye in the challenge of nurturing strong social bondings within organizations for superior competitive performance.

Three Hs of the Common Glue: Harmony, Holism, Holograms

George had also emphasized other constituent parts of this sort of "Common Glue" of strong social bondings that unleashed Medtronic's superior competitive performance results. He had described managers rallying around a challenging *company-wide business initiative* that was strongly connected to the company's mission. Joaquín Coronado Galdós, CEO of Iberian electrical utility HidroCantábrico, explains the reason for this connection:

> Strong bondings and stretch business goals are the two sides of the same coin. When you are asking people to establish strong bondings across organizational silos or cultural boundaries, you are encouraging them to get out of their comfort zone. They need to have an incentive. You need to challenge them with stretch business goals that are organization-wide and involves them emotionally. You also need to rotate managers around, communicate to them, so you build on the excitement, you inspire them, make it worth for them. You can reason the other way around and you will reach the same conclusion. Some organizations are in a very critical state when they finally come to the realization that they need to get

together strongly and tear down barriers inside the organization. So this calls for a radical transformation inside as well as for very challenging business goals to turn the organization around.

Not only the company-wide stretch goals — what I later termed a "company-wide business case" — are strongly connected to the mission of the organization, but the leadership cadre in charge of attaining those goals also had to be *emotionally* and *passionately* connected to the organization's mission. George explains how this was achieved in Medtronic:

> [In 1990 when I arrived to Medtronic] we promoted several [functional managers] who were in their 40s to general management jobs. And in addition to that we went out and recruited a number of general managers from other companies. Now, one of the key criteria was whether they saw the [Medtronic] mission as something they would really buy into, whether they were really interested in that. And I know I told a couple of them: *Look, if [our company mission] did not turn you on, don't come here.*

During the decade of the 1990s, Medtronic exemplified what I call the *harmonic* character that any organization's Common Glue has to have in order to drive superior competitive performance. There is a synchronizing undercurrent fitting all the pieces of the 'glue' together with the harmony of an organic work of art. At Medtronic, for example, people disregarded any initial discomfort they might have felt to bond with diverse people across boundaries, because they saw that *together* they could achieve challenging business initiatives that embodied the company's mission which they *all* felt passionate about: *restoring people to full health*. This is a common thread I saw at work in other companies as well. When Novartis was formed in March 1996 from the US$ 36 billion "merger of equals" between Ciba-Geigy and Sandoz, a competitor noted that neither company on its own had been at the very top of the global pharmaceutical leagues. It sarcastically commented, *"two crows do not make an eagle."* However, first Novartis CEO, Daniel Vasella, immediately set about building the new company's Common Glue:

> Together with a dozen key managers, in only nine months Vasella appointed the company's 300 "global managers" from both merging companies, designed a common organizational blueprint, and set a global re-engineering program in motion with aggressive financial targets. About two thirds of Novartis global managers

experienced international rotation or job transfers within the first two years of the merger. Building blocks were also established: a common company language (English), three global performance measurements (market share, profitability and return-on-assets), a unified reporting and control system, a common career policy and performance evaluation for the global managers and a single "book of values." The latter highlighted behaviors such as entre-preneurship, self-reliance, integrity and speed. The company's annual budgets became a key tool for bringing some of these values alive, with Vasella stretching his global managers with impossibly high business goals in order to foster proactive, risk-taking behavior and world-class performance.[5]

By 2003 Novartis was widely regarded as one of the very few truly successful "mergers of equals", based on earnings, revenue and profitability growth. As described in detail in the next section, one crucial selection criterion for Novartis' 300-strong leadership cadre had been a strong track record and commitment to high performance. These were the kinds of managers that raised to the challenge of Vasella's company-wide stretch goals with a strong emotional pledge and went on to prove their competitors' denigrating comments wrong. But Novartis' undertakings also illustrate the *holistic* characteristic of the Common Glue. This involves two crucial aspects. First, as systems theory suggests, *holistic* phenomena — those where the total entity is greater than the sum of its constituent parts — are characteristic of living and organic entities. The companies I examined that were intent on building robust "common glues" strongly resonated with this notion. Says Vasella:

> [The 1996 Novartis merger was] not about the mechanistic jamming of two companies together. It was about building a global leader with a common purpose. We are reaching for the slightly impossible. We want to graft a truly global, high-performance corporate culture onto the company's Swiss roots.[6]

Second, company managers made it clear that nurturing a strong Common Glue was about working on a series of diverse elements at the same time, *all* of which had to be in place and functioning properly. As described in the previous chapter, all these elements could be grouped in five logical clusters which I termed *social capabilities*. What is important to highlight here is that the resulting Common Glue was portrayed as being greater than the sum of its constitutive elements. And this "more" was variously described as: coherent execution, mutual trust, emotional commitment, shared behaviors and a common language that turned differences into advantages and cohesively amalgamated the entire organization around the common pursuit of challenging business goals. As Vasella observes:

> In the beginning of the [1996 Novartis] merger it was not legitimate [for me] not to know or to just let go [of things]. There are too many risks involved if you do that. But now [In 2003] there are many things I don't know. But the difference is that today there are many more people who do know and would act in a similar way as I would probably act. And certainly with the same intentions. And so I think it is absolutely legitimate [today, for me, not to know and to let go of certain things].

Vasella's statement highlights another key characteristic of the Common Glue that was repeatedly mentioned by the managers I talked to. Similar *enacted* behaviors and common decision-making patterns were described as rendering a cohesive leadership cadre to something akin to a collective brain. In other words, a collective brain made out of a group of individuals where each individual holds a different piece of the corporate neurons, but where *all* individuals share a common set of images and beliefs guiding their individual actions. This characteristic is reminiscent of the remarkable properties of laser photographs called *holograms.*

A hologram is a three-dimensional photograph made with the aid of a laser. To make a hologram, the object to be photographed is first bathed in the light of a laser beam. Then a second laser beam is bounced off the reflected light of the first and the resulting interference pattern (the area where the two laser beams commingle) is captured on film. When the film is developed, it looks like a meaningless swirl of light and dark lines. But as soon as the developed film is illuminated by another laser beam, a three-dimensional image of the original object appears. The three-dimensionality of such images is not the only remarkable characteristic of holograms. If a hologram of an orchid is cut into half and then illuminated by a laser, each half will still be found to contain the entire image of the orchid. Indeed, even if the halves are divided again, each snippet of film will always be found to contain a smaller but intact version of the original image. Unlike normal photographs, *every part of a hologram contains all the information possessed by the whole.* Neurologists have discovered hologramic properties in the human brain. Some people who had affected parts of their brains surgically removed did not lose the body functions governed by the part of the brain they had lost. These functions were later found to have spontaneously moved to other parts of their operated brains. Moreover, in 1982, physicist Alain Aspect found hologramic properties at the subatomic level, showing that electrons were able to instantaneously communicate with each other regardless of the distance separating them.

When imbued with a strong Common Glue, an organization's leadership cadre was likened to a collective brain with hologramic properties. On the one hand, this means that each individual member of this collective brain holds different and unique technical knowledge but, from the perspective of certain images, social relationships, enacted beliefs and emotional commitments, each separate individual represents *all the information possessed by the whole group*. On the other hand, although each constituent social capability of the Common Glue was described as being distinct from one another, it was suggested that, when examined separately, each of them should clearly *include and delineate clearly all the essential elements of the remaining four social capabilities.*

The harmonic, holistic and hologramic properties of an organization's Common Glue are important to understanding how superior organizational performance is actually achieved by transcending all kinds of boundaries. In fact, organizations intent on nurturing strong "common glues" demonstrated an ability to decentralize decision-making and knowledge management — to *just let go of things* as Vasella put it — more as a result of the social bondings and emotional committments that were being created within the leadership group than in relation to any specific set of cultural norms or to the characteristics of the organizational structure. Says George:

> I like to think of cultures as values and norms. The values can be the same but the norms are different: what time you came to work, how you dressed, how you interacted with people. And what people learned is that when they went to Medtronic Japan [for example] it was the same set of values even if people had cultural norms that were different. They had the same belief. They believed in: *Restoring People to Full Life and Health.*

Nurturing Cohesive Worlds in the Edge of Stability

The managers I spoke to referred to the Common Glue as a dynamic phenomenon made up of a network of cohesive relationships that was nevertheless in a constant flux of tumultuous changes, always moving, always transforming, either to introduce new ideas and undertakings into the surrounding environment, or to timely adapt the organization to sudden changes stemming from it. Their descriptions of the Common Glue sounded to me, at times, like an oxymoron: the portrayal of a stable organizational phenomenon which was nevertheless generating continuous organizational upheaval. This odd organizational phenomenon was set within the context of an open-ended journey, where past changes reinforced and gave impetus to new ones continuously over time. This was far from the idea of organizational equilibrium as embraced by the early classical economists (as well as by many management scientists to this day). Instead, their portrayal fitted rather well with the notions of *critical state* in organizations, developed within non-equilibrium physics:

> The key idea is the notion of the *critical state,* a special kind of organization characterized by a tendency toward sudden and tumultuous changes, an organization that seems to arise naturally under diverse conditions when a system gets pushed away from equilibrium. This is the first landmark discovery in the emerging science of nonequilibrium physics — what we might equally call the field of *historical physics* [...] I should point out that in recent years this field has also gone under another name: complexity theory. After all, when things are out of equilibrium they tend to be complex — the intricately knitted structure of a food web, the irregular surface of a fractured brick, the infinitely detailed shape of a snowflake. But *history* reveals the essential elements that underpins complexity in all these cases.[7]

Non-equilibrium physicists have demonstrated that *critical state* is inherent to cosmic phenomena that are organized as *connected systems.* The latter are systems made up of a set of extremely *similar elements* that are *connected* via functional networks (where the functions can be physical, biological or social). Examples of connected systems are: pine forests, a beach made up of billions of similar grains of sand, the subatomic particles of a piece of enriched uranium or *social communities* made up of human beings such as the ones we find in cities, states or organizations. Within connected systems, upheavals that are provoked by sudden external changes — in other words: critical state — result from the propagation of physical, biological or social forces through the connecting networks that are inherent to the system. The key idea here is that the way in which upheavability — or critical state — is achieved within the system *has little to do with the details of the things involved.* Thus, the way in which a fire spreads within a pine forest, sand dunes are formed in the beach, atomic fusion is reached or a strong Common Glue is nurtured within a social community follows *the same, simple set of geometric rules.* These are the rules driving complexity and critical state within the system.

   The managers I spoke to described their organization's Common Glue journeys in ways that followed the key notions behind *critical state* with amazing precision.

George provided a good example of this when describing Medtronic's Common Glue:

> I believe that the most important thing is when you have this Common Glue, which for Medtronic was the mission, vision, the values, the relationships between people, when you have that Common Glue, then people can accept change as a way of life. Shortly after I became CEO [in 1990] I wrote a paper called *Reinventing Medtronic* that said we will be a totally different company every five years, but what will never change is the mission and the values. So that gave people a certain confidence that, yes, the strategy may change, the businesses may change, we may do things differently, but we know it's Medtronic.

The Common Glue was thus described as placing an organization in a situation akin to *critical state*. The way in which the managers portrayed this was by highlighting five key notions that are fundamental tenets in this branch of non-equilibrium physics. First, the idea that *history counts*. The Common Glue was described as an open-ended, evolving journey over time, where past initiatives, events and transformations are essential reinforcements of the next ones and constitute the seeds for new transformational initiatives and events. Second, the seemingly contradictory notion of *tumultuous changes being an inherent aspect of the stability of the organization*. In other words, the Common Glue was described as a stable core of cohesive relationships and organizational identity that *pushes* the organization *away* from static equilibrium and *into* a dynamic of constant, sudden and tumultuous changes and flexible adaptations. Third, the idea that *nothing reaches the critical state by itself*. To put any connected system in the edge of stability you require an initial thrust and continuous adjustment. Thus, a forest fire requires an external source of fire provided either by natural phenomena or by careless or pyromaniac hands. It also requires determined containment actions lest the fire can spread out of control with catastrophic consequences. The gentle action of the wind or the playful hands of beach bathers are needed to form sand dunes. But very strong winds make sand dunes turn into sand storms. Atomic fusion requires nuclear reactors that need to be constantly monitored to avoid the risk of nuclear leaks or an outright atomic explosion. And, as pointed out by the managers interviewed, nurturing a strong Common Glue within organizations requires *deliberate leadership actions* that need to be carefully monitored and adjusted over time in order to ensure that they lead to the intended performance results. Fourth, following the initial thrust, any connected system will reach critical state in a *self-organizing* way, in other words, by following the connecting patterns that are inherent to the system. The way in which falling sand grains *always* form sand dunes on landing, or the seemingly random way in which informal networks and social bondings spread within organizations intent on building a strong Common Glue, are good examples of the self-organizational characteristics of connected systems working toward critical state. Finally, the concept that *organizational complexity and upheaval arises from very simple structures and patterns* that control how influences propagate within connected systems. In other words, the way in which the intrinsic structure of the Common Glue was described resonated strongly with extremely simple features of geometry which, within non-equilibrium physics, lead to the complex patterns of *critical state*. This latter point deserves attention as it was described in connection with the Common Glue's capability to create strong social bondings that *transcended* the formal organizational structure as well as boundaries of culture, functions, geographies and the like.

As described by the managers interviewed, the propagation of the forces leading to complexity and critical state within organizations followed configurations that were similar to the *simple patterns of non-equilibrium geometry*. One of these patterns is known as 'small world graphs', and describes with stunning accuracy what the managers told me about how social cohesiveness is formed within organizations through the workings of formal and informal networks. As illustrated in Figure 9, a 'small world graph' is halfway between an ordered graph and a random graph. An organizational chart looking like a chess board, where people are represented by dots, and each dot is connected by straight lines with a minimum of two and a maximum of four other dots, provides a good example of an ordered graph. Replace the links in the ordered graph by a random set of connections, and you will obtain a chaotic figure of dots, straight, diagonal and curved lines which is typical of random graphs. The key idea here is that while you can connect any two dots with a few steps in a random graph, *it takes many more steps to move about on an ordered graph.* Now, small-world graphs are between these two extremes: they are made up of an ordered pattern of connections between the dots of the system together with a number of random connections between the dots. The random connections can link a set of physically close dots (in which case they are called 'short links') or can connect dots that are quite far away (this is termed a 'long link'). Not less importantly, some dots might turn into something like "web portals" in that they can show many more random links than the average number of connections in the network.

The Common Glue was described by managers as closely following the geometry of a 'small-world graph'. In other words, by wisely enacting company-wide communications and business inititatives as well as cross-boundary

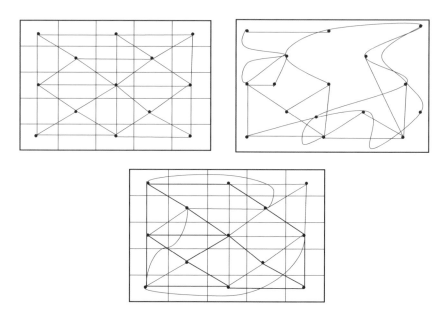

Figure 9: The 'small-world graph' in the center is a combination of the 'ordered graph' and the 'random graph' patterns seen at each side.

rotations, an organization was described as nurturing the development of *both* formal and informal social networks, and fostering the spontaneous emergence of bondings, relationships and contacts across boundaries. Not less importantly, it was highlighted that the informal social networks that are randomly created through these company-wide undertakings, provide the organization with a much more compact network of social relationships that allows for a much faster transmission of ideas and resources than what the formal organizational structure does. International assignments in far-away locations, for example, were likened to the 'long links' of a small-world graph, connecting people far apart within the organization in much faster and effective ways than the formal reporting lines. Similarly, some people in the organization who were particularly gifted at facilitating multiple informal connections among other people were referred to — and used — as 'portal people'. Indeed, it was often remarked that the patterns of the informal networks that are thus nurtured within an organization achieve their effectiveness by *transcending* the formal organizational structure as well as the associated cultural, professional and geographic boundaries.

Common Glue is about the Journey, not the Destination

As already hinted, when describing the nurturing of the Common Glue, the managers I talked to unanimously referred to it as a long-lasting organizational journey, involving the top leadership cadre first and then gradually embracing the whole organization. This was not, however, portrayed as a hopeless and never-ending pursuit. Rather, it was explained that by nurturing a strong Common Glue, an organic, evolving and living collective asset was being modeled within the organization. In 2003, Vasella remarked this aspect:

> It is an evolution, and [if] you fail then you have to re-start [again]. It is probably never entirely finished. Which is good, otherwise I would be out of the job.

This meant, for example, that once a set of company-wide stretch goals were achieved, another set of business goals and initiatives was immediately in store to renew the organization's impetus and continue to strengthen the corporate glue. It was also highlighted that, once an organization sets itself in the path of nurturing a Common Glue, it ought to follow it through *relentlessly*. George explains:

> If you are going down a direction don't change the path. In other words, stay with it. I think a lot of companies do change. A new CEO, a new leader comes in, they get into operational or financial problems and they start changing. And people become very cynical. So you have to stay the course. I think that is really very important.

The Common Glue journey was also portrayed as being rich in communications. Within the organizations I examined, these took several forms but — as mentioned — followed a common pattern of implementation. Initially, communications to nurture strong social bondings would clearly involve the top leadership cadre of the organization. Then, the members of this cadre would go out to their organizational units and lead the nurturing of similar bondings inside them. This seemingly simple, "trickle-down" type of approach to communications was especially followed by the larger and more complex organizations I looked at.

In short the Common Glue journey was seen as both long-lasting and challenging to go through. However, this was in itself portrayed as a competitive advantage by the managers I talked to. In their view, as any organization operating within complex environments has to face the detrimental effects of cultural boundaries and the like, over time they will also need to face the challenges of creating a strong Common Glue. Organizations that move and learn fast how to create this corporate glue will therefore get advantages over slower and less knowledgeable competitors.

Moving fast and decisively to build a strong Common Glue was therefore described as critical for organizations intent on achieving superior competitive performance across boundaries. This meant embarking on a journey where a number of activities had to be carried out simultaneously. These activities were quite varied in scope and nature but could be neatly clustered around five aspects. The latter were aspects that led to the organization developing certain capabilities to establish strong social bondings across cultural, organizational and geographic boundaries. We will examine these five social capabilities in more detail in the following sections.

Nurturing Leaders Who can Span Boundaries

The first cluster of activities managers typically talked about had to do with an organization's capability to identify, attract, develop and retain a leadership cadre with certain character traits that I termed: *boundary-spanning*. This was the first issue that Carlos Ghosn addressed in June 1999 when he left his executive position at French carmaker Renault to become COO of Nissan, then an ailing Japanese automaker where Renault had just acquired a controlling stake within the context of a broad strategic alliance between the two companies.

When Ghosn arrived at Nissan's Japanese headquarters he found the company in a nearly bankrupt state. Since 1991 it had been losing money and market share continuously, and car production had dropped by 600,000 units. The latter meant that Nissan's factories were running at a 53 percent capacity utilization. The company's product portfolio was aging, and it had 10 times the number of suppliers and four times the number of manufacturing platforms as Ford and Volkswagen respectively. Its US$20 billion debt mountain was more comparable to that of a medium-sized developing country, than that of a large automaker. Five years later, in 2004, following one of the most successful turnarounds in corporate history, Nissan's annual profits of US$7.6 billion and 11 percent operating margins were the highest in the automotive industry. Debt had been all but eliminated, and the company had launched a record 22 new car models over the previous 3 years.

From the outset, Carlos Ghosn, a South American of Lebanese descent and French education had provided an example of boundary-spanning leadership traits at work in Nissan. At the time of his COO appointment Carlos Ghosn did not speak Japanese, but he addressed the people in Japan directly, without pre-existing mental models, cultural prejudices or preconceptions. Said Ghosn:

I am not going [to Japan] with any preconceived ideas.[8]

Ghosn encouraged the expatriates he brought with him to Japan to do the same thing:

> [In July 1999] I handpicked 17 [French executives] from Renault and brought them to Nissan. I chose people who were around 40 years old, experts in their field, very open minded and coaches, not people who wanted to play it solo [...] [Before coming to Japan I told them:] we are not missionaries. We are not going there to teach the Japanese [about] the role of women in Japanese business. We are there to help fix Nissan, that's all. Any issue that does not contribute to that is of no concern to us.

Amongst the 17 Renault expatriates that Ghosn brought to Japan were Patrick Pelata and Thierry Moulonguet whom, as heads of Nissan product development and finance, respectively, would play a critical role in Nissan's revival. Once in Japan, Ghosn formed the company's boundary-spanning leadership team:

> I requested that 1,500 profiles of Nissan employees be posted in headquarters to select about 200 people for nine cross-functional teams. I was looking for young mavericks who would be the backbone of the next Nissan leadership generation. Multicultural experience was not considered an absolute requirement for success, but it was a value-added. I think that the basic personal qualities of an individual can always overcome any lack of experience. It is important how you handle small frustrations. And when you have taken time to understand and accept that people don't think or act the same way in France or in Japan, then the cultural differences can become seeds for innovation as opposed to seeds for dissention.

In early 2000, Nissan's new leadership cadre was in place. It was a reduced group of 200 executives not permanently housed at the company's Tokyo headquarters, as had been the case until then, but spending time there on a project-by-project basis. Together with this newly formed boundary-spanning leadership team, Carlos Ghosn began patiently crafting building blocks inside Nissan and made walk-the-talk and transparent communication his leadership trademark. As a result, the company's executive team presided over one of the fastest, most successful turnarounds ever.

As illustrated by the Renault–Nissan alliance, boundary-spanning leadership refers to the extent to which an organization's key leadership cadre — typically made up of a few hundred executives from many different nationalities — possesses traits that allow them to build bridges and establish strong social bondings between people belonging to different parts of the organization. This typically allows the flow of knowledge and ideas, and sets a transformational wave of cross-functional integration in motion throughout the organization. The boundary-spanning character traits were described as: tolerance, patience, the ability to "walk the talk" (or serve as an example through his or her actions), a giver's mentality (the generosity to give first in order to receive) and wholeness (a balanced display of 'male' and 'female' behaviors in every situation):

> Tolerance is an individual's courage, ability and humility to drop what I call his or her deeply embedded "mental models" in a cross-boundary working situation. Walk-the-talk is an individual's capacity to provide at all times a living example of what he or she advocates to others. Patience is the gift of taking time to craft a common language and make sure a common understanding has been reached in a cross-boundary working situation. A giver's mentality is the individual's innate empathy with what others are experiencing — the ability to understand them and be compassionate — and the generosity to spend time supporting and coaching them. Wholeness is an individual's balanced display of two seemingly contradictory characteristics: on the one hand, the courage to take tough decisions with decisiveness whenever the situation requires it and, on the other hand, the ability to genuinely care about others and build cooperative relationships with them across cultural and organizational divides.[9]

Carlos Ghosn and his team of 17 French expatriate executives exemplified the character of *tolerance* when — prior to their arrival to Nissan's Japanese headquarters — they worked within themselves humbly and courageously in order to get rid of their internal mental models, stereotypes and preconceptions about Japan or the Japanese. From the outset, they also provided a very good example of integrity, which most managers I talked summarized as: *walk-the-talk,* that is, an approach of leading by example. In 1999, Ghosn defined walk-the-talk behavior to Nissan employees as:

> What we think, what we say, and what we do must be the same. We have to be impeccable in ensuring that our words correspond to our actions. If there are discrepancies between what we profess and how we behave, that will spell disaster.

Patience is critical for the crafting of a common language and mutual understanding amongst a company's leadership cadre, and thereon amongst all of a company's employees. CNH Global, the European leader of construction and agricultural equipment formed through a string of cross-border mergers, acquisitions and joint ventures over the 1991–1999 period between Italian Fiat, U.S.-based New Holland, Case Corporation, German Orenstein & Koppel (O&K) and Japanese Hitachi as well as Kobelco provided a good example of patience at work to form a common language and understanding. In 1999 the construction equipment business of CNH Global created a series of 20 cross-funtional project teams in order to transform its multi-cultural corporate elements into one diverse but cohesive operation. Each of the 20 project teams included members of all of CNH's merger, acquisition and alliance partners, and organized itself as it wished. CNH Global had decided to follow a "multi-brand" strategy, meaning that it would sell its construction equipment under the Case and New Holland brands in the US, under Fiat–Hitachi, O&K, New Holland Light and Case in the European Union, and under both the Case and the New Holland-Allis brands in South America. Maintaining these different brands allowed the company to use all of its existing dealership networks. Thus, "multi-channel" distribution meant that CNH Global could reach different CE customers through different dealership networks offering their distinct brands.

At the beginning some teams had problems understanding CNH Global's "multi-brand and multi-channel" strategy for the construction equipment business. Former Case and New Holland employees, for example, were used to the concept of a single global brand and found it difficult to understand how the company would execute a multi-brand strategy. Therefore, the project team looking after multi-brand strategy implementation went into great detail, looking at every single product line and model, discussing and deciding what components could be shared with which product line and what components had to remain different. Moreover, it analyzed and decided which distribution channels would be allocated to each product line, targeting different customer segments with different dealership networks, marketing mixes and marketing tools. One project team member said:

> The strength [of our approach] was that the way in which product differentiation, multi-brand and multi-channel strategies were implemented was born within and across our 20 project teams. It was not a top-down process.[10]

The project teams also developed a common vocabulary for key terms. The word "logistics", for example, had different meanings for different people. For some former New Holland managers this meant the operational flow of materials along a specific supply chain, i.e. for manufacturing trucks. However, for a number of former Case executives "logistics" meant "transportation services". There were similar differences across many other terms such as "product marketing", "brand management" and so on. These could be found not only along national or corporate lines within CNH Global but also along professional and functional lines — even within the same corporation.

The character trait of *wholeness* is also central for leaders intent on transcending boundaries of any kind, and it is reminiscent of ancient Peru's myth of Wiracocha. As vividly portrayed in this myth, wholeness, in fact, stands for the harmonic blending of an individual's male and female traits in his/her leadership behaviors and actions. This was encapsulated by Vasella's description of the characteristics that were sought after in the selection of Novartis' initial group of 300 leaders:

> [In March 1996] we nominated [Novartis top 300 managers] based on our knowledge of the people and a clear criteria: we wanted performance, we wanted integrity, we wanted people with a certain experience. For us it was important to identify people that were willing to 'make cuts' even if they hurt. So, on the one side, these were people that needed to be very cool headed and very cool blooded. On the other side, these people also needed to be compassionate and have empathy, and react to what others were experiencing and support and help them.

To be able to alternate determined assertiveness and compassionate empathy, and to have the experience and wisdom to *know* when to display these seemingly contradictory facets, is what best describes the leadership trait of wholeness.

Both Vasella's description of Novartis leadership traits and Ghosn's portrayal of the 17 French expatriates he brought from Renault to Nissan's Tokyo headquarters highlight a bias for coaching others and spend time to support them when they are facing tough times or going through difficult challenges. This quality of empathy and willingness to support and nurture others is a character trait that I termed *giver's mentality*. One important thing to highlight is that companies such as Medtronic, Renault–Nissan and Novartis look for and encourage a strong giver's mentality in *all* members of their leadership cadre. Again, this is strongly reminiscent of the ancient Peruvian notion of *collective reciprocity,* described in Chapter 1. That is, the situation where every individual within a group agrees to and *enacts* the principle of *giving first in order to receive.*

It is important to mention that the managers I spoke emphasized continuously on these qualities as being character traits rather than technical competencies. And they were described in ways that denoted a certain sensibility, a certain intuition on those gifted with them. These notions resonate well with the management literature on leadership. For example, the difference between managers and leaders has been highlighted by Zaleznik in the following terms: "Managers relate to people according to the role they play in a sequence of events or in a decision-making process, while leaders, who are concerned with ideas, relate in more intuitive and empathetic ways."[11] Similarly, Kotter noted that while management is about coping with complexity, leadership is about coping with change: "leading an organization to constructive change begins by setting a direction — developing a vision of the future along with strategies for producing the changes needed to achieve that vision." In order to effect change and to act a as force for integration, the key leadership cadre needs to be managed as a global, cohesive and trusting group.[12]

A number of studies have in fact found that forming an effective cadre of key managers requires mutual cohesiveness, trust and integrity, in addition to the ability to empower and respect people as well as to communicate and to assume responsibility for the entire company. As noted by Bartlett and Ghoshal, transnational companies depend on leaders to manage complex interactions between an integrated network of specialized yet interdependent units. These leaders or corporate managers act to identify and develop talented business, country and functional managers and balance negotiations between the three: "A company's ability to identify individuals with potential, legitimize their diversity, and integrate them into the organization's corporate decisions is the single clearest indicator that the corporate leader is a true global manager — and that the company itself is a true multinational."[13]

The relevant literature also highlights that an organization needs to cultivate its key leadership cadre in order to allow it to effectively span boundaries. Continuous identification of a key pool of managerial talent means that the profile of this group of leaders is actively planned. Top leaders are constantly involved in the developing, attracting and retaining this key group of managers, as well as clearly communicating with them on a continuous basis.[14] As noted by Evans, Pucik and Barsoux, leadership development has to be viewed as a global and long-term process that goes side-by-side with the operational process of performance measurement and includes three sub-processes: (1) a process of identifying talent, (2) a process for planning the development of potential through appropriate assignments, coaching and training and (3) a decision-making process on who gets the job, ensuring follow-through on development plans. The leadership group is cohesive, acting as a well-defined unit, encouraged to have rich and numerous interactions across functional and geographic divides, highly supportive of one another, freely sharing information amongst one another in teams and across functional and geographic boundaries.[15] According to Hambrick, "team qualities are the essential foundation for a successful strategic process within the firm," since "the amounts of open-mindedness, perseverance, communication skills, vision, and other key characteristics that exist within the team clearly set the limit for how well the team — and in turn, the firm — can operate.[16] Equally importantly, when the leadership group is seen as possessing integrity, it "significantly increases the overall levels of trust and commitment throughout the organization, needed for great execution of strategy,"[17] and it inspires trust, which is "the emotional glue that binds followers and leaders together."[18] According to these authors, this is reinforced when the group leads by example and has close relationships with external partners, including customers and suppliers.

Building Blocks: The "Forrest Gump" of Management

A second cluster of activities managers often described referred to an organization's capability to enact what I termed *company-wide building blocks*. Taken together, an organization's building blocks represent a common stock of social and organizational knowledge amongst its boundary-spanning leaders that is constantly enacted and disseminated throughout the entire organization. Five fundamental building blocks were described by managers: (1) a common language, (2) a set of articulated beliefs that are shared organization-wide, (3) common career development paths for the organization's boundary-spanning leadership cadre, (4) unified performance measurement systems and reporting controls and (5) one set of common company-wide performance measurements.

A company's building blocks are such obvious enablers of global co-ordination that I often refer to them as "the Forrest Gump of management." However, herein lies a curious managerial paradox: although these building blocks are obvious to the intellect, they were very hard to find in a functioning state across most organizations I examined. For example, although most multinational companies I studied had an official internal company language such as English, the same companies demonstrated extremely weak levels of mutual understanding across organizational and cultural boundaries. One of the key reasons behind these kinds of inconsistencies is that these building blocks really are about common principles of corporate behavior. In other words, they are about establishing explicit, common rules, parameters and measurements in order to instill the specific kinds of behavior a company wants their people to live by. The crucial test of how effectively these building blocks have been implemented in a company therefore lies on how much they are reflected in the actual behavior of their employees. Establishing building blocks is especially difficult in the case of large organizations competing internationally. Here, even if one were to consider only the key leadership cohorts, these will typically number a few hundred individuals with different professional orientations, national cultures and functional attitudes. Establishing a common set of "obvious" building blocks across these differences constitutes a major challenge for even the most seasoned company leaders.

One of the first things that Nissan's boundary-leadership team did in 1999 was to set company-wide building blocks such as a common language in place. Says Ghosn:

> I told the old guard [of Nissan managers from the outset]: You speak English. Learn it immediately if you must or you're out. But some key words were not understood in the same way by different Japanese people or even different French people. So I asked a mixed Renault–Nissan team to establish a dictionary of essential terms. The 100 or so entries included clear definitions for terms like 'commitment', 'authority', 'objectives', 'transparency' and 'targets'.

A common language helped Nissan's work in "cross-functional" and "cross-company" teams effectively, with Renault and Nissan executives from different functions and nationalities working together to achieve challenging business objectives. Examples of the latter include: "launch 22 new car models in the next three years," "improve manufacturing capacity utilization in Japan from 53% in 1999 to 82% in 2002" and "cut automotive debt in half, to US$5.8 billion net in the next three years." George also provided several examples of the delicate interplay of setting common building blocks in place within an organization in ways that do not eliminate diversity but builds bridges to unleash the performance potential stemming from it:

> One of the important things that was made common [in Medtronic] was the accounting system, and [as we speak, in 2003] we are moving toward making the IT [information technology] common. But each individual unit gets to use their own system to operate their management process. All these individual units had to buy into the [company-wide business] goals we would set for the corporation.

In the case of CNH Global, its "multi-brand and multi-channel" strategy for construction equipment relied heavily on managing multiple brands, product differentiation and brand-based distribution channels all over the world. In order to manage this complexity the company created a "book of brands." The substance of each brand — its DNA, as managers at CNH Global called it — was to be identified, understood and codified in this "book of brands," which was accessible to all company employees.

The "book of brands" provided clear guidelines that reflected a proper understanding of the value inherent in each of the company's brands. Once the "DNA of a brand" had been explicitly defined and managers understood it, modifications to the brand could be undertaken. In turn, this helped managers determine the right degree of product differentiation across the company's full range of product lines. If product differentiation was too low, the brands risked converging and separate dealer networks could find themselves competing for the same customer segments. However, if product differentiation was too high, the potential for cost efficiencies and scale economies in purchasing, manufacturing and the like might be lost.

The management literature has emphasized many aspects of company-wide building blocks as addressing the ability of an organization to develop a set of shared commonalities among its members. A number of authors highlight that central to developing this common ground is a common language, which is used comfortably and consistently by the boundary-spanning leaders. Marschan, and Welch and Welch, for example, underscore the importance of a common language to multinational companies: "language affects the ability of companies to function in the international arena;" and "a shared company language is a common tool used not only for formal reporting but also as a part of the general process of communication at all levels."[19]

Another commonality underscored in the relevant literature is a set of shared business values, which is understood by upper and middle managers around the world as well as employees. This can also be expressed as the idea of corporate culture, which "represents an interdependent set of values and ways of behaving that are common in a community and that tend to perpetuate themselves, sometimes over long periods of time," in the words of Kotter and Heskett, who also note that in firms with strong corporate cultures, managers are excited about the shared vision and goals, and "managers tend to march energetically in the same direction in a well-co-ordinated fashion."[20]

Additionally, a number of authors highlight that companies with strong building blocks have a vision, mission and values which are evident in goal-setting and strategy-making, as well as most operational management. According to Schoemaker, a firm's strategic vision is "the shared understanding of what the firm should be and how it must change."[21] This vision is different from a strategy per se since, according to Collins and Portas, companies that have enduring success have core values and a core purpose that remain fixed while their business strategies and practices endlessly adapt to a changing world."[22] As such, a vision is stable, aligning the company over the long term. But formulating and communicating a vision is insufficient, according to Bartlett and Ghoshal: "central to effectiveness of a shared vision is the ability of individual organization members to understand and accept the goals and objectives articulated."[23] Thus the degree to which the vision is internalized by company members is of critical importance, according to these authors.

"Company-Wide Business Cases" Driving Knowledge Sharing

A third cluster of activities described by the managers had to do with the creation and the implementation of what I call *company-wide business cases*. A "company-wide business case" was described as a business initiative with challenging and clear quantitative and qualitative targets, which requires the involvement of — and has a significant impact on — most of an organization's component areas, and which the company employees feel passionate about because of its strong connection with the company's mission. An executive of a company that participated in my research summarized it as: *"An exciting business initiative that connects everybody and brings forward the performance of the entire organization."* The key idea here is that, by rolling out a continuous sequence of company-wide business cases, organizations compel people to get together to blend their specialist knowledge and create new knowledge around the attainment of very challenging and specific business goals.

Sometimes a "company-wide business case" integrates a company's diverse businesses toward the customer. This was the case with Accenture during the late 1990s. Made up of four different consultancy businesses — strategy, systems, processes and change management — Accenture started to form "service delivery platforms" worldwide. Each of these platforms, with names such as "e-commerce", "strategic alliances" and "outsourcing", offered global customers integrated solutions that involved all of Accenture's consultancy businesses. These platforms also had ambitious and clear quantitative sales and market goals as well as dedicated teams and resources spanning most of the company's locations worldwide. Accenture's "service delivery platforms" were one of the key reasons behind its rapid revenue and profitability growth during the late 1990s, which led it to outperform most of its competitors internationally.

In other cases, a "company-wide business case" operates behind the customer, across specific areas of a company's businesses that are, however, central to customer delight. One example of this was "six sigma", an approach to zero-defect quality that General Electric (GE) applied to all of its highly diverse divisions — encompassing financial leasing, aircraft engine manufacturing and specialty plastics production — throughout the 1990s. By enthusiastically applying "six sigma" to all of its activities, this conglomerate achieved astonishing customer satisfaction, cash flow and productivity improvements company-wide, and greatly fostered the sharing of business knowledge and best practices across its highly diverse set of activities.

As described by the managers interviewed, "company-wide business cases" share five fundamental characteristics. First, company-wide business cases focus *externally* on the end-customer. For example, Medtronic's unprecedented increase of their product release frequency was explicitly driven as a way of saving the lives of the end-customers. GE's six-sigma company-wide business case was also portrayed as making end-customers happy through a much better quality of manufacturing and flawless customer service. Secondly, employees feel a strong emotional connection with achieving the goals of their "company-wide business case" because of its embodiment of the company's mission. For example, Medtronic's increased ability to save people's lives by accelerating product release frequency considerably was seen as a very visible way of realizing the company's mission of *restoring people to full life and health*. Third, "company-wide business cases" crystallize in a very concrete way to employees, customers, suppliers and company analysts alike, the balance of strategic choices made by the organization's leadership. For example, GE's six-sigma initiative showcased the organization's strategy of delighting the customer (via better quality and zero defects) while gaining cost advantages over competitors (through an increased productivity and the elimination of defect-related costs), in ways that leveraged on the sharing of knowledge across the conglomerate's very diverse businesses. The same thing can be said of Medtronic's dramatic increase of product release frequency, except that in their case customer delight was also due to faster availability of better products, and cost-advantages stemmed from product release speed stemming from radical process and product innovations. Nissan's 1999 "Revival Plan" also encapsulated the twin aims of delighting the customer through much faster development of more exciting and innovative cars, while driving unprecedented cost-cutting and restructuring initiatives. Fourth, "company-wide business cases" without exception pursue very challenging business targets that stretch the employees innovation capabilities to levels of performance they previously thought impossible to reach. Thus, Medtronic's product release targets meant that the company became the world's benchmark in innovative product portfolio. Likewise, Nissan's "Revival Plan" objectives turned the organization into the world's most profitable carmaker with one of the highest levels of market share growth and new product design and development. Finally, "company-wide business cases" are a *permanent feature* of the better-performing organizations I examined, and they drive continuously and effectively the *sharing of knowledge* and other critical resources *company-wide*. Thus, for example, after achieving all the business goals in their "Revival Plan" ahead of time, Nissan introduced a new "company-wide business case" named "180" (1=1 million more cars by 2005; 8=eight percent margin or higher every year; 0=zero debt by the end of 2005). By its very nature, the "180" initiative also involved all employees throughout the organization and compelled them to join efforts and share knowledge across all kinds of boundaries in order to achieve their challenging business goals on time.

The connection between an organization's ability to create and transfer knowledge, and its competitive performance, has been highlighted in the management literature. For example, a number of authors maintain that central to a firm's ability to compete is its creation and internal transfer of knowledge. As noted by Nahapiet and Ghoshal, "increasingly, the special capabilities of organizations for creating and transferring knowledge are being identified as a central element of organizational advantage."[24] This is critical for the multinational, since it is "an economic organization that evolves from its national origins to spanning across borders" and "the cornerstone of this evolutionary approach is the treatment of the firm as a social community whose productive knowledge defines a comparative advantage."[25]

According to Bartlett and Ghoshal, "to operate as an effective strategic whole, the transnational must be able to reconcile the diversity of perspectives and interests it deliberately fosters, integrate the widespread assets and resources it deliberately disperses, and co-ordinate the roles and responsibilities it deliberately differentiates."[26] This is achieved in large part by a firm's ability to co-ordinate a large number of complex knowledge interactions at different levels, as well as the strategic roles of managers since "managers at the corporate and subsidiary levels will have sophisticated responsibilities, and the management processes linking the various organizational units will be complex."[27] The strength of a company's knowledge interactions is seen by some authors as being determined by the degree of co-ordination across different types of boundaries, interactions across businesses and business units. For example, cross-border co-ordination is regarded as a central component of the co-ordination of knowledge interactions, involving interactions across international boundaries as well as the processes and mechanisms which ensure smooth co-ordination across countries and regions.[28]

Rituals that Bond People Together Across Boundaries

A fourth cluster of activities described by the managers had to do with the roll-out of a series of *communication rituals* in a continuous and relentless way. As the name indicates, these communication undertakings were portrayed as being pregnant with symbolic content that involved organizational members both rationally and emotionally. There was a range of communication rituals described by these managers, ranging from company-wide events, to events involving the boundary-spanning leadership cadre, all the way down to individual behaviors and attitudes that sent powerful signals to the entire organization. What all these communication rituals had in common was an emphasis on frankness, transparency and an openness to turn these rituals into events that showcased the values of the company, its company-wide business case, or its opportunities for improvement through honest, fact-based and competent feedback.

Bill George set a powerful set of communication rituals in motion within Medtronic since his arrival there as CEO in 1990. Says George:

> We had some symbolic events which are very important to the company. For forty years we had a "Holiday Party" that comes across during December in which we bring patients in and they tell stories about how Medtronic products have saved or enhanced their lives. People are amazing, they run marathons with our defibrillators, they do the Iron Man Triathlon, they compete as master swimmers. These are some of the amazing things that people do with our products implanted in them. In addition to the Holiday Party, we also have a "Mission and Medallion" ceremony for every new employee. One year, I gave out medallions to eight thousand employees individually. Called them up, shook their hands and said: *Thank you very much for what you are doing for Medtronic.* And these are all employees. But the important thing is that it sends a powerful message. It is easy to delegate. It is easy to say: *Would you like to take care of this for me?* It doesn't have the same impact.

Likewise, Carlos Ghosn provided a good example of powerful communication rituals at work within Nissan. From the outset, in 1999, he embarked on communication efforts to instill a culture of extremely transparent, open, precise and factual communication, both inside Nissan and with outside parties such as the media. In 2002, Ghosn reflected back upon what Nissan's leadership set out to do in this area:

> If you want to mobilize 130,000 people, in different cultures and different countries you have to be precise, you have to be factual, and you have to base everything you say on hard evidence that people can measure.

In 2001, Thierry Moulonguet — a former Renault executive who became Nissan's VP of Finance in June 1999 — characterized this new approach to communication further:

> With Carlos Ghosn the rules of the game are simple and clear. That was perfectly understood by the young generation of Japanese managers. He is very approachable. Anyone can send him an e-mail, he looks at all of them. He reacts in an open and straightforward way.

A year later, addressing an audience of business school students, Ghosn provided additional arguments supporting the need for total clarity in communication:

> If people don't know the priority, don't understand the strategy, don't know where they're going, don't know what is the critical objective, you're heading for trouble. Confusion is the first sign of trouble. It's [the leader's] duty to clarify the environment, to make sure there is the maximum light in the company.

Nissan's new culture of transparent and factual communication was instilled by its top leaders' habit of 'walking-the-talk'. In other words it was made alive within the company through their top leaders' daily behavior, interactions and practices. In 2001, Ghosn's response to a journalist summarized this approach. Asked how much time he spent in communication he replied:

> Even in brainstorming sessions, even when we elaborate strategy, you communicate all the time.

Some of these daily events and practices became powerful and visible rituals that made the new walk-the-talk approach to communications come alive within the company. For example, in order to communicate his conviction that the solutions to Nissan's problems were inside the company, Ghosn would make surprise visits to Nissan's research facilities and production plants, gathering input from senior managers and line workers alike. The decision to make English Nissan's common, official language was backed up with intensive language courses for all the company's employees, regardless of level. In spite of the company's critical state in 1999, Ghosn also started the practice of inviting the media to Nissan's annual shareholder meetings and gave them complete freedom to report what they saw. He explained the rationale behind this new transparency:

> [People say] you cannot criticize your own company, but if you don't look at reality as it is, even being harsh at yourself, you'll never fix it.

Ghosn's reactions to critical observations by journalists and other similar outsiders often puzzled them. Far from being defensive, Ghosn would talk candidly about the company's shortcomings while pointing the way out of them. For instance, a journalist who in 1999 expressed disbelief that Nissan lacked even the most basic competitive marketing data, received the following reply from Ghosn:

> You laugh, [but] it's real. We had no substantial analysis, segment by segment [of] what was going on.

His choice to communicate the NRP to the outside world *at the same time* that Nissan employees were learning about it, in the Tokyo Motor Show on October 18, 1999, was a powerful sign of the company's determination to establish transparent, reliable goals and achieve them in a no-nonsense fashion. Ghosn explained:

> Credibility has two legs [...] the first is performance, but [we had nothing to show at the start, in 1999]; the second leg of credibility is transparency — what I think, what I say, what I do is the same thing. So we have to be extremely transparent.

Supporting this, following the public announcement of Nissan's revival plan (NRP) in October 1999, Ghosn stuck to its ambitious goals even though these were regarded as unrealistic by an overwhelming majority of competitors, industry experts, the international media and most qualified observers. Said Ghosn:

> The big risk is that if you announce ambitious [goals], people will not believe you. They'll say, 'He said 100 percent, but if he gets 50 percent he'll be happy'... Well, we want 100, and we're going to get 100. If we don't get it next year [2000], that's it. We will resign.

Instilling this new culture of transparent communications was not easy. In 1999, Ghosn had found a rather compartmentalized culture within Nissan that prevented the flow of communication across the company's various functions, borders and hierarchical lines. He observed:

> Country organizations were not talking to each other, people were not talking to each other. I want to destroy this spirit.

The "cross-functional teams" were crucial to turn the prevailing culture into a more open spirit that fostered cross-boundary communications. But there were other organizational changes that provided further support to the new culture. In late March 2000, Ghosn — in one of the few unilateral decisions he made since his arrival in Japan — replaced the company's divisional presidencies in North America and Europe with four cross-functional management teams that met monthly. He remarked:

> Each time you have a regional president, you start to have problems of communication and retention of information, either from headquarters to the region or from the region to the headquarters.

We don't want that. This is a killer for the global performance of the company.

There is a vast management literature supporting the notion that an organization's ability to carry out a set of frank, compelling, regular and company-wide communication interactions is crucial to instill a common leadership behavior in its key leadership cadre. The degree to which a company has informal communication networks across its worldwide organization is seen as an indicator of the health of its communication network. In the words of Ghoshal, Korine and Szulanski: "Interunit activities such as joint work in task forces and meetings play a powerful role in building the interpersonal relationships which, in turn, facilitate ongoing communication among people in different parts of the company."[29] Additional indicators of this network's effectiveness is the number of communication events and the effectiveness of these events.[30] The use of direct communication lines by top executives, key managers and shareholders, as well as the degree of mutual understanding between diverse organizational cultures is highlighted as another important component of communication mechanisms. The degree of internal communication quality is also important, and is characterized by a frank, clear and realistic communication style by top management which promotes proactiveness and opinion-sharing among key managers, and which also promotes shared values and goals and informs managers of the business situation and policies. Kaplan and Norton summarize the central importance of communication: "Communication is a major lever for organizational success. If employees don't understand the vision, they are even less likely to understand the strategy intended to realize that vision."[31]

Valuable Networks that Bridge Organizational Divides

Finally, a fifth cluster of activities described by the managers had to do with an organization's ability to use global personnel policies in order to foster *cross-boundary rotations* continuously. The key idea here is the capability of organizations to use a variety of such policies — ranging from expatriate and repatriate policies, incentive systems, evaluation and career growth programs, all the way to executive development policies and international assignments — in order to create valuable networks of relationships amongst key managers and across cultural, organizational and geographic divides. Once more, during the 1999–2004 period, Nissan provided a good illustration of cross-boundary rotations at work in support of the creation of a strong Common Glue.

Nissan used personnel and career growth policies effectively in order to break boundaries, rotate key executives around and create a truly global leadership cadre inside the company. The initial thrust was provided in June 1999 by the incorporation of Carlos Ghosn and seventeen other expatriate managers from Renault's Paris headquarters, to very senior positions inside Nissan. But high-level rotations were not the only means used by the company to foster the development of formal and informal networks across boundaries. For example, a new stock option plan for all of Nissan's managers worldwide was set in place in July 1999. It helped in moving key development, design and purchasing executives to centralized, global locations that facilitated cross-functional knowledge interactions. To support this further, in 2000, a new global promotion and compensation system was rolled out. Based on the employees' profit contribution, it broke an old tradition of incentives based on seniority at Nissan and throughout corporate Japan. Nissan also established and led a Nomination Advisory Committee to review promotion recommendations. Since 2000, no leadership promotions have been made at Nissan without a performance review by this Committee, which used a performance rather than seniority criterion to endorse its recommendations.

However, preparing the mindsets and attitudes of its employees was a key step that *preceded* the rollout of Nissan's sweeping changes in personnel, career growth and incentives policies. Ghosn had made this clear when unveiling the NRP in October 1999:

> Performance-based career advancement will be established at the latest by the end of 2000 to make sure we act in a coherent manner across the company. Concretely, some of the changes will not be implemented before ensuring that the people in charge have changed their attitude, and that the clear performance indicators for which they are accountable exist.

Nissan's new global promotion criterion put into place in 2000 — based on performance — was ruthlessly showcased in March 2001. On that day, Nissan announced a series of high-profile casualties affecting executives who had failed to meet their targets repeatedly, including one company vice president and twenty subsidiary presidents. Said Ghosn:

> Accountability has to start at the top [otherwise] it is very difficult to push a company at all levels [and] make sure everybody is committed to the subject.

However, the benefits of the new personnel and career growth policies were showcased in other ways as well. Challenging long-dated boundaries of gender, in 2001 a high-profile female Japanese executive was hired from JP Morgan

Securities to head Nissan's communication department, becoming the first woman ever to lead a function within the company. The move grabbed widespread attention from the Japanese media, who commented that up until then ambitious Japanese female executives had had to switch from domestic to foreign-owned companies in order to make progress in their careers. Boundaries of age and seniority were also challenged by Nissan's new policies. In 2000, Nissan executives in their early forties had for the first time been promoted to very senior positions based on their profit-contribution performance rather than their seniority. Likewise, many of the best-performing heads of Nissan's cross-functional teams were promoted rapidly. Said one of them:

> In the old system everyone could be promoted, so there was no pressure […] For many employees it was a good system but for those with good skills, it was no good. If I [had] been replaced by a younger man in the past I would have been shocked. But now I don't think I would care, because clearly the person has better skills than mine.

Company managers also highlighted that valuable networks can be developed across boundaries in a *virtual* fashion, through the use of communication technology. For example, CNH Global encouraged the use of video conferences and conference calls to co-ordinate critical activities across its global organizational structure. One company manager commented on this practice:

> [Within CNH Global's construction equipment business] we choose to travel relatively little, except for the top executive team. Instead, we are incredibly big users of video conferences. I believe that each of our 300 global managers in the construction equipment business has got at least one videoconference scheduled every day. To the point that in 2001 we had to install four new video-conferencing positions at [former] Fiat–Hitachi's Torino offices, which can simultaneously engage 60 people.[32]

The management literature resonates well with the notions described by the managers interviewed. The human resources literature has devoted quite a lot of attention to expatriate and repatriate policies in connection to the development of cross-boundary networks within organizations. The potential of other kinds of global personnel policies to foster these types of networks have received relatively less attention. According to Black et al, for example, international assignments are one of the most powerful international management development methods.[33]

Edstrom and Galbraith posit that the international transfer of managers can "increase knowledge of the network, develop multiple contacts within it and increase the likelihood that these contacts will be used in collecting information to support local discretion."[34] In the words of Stahl, Miller and Tung, "expatriate assignments play an increasingly critical role in the execution of international business strategies and the development of global managers," since they "provide expatriates with an opportunity to improve their general management skills and intercultural competencies," and shape "the perspectives and capabilities of effective global leaders."[35] Also important are repatriate programs, according to Black and Gregersen et al, who note that companies that manage their expatriate employees effectively, combine expatriate programs with a deliberate repatriation process.[36] Cross-cultural training and coaching for the firm's expatriates and their families are seen as central components of cross-boundary rotations, as is the frequency of such rotations.[37] Mendenhall and Stahl highlight three areas that are emerging for human resource managers who work in the international human resources area: (1) in-country real time training, (2) global mindset training and (3) CD-rom an internet-based training.[38] The rise of virtual teams has also been highlighted as increasing the strength of organizational networks. According to Maznevski and Chudoba, "Managers from around the world must build close networks and interact intensively to achieve a global strategy's potential, functions served well by global virtual teams".[39]

Ascending "From Lesser Things to Higher"

The managers I interviewed described an organizational journey to nurture a strong Common Glue leading to superior competitive performance across cultural, functional and geographic boundaries. This Common Glue was portrayed as a collective asset of sorts. It is an organic asset made up of five *social capabilities,* all of which have to be in place in holistic fashion in order for the Common Glue to be attained. Moreover, the Common Glue was likened to a sort of organizational hologram, where each of its constituent social capabilities is distinct from the others but includes and delineates clearly all the essential elements of the remaining four. There were more remarkable characteristics of this collective asset as portrayed by the managers. At one level, the Common Glue was described as representing a stable core of strong social bondings and cohesive relationships amongst key organizational members, that transcend all the boundaries of the organization. At the same time, it was depicted as a dynamic asset that sets the organization into *critical state:* a constant flux of tumultuous changes, constantly transforming the organization either to achieve new goals that will change the surrounding environment, or to timely adapt it to sudden changes stemming from the external milieu. What was described was in fact an evolutionary process of continuous and positive transformations, where the important thing was the journey itself rather than the occasional destinations merely signalling that yet another step of the organizational trek had been reached.

Each of the constituent capabilities of the common glue had a distinct flavor that resonated well with existing notions in the relevant management literature. First, there was the boundary-spanning leadership cadre of the organization, possessing five character traits that allowed them to bridge divides and blend differences: tolerance, patience, walk-the-talk, wholeness and a giver's mentality. Then there were the company-wide building blocks — such as a common language, a unifying organizational mission and a single set of performance measurements — providing the commonalities that allowed organizational diversity to flourish. The power of knowledge interactions was described in connection to company-wide business cases that compelled people to reach out across boundaries in order to share knowledge for the attainment of challenging and exciting business goals that encapsulated both their organization's mission and its strategy. There were also events, dialogues, initiatives and attitudes that were carried out in a way that provided the organization with unifying symbolic rituals of communication, which had a strong impact and held a deep meaning to the employees. Not less importantly, it was mentioned that global personnel policies could very effectively foster cross-boundary rotations throughout the organization, thus transforming it into a "small world" of formal and informal networks — in spite of the vast geographic and cultural divides that often characterized the larger and more complex organizations.

These were the things that were told. And herein lay the challenge for the researcher to "ascend from lesser things to higher". At this stage of the study, the challenge certainly was *not* to go back to the existing theories or to scan the relevant scientific literature in search of an overarching epistemology that could place the empirical findings within an orderly framework. Had Leonardo and Harvey done that, the ancient age of the Earth crust or the circulation of the blood would have never been discovered in their times, as these things were nowhere to be found in their contemporary scientific literature. Rather, the challenge for the researcher at this stage is to keep his/her mind empty of pre-existing mental models and let it *ascend* to discover the underlying causes connecting the "lesser things" that were found empirically.

When I did that six things stroke me immediately about what the managers of the better-performing organizations had said. First, all of them had, *without exception,* described their organizations as pursuing the twin goals of delighting the customer while gaining cost advantages through innovation and knowledge sharing. These goals were pursued at the same time. Thus, rather than focusing on one *generic* strategy, these organizations pursued a harmonious *blending* of seemingly conflicting strategic options. Likewise, the more successful organizations I studied typically carried out a harmonious *blending* of external (i.e. via mergers, acquisitions, joint ventures and alliances), and internal — in other words, organic — approaches to top-line growth. Thirdly, these company managers clearly saw their organizations as having a positive mission toward the end customer. Fourth, these managers described both their organizations' strategic aims and its mission in connection to concrete company-wide business cases that brought them to life. Fifth, they all had talked about managing conversations. Meaningful, positive and powerful conversations. Conversations that created a common language bridging individual, professional, gender, generational, cultural and organizational divides. Conversations that created networks, bondings, strong relationships, trust and excitement amongst diverse people. Conversations that led to profound organizational transformations, innovations and knowledge exchanges. Conversations that opened up new possibilities, opportunities and challenges. In short, conversations that created common grounds for diverse people to blend their experiences and transform them into valuable organizational outcomes. Finally, these managers obviously saw superior competitive performance as a result of what they did. But what they did was described in terms of co-operation, collaboration, blending diversity of resources and view-points, crafting a common language, integrating knowledge, working together inside toward the customer, the suppliers, the allies. There was no obsession with competitors in what they did. Rather, a sort of awareness that by doing what they did, superior competitive performance was to be the inevitable end-result.

All of this called for a theory of harmonious social blending of diverse resources leading to superior organizational performance. A theory that was organic and evolutionary in nature, transformational in character, social in essence and multi-disciplinary in quality. A theory where the notions of social conversations, relationships and bondings forming collective goods were the centerpiece. A theory that expressed all the key inherent characteristics of the phenomenon at hand in one powerful metaphor of organizations. Metaphors looking at organizations as machine-like or mechanistic were out of the question. Those looking at organizations as systems of a kind were closer to the mark, but their abstraction sat oddly with the living, vivid images that the managers had described to me. Some organic metaphors, i.e. organizations as "brains" left outside the dynamicity of the social blending that managers had so emphatically portrayed as being critical to organizational performance. Others, i.e. organizations as functioning parts of the larger clock wise mechanism of the marketplace did not reflect the notion of critical state and sudden upheavals that the managers had so clearly described in connection with the Common Glue.

And so I was, having discarded all these metaphors as inadequate, pondering some ideas during a break in an international women's conference in Lausanne, when the thought arrived swiftly to my mind. The simplest metaphor was to reveal itself as the most insightful. The Harmonic Fusion of the Male and the Female, transcending that primordial divide in order to blend into a unifying whole with the cosmic order. This was slightly more than a metaphor. It was a most ancient and universal archetype grounded in mythical accounts — such as the timeless Peruvian story of the *Pacha-Yacha* — as well as on hard scientific data. Its blending power seemed to work at the very epistemological level, as the supporting evidence for the archetype not only integrated different branches within the management field but also disciplines as far apart as cultural anthropology, neurology and behavioral science. This was to be the *causa prima* that connected all the stories I had heard. It was in fact an organic and intrinsically holistic archetype providing an evolutionary account of the unfolding universe. When applied to social phenomena such as organizational performance, it provided an explanation for all the social, harmonius, hologramic and transformational characteristics I had heard from the managers as driving superior organizational performance across boundaries. An account of this archetypal framework has already been offered in Chapters 1 and 2. It provides the theoretical notions behind social capabilities and the Common Glue as the female-like blending power of organizations that acts both at the strategic and the transformational levels to drive superior competitive performance across boundaries. The next step in the research was to validate these theoretical tenets with quantitative rigor. In order to do this, I had to elicit some hypotheses based on my qualitative research findings, collect relevant data systematically across a sample of diverse organizations, and test the hypotheses with the aid of statistical analyses. After all these steps were carried out, I made additional findings on the link between *blending* strategies, *blending* approaches to top-line growth, Common Glue and competitive performance — this time grounded on quantitative statistics. The approach I followed as well as the findings stemming from this part of the research are all described in detail in the following Chapters 4 and 5.

Notes and References

[1] Sherwin B. N, (2000) *The Manuscripts from Leonardo da Vinci*, Viking Penguin, U.S.
[2] Morosini, P. (2004) "Competing on social capabilities". In: *Next Generation Business Handbook*, S. Chowdhury (Ed.), Wiley, New Jersey, pp. 248-271.
[3] See Glaser, B.G. and A.L. Strauss, (1967) *The Discovery of Grounded Theory: Strategies for Qualitative Research*. Aldine, Chicago. Glaser, B.G. (1978) *Theoretical*

Sensitivity. Sociology Press, Mill Valley, CA. Glaser, B.G. (1992) *Basics of Grounded Theory Analysis.* Sociology Press, Mill Valley, CA.

[4] Bill George's quotations come from a video-case I made based on our 2003 interview. The video-case is entitled: "Building a Common Glue for Extraordinary Company Transformation", and can be found in the European Case Clearing House (ECCH).

[5] See Reference 2, pp. 266-267.

[6] Daniel Vasella's quotations come from a video-case I made based on our 2003 interview. The video-case is entitled: "Building a Common in a Merger of Equals", and can be found in the European Case Clearing House (ECCH).

[7] Buchanan, M. (2000) *Ubiquity*, Crown Publishers, New York.

[8] All of Carlos Ghosn quotes can be found in Morosini, P. (2005) "Nurturing successful alliances across boundaries — lessons from the Renault–Nissan case". In: *The Strategic Alliances Handbook,* O. Shenkar (Ed.), Sage Beverley Hills, CA.

[9] See Reference 2, p. 267.

[10] Morosini, P. (2004) "Building social capabilities to win in global acquisitions, joint ventures and alliances — The CNH global case". In: *Managing Culture and Human Resources in Mergers and Acquisitions*, Stahl, G K. and M. E. Mendenhall (Eds.), Stanford University Press, Stanford.

[11] Zaleznik, A. (1977) "Managers and leaders: Are they different?" *Harvard Business Review* 55 (3): 67-77.

[12] Kotter, J. (1990) "What leaders really do," *Harvard Business Review* 79(11): 85-90.

[13] Barlett, C.A. and S. Ghoshal (1994) "What is a global manager?" In: *Global Strategies: Insights from the World's Leading Thinkers,* P. Barnevik and R.M. Kanter (Eds.), Harvard Business School Press, Boston, MA.

[14] Conger, J. (1991) "Inspiring others: the language of leadership," *Academy of Management Executive,* 5 (1): 31-45.

[15] Evans, P.V. Pucik and J.L. Barsoux (2002) *Leadership development,* McGraw-Hill, New york. Also see: Evans, P.A. (1992) "Developing leaders and managing development," *European Journal of Management* 10:1

[16] Hambrick, D.C. (1987) "The top management team: Key to strategic success," *California Management Review* 30(1): 88-108.

[17] Gregersen, H.B., A.J. Morrison and S.J. Black (1998) "Developing leaders for the global frontier," *Solan Management Review* 40(1): 21-32.

[18] Bennis, W. and B. Nanus (1985) *Leadership: The Strategies for Taking Charge,* Harper & Row, New york.

[19] Marschan, R., D. Welch and L. Welch (1997) "Language: The forgotten factor in multinational management," *European Management Journal* 15 (5): 591-198.

[20] Kotter, J.P. and J.L. Heskett (1992) *Corporate Culture and Performance,* Free Press, New York.

[21] Schoemaker, P.H. (1992) "How to link strategic vision to core capabilities," *Sloan Management Review* 34(1): 67–81.

[22] Collins, J.C. and J.I. Porras (1996) "Building your company's vision," *Harvard Business Review* 74(5): 65–77.

23 Bartlett, C.A. and S. Ghoshal (1998) *Managing across borders: The transnational solution*, Harvard Business School Press, Cambridge.

24 Nahapiet, J. and S. Ghoshal (1998) "Social capital, intellectual capital and the organizational advantage," *Academy of Management Review* 23(2): 242–266.

25 Kogut, B. and U. Zander (1993) "Knowledge of the firm and the evolutionary theory of the multinational corporation," *Journal of International Business Studies* 34(6): 516–529.

26 Bartlett, C. A. and S. Ghoshal (1989) *Managing across Borders: The Transnational Solution*, Harvard Business School Press, Cambridge.

27 Doz, Y. and C.K. Pralahad (1981) "Headquarters' influence and strategic control in MNCs," *Sloan Management Review* 23(1): 15–29.

28 Evans, P., V. Pucik and J.L. Barsoux (2002) *The Global Challenge: Frameworks for International Human Resource Management*, McGraw-Hill, New York.

29 Ghoshal, S., H. Korine and G. Szulanski (1994) "Interunit communication in multinational corporations," *Management Science 40(1)*: 96-110.

30 See Reference 15.

31 Kaplan, R.S. and D.P. Norton (2001) *The Strategy-Focused Organization: How Balanced Scorecard Companies Thrive in the New Business Environment*, Harvard Business School Press, Cambridge.

32 Morosini, P. (2004) "Building social capabilities to win in global acquisitions, joint ventures and alliances — The CNH global case", in: *Managing Culture and Human Resources in Mergers and Acquisitions,* Stahl, G.K. and M.E. Mendenhall (Eds.), Stanford University Press, Stanford.

33 Black, S.J., H.B. Gregersen and M.E. Mendenhall (1993) *Global Assignments: Successfully Expatriating and repatriating International Managers*, Jossey-Bass, San Francisco.

34 Edstrom, A. and J.R. Galbraith (1977) "Transfer of managers as a coordination and control strategy in multinational organizations," *Administrative Science Quarterly* 27: 248–263.

35 Stahl, G.K., E.L. Miller and R.L. Tung (2001) Towards the boundaryless career: A closer look at the expatriate career concept and the perceived implications of an international assignment, INSEAD Working Paper, Fontainbleau.

36 Black, S.J., H.B. Gregersen (1999) "The right way to manage expats," *Harvard Business Review* 77(2): 52–59.

37 Mendenhall, M. and G. Oddou (1985) "The dimensions of expatriate acculturation: A review," *Academy of Management Review* 10(1): 39–47; Forster, N. (2000) "Expatriates and the impact of cross-cultural training," *Human Resource Management Journal* 10: 63–78; Mendenhall, M. and G.K. Stahl (2000) "Expatriate training and development: Where do we go from here?" *Human Resource Management Journal* 39(2 and 3): 251–265; Caligiuri, P., J. Philips, M. Lazarova, I. Tarique, and P. Bürgi (2001) "The theory of met expectations applied to expatriate adjustment: The role of cross cultural training," *International Journal of Human Resource Management* 12(3): 357–372; Tung, R.L. (1981) "Selection and training of personnel for overseas assignments," *Columbia Journal of World Business* 16(1): 35–49; Harris, H. and C. Brewster (1999) "International human resource management: the European contribution,"

In International Human Resource Management: Contemporary Issues in Europe, Routledge, London; Murray, F.T. and A.H. Murray (1986) "SMR Forum: Global managers for global businesses," *Sloan Management Review* 27: 75–80; Morosini, P. (1998) *Managing Cultural Differences*, Pergamon Press, Oxford; Evans, P., V. Pucik and J. Barsoux (2002) *The Global Challenge: Frameworks for International Human Resource Management*, McGraw-Hill, Boston; Harris, H. and C. Brewster (1999) "The coffee-machine system: how international selection really works," *The International Journal of Human Resource Management* 10(3): 488–500; Black, J.S. and G.K. Stephens (1989) "The influence of the spouse on expatriate adjustment and intent to stay in assignments," *Journal of Management* 15: 529–544; Stephens, G.K. and S. Black (1991) "The impact of spouse's career-orientation on managers during international transfers," *Journal of Management Studies* 28(4): 417–428.

[38] Mendenhall, M.E. and G.K. Stahl (2000) "Expatriate Training & Development: Where do we go from here?" *Human Resources Management* 39 (2/3): 147-157.

[39] Maznevski, M.L. and K.M. Chudoba. (2000) "Bridging space over time: Global virtual team dynamics and effectiveness," *Organization Science* 11(5): 473-492.

Chapter 4

Measuring The Blending Power of Organizations

> Things should be made as simple as possible, but not simpler.
>
> Albert Einstein

The company managers of the better-performing companies I interviewed during the initial, qualitative stage of my research study described a balance of strategic choices characterized by, at the same time, delighting the customer through product and service differentiation, and gaining cost advantages via knowledge sharing and innovation. Rather than *generic* strategies, their strategic choices could be better characterized as a harmonious *blending* of seemingly conflicting strategic options. Similarly, top-line growth was described as a balanced mix of external (i.e. via mergers, acquisitions, joint ventures and alliances), and internal — that is, through organic growth approaches. These *blending* strategies and approaches to top-line growth were portrayed by the managers as being just specific facets of the blending power at work of an organizational asset of sorts: the Common Glue.

As explained in the previous chapter, the Common Glue was described as a collective asset that organizations nurtured harmoniously in order to attain superior competitive performance across cultural, organizational and geographic boundaries. And nurturing a strong Common Glue meant working relentlessly on five *social capabilities* at the same time, *all* of which had to be in place and functioning properly. These social capabilities were termed: boundary-spanning leadership, company-wide building blocks, knowledge interactions, communication rituals and cross-boundary rotations. In addition, the Common Glue was described as being *holistic* in nature, that is, as being more than the sum of its constitutive elements. And this "more" was variously portrayed as coherent execution, mutual trust, emotional commitment, a common language and shared behaviors. All these aspects allowed the organization to turn differences into advantages by cohesively amalgamating it around an exciting company mission and the pursuit of a common set of challenging business goals. Moreover, there were *hologramic* properties associated with the five elements of the Common Glue. In other words, although each constituent social capability of the Common Glue was described as being distinct from one another, it was suggested that, when examined separately, each social capability *included and delineated clearly all the essential elements of the remaining four.* Equally importantly, the nurturing of a strong Common Glue was described as an open-ended journey characterized by continuous work around the five social capabilities, the attainment of numerous challenging business goals on the way and the succession of sudden and tumultuous internal transformations vis-à-vis a continuously changing milieu.

An attempt to capture all these characteristics in rigorous predicaments is provided in the five propositions below:

Proposition 1. *Blending strategies are combinations of the generic strategic options of: delighting the customer, cost leadership and innovation.*

Proposition 2. *An organization's blending approach to top-line growth is a combination of external (i.e. via mergers, acquisitions and strategic alliances) and internal (i.e. organic) growth.*

Proposition 3. *An organization's Common Glue is represented by the holistic interaction of five social capabilities: boundary-spanning leadership, company-wide building blocks, knowledge interactions, communication rituals and cross-boundary rotations.*

Proposition 4. *An organization's Common Glue is made up by five social capabilities which are, at the same time, distinct from one another but closely interrelated amongst themselves.*

Proposition 5. *The strength of an organization's Common Glue is nurtured over time.*

Within the management literature, the kind of harmonious, holistic, hologramic and evolutionary qualities attributed to the Common Glue by the managers interviewed have been ascribed to other organizational phenomena. A good illustration of this is provided by Nahapiet and Ghoshal's notion of a firm's social capital as comprising relational, structural and cognitive dimensions that evolve over time.[1] *Relational* social capital refers to the networks of mutual acquaintance and recognition within a firm's relationships together with the critical knowledge and other resources that can be mobilized through those networks. *Structural* social capital comprises the overall, personal patterns of connections between the members or actors of a relational network — "that is, *who* you reach and *how* you reach them". *Cognitive* social capital consists of key knowledge and other resources that provide a system of meaning, purpose, identity and social belonging, as well as shared representations, beliefs and interpretations to a group of individuals within a firm.

Social capital theorists describe these three dimensions of social capital as being *distinct but highly interrelated*. Furthermore, these authors highlight two important ways in which a firm's social capital can act as a holistic organizational phenomenon. First, applied social capital increases the efficiency of action. Especially in the case of critical firm-wide activities where knowledge integration is required across professional, cultural and functional boundaries, social capital can increase the efficiency of information diffusion and reduce the costs of transactions.[2] Second, applied social capital encourages trust, creativity and learning between the members of a social network. This in turn leads to the development of innovative forms of association and organization that create value for the firm.[3]

Interestingly, some connections are apparent between the dimensions of a firm's social capital and specific aspects of some the social capabilities that the managers described. For example, some areas of knowledge interactions, i.e. formal and informal know-how networks, are similar to the *relational* dimension of a firm's social capital. Some aspects of cross-boundary rotations as well as communication rituals, namely the 'small-world' network of social relationships and communications within organizations, are also akin to the *structural* dimension of a firm's social capital. Some elements of company-wide building blocks such as a common language as well as a shared mission, vision and beliefs are also similar to the *cognitive* realm of a firm's social capital.

The Blending Power that Unleashes Superior Performance

The first hypothesized relationship stemming from the qualitative data is what I called the hypothesis of *the blending power of organizations*. It postulates a positive link between, on the one hand, *blending* strategies, *blending* approaches to top-line growth and the Common Glue, and, on the other hand, competitive performance. This hypothesis, in fact, represents the cornerstone of this whole 'female' theory of organizational performance, simply expressing that it is the power of blending an organization's 'male' and 'female' characteristics *together* — at the strategic and the implementation levels — *what* explains its level of competitive performance across boundaries. This hypothesis was, in fact, often made explicit by many of the managers interviewed, more or less in the following terms:

H1 — The blending power of organizations

An organization's blending strategies and blending approaches to top line growth, together with its Common Glue, positively explain its level of competitive performance across cultural, organizational and geographic boundaries, and the strength of this link is greater than the links between each separate element and competitive performance.

In Hypothesis 1, the phrase "positively explains" means that, on the one hand, blending strategies and approaches to growth as well as the Common Glue are expected to be positively correlated with competitive performance. In addition, it means that the model that *altogether* includes blending strategies and approaches to growth as well as the Common Glue, is expected to be better at explaining differences in competitive performance vis-à-vis alternative models that include only a subset of these elements. In other words, the hypothesis of the blending power of organizations postulates that *each and all* of these elements are useful at explaining *what* drives an organization's competitive performance across boundaries. Conversely, were we to take one of these elements out, the hypothesis maintains that we would end up with a less powerful explanation of competitive performance within organizations.

The second hypothesis gets us closer to the Common Glue itself, linking the strength of its holistic *and* blending power to superior competitive performance. This hypothesized link was highlighted very obviously by the managers I interviewed. There were insistent remarks that, although each social capability on its own could lead to positive competitive performance results, it was addressing all five that worked the magic. The strength of an organization's Common Glue was therefore described as having a positive and holistic impact on its competitive performance:

H2 — The common glue hypothesis

The stronger a firm's Common Glue the better its competitive performance; and the strength of this link is greater than the links between each separate social capability and competitive performance.

The Common Glue hypothesis resonates well with some arguments and empirical evidence that have been advanced in the management literature. Although the empirical evidence remains fragmented, it suggests that firms with a well-assembled and mobile cadre of leaders that are capable of spanning organizational boundaries, together with a common language, shared beliefs and well-functioning communication and co-ordination mechanisms innovate more, develop products faster, have higher sales growth, achieve a better reputation in the marketplace and show stronger productivity and profitability levels than their competitors.[4] Equally importantly, it has been highlighted that these performance results are often obtained across challenging cultural, organizational and geographic divides.[5]

Linking Strategies, Approaches to Top-Line Growth, Social Capabilities and Performance

As mentioned, although the managers remarked the *blending* organizational function as driving superior competitive performance, this did not mean that the strategic choices and social capabilities had no value when approached individually. Rather, they were also seen as positively influencing competitive performance, though not as powerfully as when taking all these elements *together*. It is therefore important for the completeness of the quantitative analyses to include these aspects managers also referred to. From the perspective of *generic* strategic options, this leads to the following hypothesis:

H3 — Generic strategies and competitive performance

3a) *Delighting the customer is positively correlated with competitive performance.*

3b) *Cost leadership is positively correlated with competitive performance.*

3c) *Innovation is positively correlated with competitive performance.*

A very interesting aspect described by the managers of the better-performing companies was the interplay between generic strategies and competitive performance, as well as between social capabilities and generic strategies. Regarding the former, although an organization was seen as following a blend of generic strategic options at every point of time, each of them had a differential impact on competitive performance. A female-like innovation strategy was described by managers as the crux of superior competitive performance. Innovation — applied to new business opportunities, processes, technology, managerial approaches or products and services — was seen as what keeps an organization's superior competitive performance in the long-run. Delighting the customer was also seen as having a very powerful impact on superior competitive performance in the long term. However, cost advantages *per se* were regarded either as a positive collateral effect of an innovation strategy or — in its more pure form, entailing continuous cost-cutting, restructuring, delayering and the like — as a necessary strategy in certain phases of the business cycle (i.e. low economic growth), local geographies (i.e. countries under socioeconomic crises), or as a useful reactive or preventive tactic (i.e. whenever price or product wars against competitors unfold). It was also mentioned that organizations intent on developing social capabilities had a "natural" bias to adopt innovative and customer-focused strategies because of the outbreak of new ideas that typically followed the development of cross-functional networks and also as a result of the strong customer orientation embedded in their "company-wide business cases" and organizational missions. These arguments lead to the following hypothesis:

H4 – *Generic* strategies, social capabilities and performance

4a) *Innovation and delighting the customer have a stronger positive correlation with competitive performance than cost leadership does.*

4b) *Innovation and delighting the customer have a stronger correlation with social capabilities than cost leadership does.*

The relationships hypothesized above have a number of supporting connections with the academic and anecdotal management literature. Companies have demonstrated an increasing understanding of the importance of innovation to achieving improvements in performance. In a survey of 50 companies by Booz Allen Hamilton in early 2004, after 5 years of cost-cutting and retrenchment, over 90% of top managers at those firms, in fields such as aerospace, automotive products, pharmaceuticals and telecommunications, cited innovation as critical to the achievement of their strategic objectives.[6] Five years earlier, in their volume entitled *The Innovation Premium*, Jonash and Sommerlatte had written:

> Wall Street places a higher value on innovation than on any other approach to generating bottom- and top-line growth […] more than a change in leadership, more than a merger or acquisition, more than a renewed commitment to cost reduction.[7]

The authors conducted a survey of Wall Street analysts, and reported their findings: 95% said that more innovative companies enjoyed a share-price premium over less innovative counterparts, 90% thought that innovation had become more important in the last 10 years and around 70% said that innovation was a key driver of market valuation of companies. The authors also found that companies in the top 20% of *Fortune*'s innovation ratings received twice the shareholder returns of the other companies in their industries.

On the other hand, as mentioned in Chapter 2, the management literature defines a strategy of delighting the customer as one that makes an organization focus on building positive relationships with customers. It achieves this by surpassing customer expectations consistently — either through differentiated products or services or through exceeding customer service standards — in order to create customer enthusiasm and loyalty. Companies pursuing this archetypally female strategy work hard to understand the customer's present requirements, as well as to anticipate future requirements. An archetypal example of this type of strategy in the management literature is offered by Jan Carlzon, a former CEO of commercial airline SAS, and a pioneer in the field of delighting the customer. Under Carlzon's leadership, in 1981 SAS went from sustaining heavy losses to turning a profit in a year's time. In a book he wrote on his experience as company CEO, he made the following claim:

> We have reoriented ourselves to become a customer driven company — a company that recognises that its only true assets are satisfied customers, all of whom expect to be treated as individuals, and who won't select us as their airline unless we do just that.[8]

On the other hand, one-sided cost leadership strategies do not seem to enjoy a positive track record of long-term competitive performance neither in the academic nor in the anecdotal management literature. As mentioned, these types of strategies are often seen as effective in the short- to medium-term, or as a first-step measure when companies are doing badly because of internal or market conditions (or both), but are not looked upon as particularly sustainable strategies over the long term. Good examples of this are provided by the corporate careers of turnaround specialists such as Albert Dunlap. This CEO, nicknamed "Chainsaw Al", was able to implement a radical turnaround at Scott Paper as well as many other troubled companies under his helm, through ruthless downsizing initiatives that turned them into low-cost leaders in their industries and increased their shareholder value quite spectacularly over the short term. Chainsaw Al would leave the companies he had successfully downsized when these were at the peak of their shareholder value, and would move on to the next troubled company that demanded his services. This type of approach was much admired by certain areas of the business community during the decade of the

1980s. However, while effective in boosting short-term shareholder value, Dunlap's restructuring initiatives were unsustainable over the long haul. When he eventually failed to implement the same approach at Sunbeam, he was fired and his corporate career ended as a result.

On the other hand, the managers interviewed also made statements on the interplay between strategic approaches to top-line growth, social capabilities and competitive performance that were summarized in the following hypothesis:

H5 – Strategic growth, social capabilities and performance

5a) *Internal growth has a stronger positive correlation with competitive performance than external growth.*

5b) *Internal growth has a stronger correlation with social capabilities than external growth.*

The managers' reasoning behind this hypothesis was as follows. On the one hand, although external growth via mergers, acquisitions, alliances and the like were seen as relatively fast ways of growing revenue, market share and customer base, in the medium and long run they were seen as making organizations too inward-oriented. That is, mergers, acquisitions, alliances and the like were described as leading the organizations toward focusing too much on internal integration processes that were often described as highly complex due to stiff cultural and organizational challenges. This often meant that organizations pursuing external growth risked losing touch with customers and devoted less resources to innovation. On the other hand, the more female-like approach of nurturing internal growth was described as perhaps slower in the short term, but leading to more sustainable top-line growth results in the long run. This was because internal growth was described as focusing the organization's resources on delighting the customer and continuous innovations. These views have a very strong resonance in the management literature[9] and lead to the additional hypothesis:

H6 – Link between female strategies and approaches to growth

Innovation and delighting the customer have a stronger positive correlation with internal growth than cost leadership does.

Finally, as already mentioned, the managers stressed that, although the five social capabilities together had the strongest impact on competitive performance, each of them could be seen as individually enhancing competitive performance results as well. There are important connections between these statements and some aspects of the management literature. For example, a number of authors suggest that a series of organizational dimensions examined here under the term knowledge interactions have a positive effect on a firm's performance.[10] In addition, in 1988, Norburn and Birley found positive links between organizational performance and the characteristics of a firm's top leadership that are similar to what has been described here as 'boundary-spanning character traits'.[11] Other authors have regarded international transfers of managers as one of the most powerful methods to develop people and increase the level of useful local knowledge within the organizational network.[12] Moreover, companies that have enduring success have been identified as having core values, a core purpose and other elements that are akin to company-wide building blocks, which remain fixed while their business strategies and practices change continuously to adapt to the external milieu.[13] Equally importantly, some authors see communication as a major lever for organizational success.[14] All these arguments lead to the next hypothesis:

H7 – Link between social capabilities and performance

7a) *The stronger a firm's boundary-spanning leadership, the better its competitive performance.*

7b) *The stronger a firm's company-wide building blocks, the better its competitive performance.*

7c) *The stronger a firm's knowledge interactions, the better its competitive performance.*

7d) *The stronger a firm's communication rituals, the better its competitive performance.*

7e) *The stronger a firm's cross-boundary rotations, the better its competitive performance.*

Developing a Method to Test the Hypotheses

The next step in the quantitative stage of the research was to develop a statistical methodology to test the hypotheses rigorously. This methodology had to take into account the holistic and hologramic properties of the organizational phenomena under examination. This meant, for example, that the statistical approach chosen to test the hypotheses had to be suited to assessing large amounts of variables and data, including statistical constructs that were expected to be well defined and separate from one another but — certainly in the case of the Common Glue's constituent social capabilities — *not* independent from one another. Moreover, as the Common Glue was described as an evolutionary phenomenon, multi-year — and possibly also multi-indicator — measurements of competitive performance were expected to be more broadly representative. Equally importantly, at this stage of the research one had to come to terms with the issue that the empirical examination of organizational capabilities usually is rendered difficult by the idiosyncratic, variegated and path-dependent processes stemming from an organization's unique history.[15]

The sample

I surveyed members of the upper managerial echelons of 11 multinational companies belonging to very different industrial or service sectors and possessing very diverse organizational characteristics as well as national cultural roots (refer to Figure 10). These companies were closely followed throughout the entire length of our research project, that is, 5 years elapsed over the 1997–2004 period. Except for Kongsberg and AVL, over most of the 1997–2004 period, each of the companies in the sample was routinely ranked amongst the top five largest outfits in the world by revenue size within their industrial or service sectors of operations. They also represented a variety of strategic orientations as well as strategic approaches to top-line growth, ranging from a preference for external growth — i.e. DaimlerChrysler and EuroRSCG — to a bias for internal growth, — i.e. DNV or Givaudan.

I chose such a diverse sample of companies for three main reasons. First, because these firms operate with very diverse organizational structures, cover dozens and even hundreds of countries individually, compete in fairly different sectors ranging from manufacturing to service to conglomerate businesses and represent both external and internal approaches to growth, this sample of companies — together and individually — convey an exceptional richness of professional, organizational, geographic and cultural boundaries at work. Second, as innovation has been consistently highlighted as central to the performance advantages driven by social capabilities, *all* of these organizations and the sectors of activity they represent can be described as fairly global and primarily driven by knowledge-based competition. Third, given that the focus of attention at this stage of the research was on the companies' upper managerial echelons — and considering the specific

Company	Industry Sector	Key 2003 figures (sales in million Euro)	Main national cultures	Key organizational characteristics
DaimlerChrysler	Automotive	Sales: 151,871 # of empl.: 362,063	Germany and U.S.	Corp. culture: Conservative, Engineering, quality values Org'l structure: Divisional
Allianz-Dresdner	Insurance, Asset Management and other financial services	Sales: 103,834 # of empl.: 173,750	Germany, Balkans, France, Italy, Scandinavia, and the US.	Corp. culture: Acquisitive, traditional, conservative Org'l structure: Divisional
Zurich Financial Services Group	Insurance and other Financial services	Sales: 45,705 # of empl.: 62,000	Swiss, US, UK	Corp. culture: Conservative, traditional Org'l structure: Divisional
Professional Services Firm*	Professional Services	Sales: over 10,000 # of empl.: over 90,000	US. and UK	Corp. culture: Conservative, professional services and customer orientation Org'l structure: Private partnership
Schindler	Elevators & Escalators	Sales: 5,505 # of empl.: 39,617	Swiss, German, US	Corp. culture: Service oriented Org'l structure: Holding company plus two divisions
Givaudan	Flavors and Fragrances	Sales: 1,787 # of empl.: 5981	Switzerland, France and US	Corp. culture: Heavy R&D focus, innovation Org'l structure: Divisional
Kongsberg Group	Conglomerate of Defence & Aerospace, Maritime Products	Sales: 833 # of empl.: 4176	Norway, Sweden, Germany	Corp. culture: Conservative, engineering Org'l structure: Holding company plus two main business areas
DNV	Quality certification	Sales: 697 # of empl.: 5,762	Norway and Scandic countries	Corp. culture: Conservative, quality and ethical values Org'l structure: Divisional
EuroRSCG	Advertisement and Communications	Sales: 669 # of empl.: 1,200	France, U.S., China, Indonesia, Taiwan, Argentina, Brazil	Corp. culture: Creative, communications/agency mindset Org'l structure: A decentralized network of local profit centers
GateGourmet	Airline catering	Sales: 461 # of empl.: 24,000	USA and Switzerland	Corp. culture: Private, innovation focussed Org'l structure: Network of local production subsidiaries with central, global co-ordination
AVL	Automotive (autoparts)	Sales: 446 # of empl.: 3150	Austria and Germany	Corp. culture: Privately owned, engineering Org'l structure: Divisional

* The identity and precise 2003 figures for this company have been kept confidential.

Figure 10: Companies surveyed during the quantitative phase of the research.

resource constraints of the project — it was decided from the outset to aim at obtaining strong response rates from a dozen of highly diverse companies, rather than spreading our efforts across a much larger sample of firms.

These organizations were invited to participate in my quantitative research usually as a result of some of their top executives having shown an interest following a presentation of the Common Glue approach, either within the context of a public event or an internal company presentation. As a next step, the cadre of "boundary-spanning leaders" would be identified within each organization, by looking at their upper managerial echelons with the help of the companies' top executives and human resource professionals. In order to do this, we typically went through the following process. First, I would share with the firm's top executives and human resource professionals the typical profile, character traits and organizational roles of the so-called boundary-spanning leaders. Second, the human resource professional of the company would usually come back to me after a few weeks with a list of people ranging from just over 50 to several hundred senior managers showing their positions within the organization. Third, the list would be revised with the help of a research assistant together with the human resource professional, checking for completeness and whether some inconsistencies needed to be addressed. Fourth, a final list with the e-mails of the boundary-spanning leaders of the organization would be put together and made available electronically.

In this way, over the February 2001 to June 2004 period 2,050 individuals were identified as being part of the boundary-spanning leadership cadres of the sample of companies. A total of 1,873 of them were top executives and senior managers of the firm, with titles such as CEOs, country managers, heads of geographic regions, general manager of local business areas vice-presidents of global business areas and global key account managers. The remaining 177 individuals had less seniority but occupied "boundary-spanning" positions within their organizations, with titles such as assistant to CEO, global center of excellence coordinator and knowledge-sharing project leader. The 2,050 boundary-spanning leaders included men and women of ages ranging from 22 years to 67 years, and belonging to over 40 different nationalities spanning all five continents.

Dependent Variable

The dependent variable under examination — competitive performance — was measured based on multiple indicators of business performance, assessed over a multi-year time horizon and utilized perceptual assessments by the respondents. Within the strategic management literature, multiple measures of business performance have been suggested as inherently superior to single (typically financial) performance measures, given the different perceptions of key stakeholders, such as employees, customers, shareholders and especially senior managers.[16] For example, in 2001, Marchand et al. included a multiple-indicator measure of competitive business performance in their empirical study linking information capabilities and organizational performance. These multiple-item types of competitive performance measurements have been found to show strong reliability and validity when the assessments are made based on perceptual appraisals by a firm's upper echelons and senior managers.[17] We adopted this type of multiple-indicator measure of competitive business performance as shown below in Figure 11.

The use of perceptual measurements of competitive business performance is due to the predictive ability of certain managerial cadres with respect to a series of organizational characteristics, as well as to the need to use uniform empirical measures of business performance. On the one hand, we adopted here the perspective of a number of authors who maintain that a firm is a reflection of its managerial upper echelons and top executives. In particular, these authors demonstrate that a firm's top executives and its upper managerial cadres have a very significant potential to assess and predict their firm's business performance and competitive advantages.[18]

On the other hand, the need to use uniform measures of business performance was important in our study due to well-known issues highlighted by several authors in the past, including substantial differences in performance reporting requirements across countries and business sectors and in accounting practices between publicly owned concerns and partnerships. According to these authors, these issues can be found even within a single large-scale multinational organization, and this certainly was the case for some of the firms under examination here, which included international partnerships as well as outfits owned by corporate

1 – Market share growth
   a) Increase of market share
   b) Ability to capture (create) new markets
      and/or customers
   c) Ability to grow the business via IT/
      e-commerce/e-business

2 – Financial performance

3 – Level of product and service innovations
   a) Number of product and service innovations
   b) Quality of product and service innovations

4 – Ability to achieve a superior firm reputation

Figure 11: Multiple-indicator measure of competitive business performance.

conglomerate, or companies made up of a vast array of — largely family- and privately-owned — acquired companies worldwide.[19] Moreover, as we were interested in a multi-year measure of past business performance, a minimum of a 3-year measurement of performance has been recommended by a number of authors in order to ensure accurate reporting.[20] Within these circumstances and constraints, perceptual multiple-indicator assessments of competitive business performance have been considered superior to either "objective" or secondary measures in previous strategic management research.[21] Equally importantly, in order to ensure the quality of our perceptual competitive business performance data, we carried out systematic checks against archival data over the relevant time periods covered by our research.

Predictive Variables

Five inductive steps were followed to define the predictive variables based on the data stemming from the qualitative phase of the research. First, I had grouped a series of key statements — stemming from my initial interviews with company managers over the course of 1997 and the early part of 1998 — into a series of predictive sub-constructs. Second, these sub-constructs were grouped logically into five constructs entitled: boundary-spanning leadership, company-wide building blocks, knowledge interactions, communication rituals and cross-boundary rotations. Next, all five constructs were grouped into one major predictive cluster entitled: social capabilities. Figure 12 shows the social capability constructs and sub-constructs, together with some connections that can be found in the management literature in support of those constructs. Fourth, two other predictive clusters were identified in addition to social capabilities. These were a basic cluster aimed at categorizing the sample of respondents based on their essential company demographics, and a strategy cluster that included generic strategies and strategic approaches to top-line growth.

The last step was to define the predictive variables themselves. This was done by following the three-cluster structure that had been defined in the initial steps of the process. Thus, there was a set of ten basic variables to categorize the sample of respondents by essential company demographics. Then there were the strategic variables, which included three generic strategies (delighting the customer, cost leadership and innovation), and two strategic approaches to top-line growth (internal growth and external growth). Last, there were the social capability variables, a total of 75 variables associated with each of the constructs and sub-constructs shown in Figure 12.

Social Capabilities: Main Sub-constructs	Some connections with literature SM: Strategic Management HRM: Human Resource Management L: Leadership M/A: Managerial/Anecdotal
I – Boundary-spanning Leadership	
• A common profile for the firm's key managerial cadre that includes the five 'boundary-spanning' character traits	**SM:** Barnard (1938), Lieberson & O'Conner (1972), Jago (1982), Hambrick & Mason (1984), Hambrick (1987), Thomas (1988) , Morosini (1998), Morosini (2004) **HRM:** Rotemberg & Saloner (1993), Noel & Charan (1988), Evans, Pucik & Barsoux (2000), Becker (1998), Simons (2002) **L:** Bennis & Nanus (1985), Doz (1991), Evans (1992a), Edstrom & Galbraith (1977), Evans, Pucik & Barsoux (2002) **M/A:** Zaleznik (1977), Kotter (1990), Day (1999), Bartlett & Ghoshal (1992), Bartlett & Ghoshal (2002), Bennis & Thomas (2002), Doz & Prahalad (1986), Zaleznik (1997), Raynor (2001)
• Level of cohesiveness of a firm's key managerial cadre	**SM:** Hambrick (1980), Dess (1987), Chandler Jr. (1991), Simon (1993), Taylor & Beechler (1996), Iaquinto & Fredrickson (1997), Lovas & Ghoshal (2000), Morosini (2004) **HRM:** Evans (1992b), Evans (1993), Ferner, Edwards & Sisson (1995) **L:** Evans (1992a), Edstrom & Galbraith (1977), Evans, Pucik & Barsoux (2002) **M/A:** Doz & Prahalad (1987), Zaleznik (1997), Raynor (2001)
• Level of mutual trust among a firm's key cadre of managers	**SM:** Barney & Hansen (1994), Davis, Schoorman, Mayer & Hoon Tan (2000) **HRM:** Jones & George (1998), Gittell (2000) **L:** Webber (2002) **M/A:** Galford & Drapeau (2003)
• Common career paths for the firm's key managerial cadre	**SM:** Bloom & Milkovich (1999), Boyd & Salamin (2001) **HRM:** Pucik (1997), Evans, Pucik & Barsoux (2002) **L:** Pucik (1992) **M/A:** Knez & Simester (2002)
• Level of coaching and development of the firm's key managerial cadre	**SM:** Wissema, Brand & Van der Pol (1981), Huselid (1995), Van den Bosch & Van Wijk (2001) **HRM:** Prahalad (1983), Doz & Prahalad (1986), Evans (1992a), Evans (1992b), Lombardo & Eichinger (1997), Conner (2000), Evans, Pucik & Barsoux (2002) **L:** Gregersen, Morrison & Black (1998), **M/A:** Schein (1977), Bolt (1985), Fulmer, Gibbs & Goldsmith (2000)
II – Cross-boundary Rotations	
• Perceived quality of expatriate policies and programs for the firm's key managerial cadre	**SM:** Beck (1988), Black, Gregersen & Mendenhall (1993), Bonache, Brewster & Suutari (2001), Yan, Guorong & Hall (2002) **HRM:** Allen & Alvarez (1998), Mendenhall & Stahl (2000), Bonache & Brewster (2001), Baruch & Altman (2002), Evans, Pucik & Barsoux (2002) **L:** Rosenzweig, Gilbert, Malnight & Pucik (2001) **M/A:** Bartlett & Ghoshal (1992), Black & Gregersen (1999), Stahl, Miller & Tung (2002)

Figure 12: Social capabilities: main sub-constructs.

Social Capabilities: Main Sub-constructs	Some connections with literature SM: Strategic Management HRM: Human Resource Management L: Leadership M/A: Managerial/Anecdotal
• Perceived quality of repatriate policies and programs for the firm's key managerial cadre	SM: Black (1991), Black, Gregersen & Mendenhall (1993) HRM: Tung (1988), Feldman (1991) L: Adler (1991), Brewster (1991), Allen & Alvarez (1998) M/A: Harvey (1989), Lazarova & Caligiuri (2001)
• Level of cross-cultural training and coaching for the firm's expatriates	SM: Mendenhall & Oddou (1985) HRM: Forster (2000), Mendenhall & Stahl (2000), Caligiuri, Philips, Lazarova, Tarique & Burgi (2001) L: Tung (1981), Harris & Brewster (1999) M/A: Murray & Murray (1986)
• Level of cross-cultural training and coaching for the firm's expatriates' families	SM: Morosini (1998) HRM: Evans, Pucik & Barsoux (2002) L: Harris & Brewster (1999) M/A: Black & Stephens (1989), Stephens & Black (1991)
• Frequency of cross-functional and international rotations among a firm's key cadre of managers	SM: Campion & Cheraskin (1994), Ortega (2001) HRM: Pucik & Saba (1998), Evans, Pucik & Barsoux (2002)

III – Communication Rituals

• Level of face-to-face and virtual, formal and informal communication networks between key managers	SM: Ghoshal, Korine & Szulanski (1994), Nobel & Birkinshaw (1998), Tsai & Ghoshal (1998) HRM: Brandt & Hulbert (1976) L: Davidson Frame (1987) M/A: De Meyer (1991), Chesbrough & Teece (1996), Davenport, De Long and Beers (1998)
• Frequency of communication events for key managerial cadre	SM: Ghoshal & Nohria (1989), Gupta & Govindarajan (2000), Morosini (2004) HRM: Evans, Pucik & Barsoux (2002) L: March & Simon (1958)
• Quality of communication events for key managerial cadre	SM: Tushman (1977), Bannister & Higgins (1991), Chakravarthy & Lorange (1991), Nahapiet & Ghoshal (1998), Moran & Galunic (1999), Kaplan & Norton (2001) HRM: Granovetter (1985), Conger (1991) L: Schein (1992), Hinds & Kiesler (1995) M/A: Sullivan Jr. & Smart (1987)
• Style of communications among a firm's key managerial cadre	SM: Roth & Ricks (1994) HRM: O'Reilly (1989), Evans, Pucik & Barsoux (2002) L: March & Simon (1958)
• Communication between a firm's top leadership and its stakeholders	SM: Morosini (1998), Morosini (2004)

IV – Knowledge Interactions

• Level of codification and articulation of explicit knowledge	SM: Kogut & Zander (1992, 1993), Hedlund (1994), Teece, Rumelt, Dosi & Winter (1994), Grant (1996b), Teece, Pisano & Shuen (1997), Galunic & Rodan (1998), Singh & Zollo (1998), Zollo & Winter (2002) HRM: Grant (1997), Von Krogh, Nonaka & Aben (2001), Evans, Pucik & Barsoux (2002) L: Kogut & Zander (1996) M/A: Nonaka (1991)

Figure 12: Continued.

Social Capabilities: Main Sub-constructs	Some connections with literature SM: Strategic Management HRM: Human Resource Management L: Leadership M/A: Managerial/Anecdotal
• Level of cross-divisional and cross-functional know-how interactions	SM: Ghoshal & Bartlett (1988), Martinez & Jarillo (1989), Bartlett & Ghoshal (1990), Grant (1996a), Szulanski (1996), Tsai (2000), Hansen (2002) HRM: Evans, Pucik & Barsoux (2002) L: Adler (1991) M/A: Takeuchi & Nonaka (1986)
• Level of cross-border know-how interactions	SM: Ghoshal (1987), Bartlett & Ghoshal (1989), Subramaniam & Venkatraman (2001), Almeida, Song & Grant (2002) HRM: Lachman, Nedd & Hinings (1994), Evans, Pucik & Barsoux (2002) M/A: Galunic & Weeks (1999), Govindarajan & Gupta (2001)
• Effectiveness of information and knowledge sharing policies and processes	SM: Edstrom & Galbraith (1977), Levinthal & March (1993), Nonaka (1994), Zander & Kogut (1995), Liebeskind (1996), Nonaka, Toyama & Nagata (2000), Teece (2000), Spencer (2003) HRM: Grover & Davenport (2001), Evans, Pucik & Barsoux (2002) L: Daft & Lengel (1986), Davenport & Prusak (1998) M/A: Hansen, Nohria & Tierney (1999), Wenger & Snyder (2000)
• Level of face-to-face and virtual know-how contacts and relationships among a firm's key managerial cadre	SM: Bartlett (1986), Bartlett & Ghoshal (1989), Brown & Duguid (1991), Burt (1992), Hansen (1999), Maznevski & Chudoba (2000), Frost, Birkinshaw & Ensign (2002) HRM: Evans, Pucik & Barsoux (2002), Harvey & Novicevic (2002) L: Granovetter (1976) M/A: Vancil & Green (1984), Gupta & Govindarajan (2000), Gratton & Ghoshal (2002)
• Level of mutual understanding between organizational functions, businesses and geographic regions	SM: Morosini (1998), Morosini (2004)
V – Company-wide Building Blocks	
• Enactment of: a common language, common codes, shared technical codes	SM: Hofstede (1980), Barney (1986), Morosini (2002) HRM: Marchan, Welch & Welch (1997), Marschan-Piekkari, Welch & Welch (1999) L: Kotter & Heskett (1992)
• Level of shared beliefs around the mission of the organization	SM: Kogut & Zander (1992), Kogut & Zander (1996), Nahapiet & Ghoshal (1998), Schoemaker (1992), Hamel & Prahalad (1994), Nohria & Ghoshal (1994), Beechler, Taylor, Boyacigiller & Levy (1999), Sussman, Ricchio, & Belohlav (1983), Kogut & Zander (1996), Morosini (2004) HRM: Evans, Pucik & Barsoux (2002), Collins & Porras (1991), Larwood & Falbe (1995), Pascale (1985), Kraimer (1997), Chew & Chong (1999) L: Evans (1992a/b), Kouzes & Posner (1987), Drucker (2001), Evans, Pucik & Barsoux (2002) M/A: Bartlett & Ghoshal (1994), Schein (1996), Collins & Porras (1996), Ghoshal & Bartlett (1996), Lencioni (2002)

Figure 12: Continued.

Social Capabilities: Main Sub-constructs	Some connections with literature SM: Strategic Management HRM: Human Resource Management L: Leadership M/A: Managerial/Anecdotal
• Common performance, incentive and reward systems for the firm's key managerial cadre	**SM:** Stonich (1981), Bloom & Milkovich (1999), Boyd & Salamin (2001) **HRM:** Milkovich & Newman & Milkovich (1996), Pucik (1997), Evans, Pucik & Barsoux (2002) **L:** Pucik (1992) **M/A:** Knez & Simester (2002)
• Common set of codifying tools and systems for organizational performance assessment	**SM:** Gupta & Govindarajan (1991), Gupta & Govindarajan (1999), Morosini (2004) **HRM:** Evans, Pucik & Barsoux (2002)
• Common set of organizational performance measures	**SM:** Bourgeois (1980), Eisenhardt (1985), Goold & Quinn (1990), Simons (1991), Simons (1994), Kaplan & Norton (1996), Venkatraman & Ramanujam (1986) **HRM:** Schneier, Shaw & Beatty (1991), Schuler, Fulkerson & Downing (1991) **L:** Kaplan & Norton (1992) **M/A:** Sihler (1971), Flamholtz (1979), Eccles (1991), Meyer (1994), Atkinson & Waterhouse (1997)

*Note: All the literature references in this figure are included in **Appendix A.***

Figure 12: Continued.

The 'Glue Test©' Survey

As mentioned, the basic clusters and constructs of predictive variables were induc-tively drawn based on a series of statements I had identified during my initial inter-views with company managers over the course of 1997 and the early part of 1998. During the first 6 months of 1998, I organized these statements as a survey for sta-tistical data-gathering purposes. The survey was called "The Glue Test" of organ-izations and was entirely written in English language. As the qualitative interviews proceeded over the ensuing 18 months, the Glue Test suffered a series of minor adjustments based on input stemming from the interviewees. In addition, from June to December 2000, I ran a total of seven focus groups with 52 senior execu-tives of international companies representing 25 different nationalities. The main purpose of these focus groups was to ensure that the survey was clearly under-standable by our target group of respondents and that it could be answered in a rea-sonable amount of time. After seven versions of the survey, each of which brought its own series of minor modifications, I ended up with a final version that was deemed highly satisfactory and could be completed in 23 minutes on average.

The survey was organized as a series of statements which the respondents were invited to assess along a Likert scale. The statements were organized along the clusters, and constructs that were described in the previous section, plus a section entitled 'competitive business performance'. Altogether, there were 104 statements in the Glue Test survey. Within the social capabilities constructs of the Glue Test, a series of statements corresponded to each of the sub-constructs shown in Figure 12. For example, within the construct entitled "company-wide building blocks", there are five sub-constructs. If one took two of these sub-constructs, for instance those named "level of shared beliefs" and "common performance, incentives and reward systems for the firm's key managerial cadre", it was possible to see that they were associated with seven and three statements of the Glue Test survey, respectively.

All the statements about an organization's five social capabilities were on a 7-point scale ranging from "strongly disagree" to "strongly agree". In total, 15 statements were about company-wide building blocks, 14 about communication rituals, 10 about knowledge interactions, 20 about boundary spanning leadership and 16 about cross-boundary rotations. Strategies and strategic approaches to top-line growth were assessed at three levels: intended options over the past 3 years, actually realized options over the past 3 years and intended options over the next three years. Because the responses were non-mutually exclusive along a 10-point Likert scale ranging from "no priority" to "very high priority", each respondent could easily articulate a *blending* strategy or growth approach for his/her organization simply by choosing a combination of responses. Similarly, there were seven statements concerning our seven-item multi-indicator multi-year measure of competitive business performance, designed on a 10-point scale ranging from "very disappointing" to "very exceptional". For example, the opening statement of the competitive business performance section read: "Relative to our competitors, our market share growth over the past three years has been….," and so on, for each of the multi-item performance indicators identified in Figure 11.

The Data Gathering

The data-gathering phase took place between April 2001 and June 2004. Each company followed a different time frame. Thus, for example, GateGourmet went through a single 'Glue Test' data-gathering process in November 2001, whereas DaimlerChrysler went through eight different data-gathering sessions between July 2001 and May 2003. This allowed me to track the performance effects of the Common Glue over time within some companies, and to control for macroeconomic phenomena that might affect the overall quantitative effects under examination over time. The data gathering would typically proceed according to the following process. First, an ad hoc web site would be designed containing the Glue Test survey and all the necessary instructions and relevant background information. It was explicitly stated that all information provided by respondents via the survey would remain strictly confidential. In fact, the Glue Test survey was anonymous, the respondents could include their names or any other personal identification only if they wished to do so. Then, the data-gathering phase was launched by sending an e-mail to all of a company's target group of respondents, with an invitation letter usually signed by both a high-ranking company executive and the author. The respondents could upload the Glue Test simply by clicking in a specific string in the end of their e-mail invitation message. After responding to the survey, the respondents would send me their data electronically by clicking on a "submit" button in the end of the survey. From the date of our first invitation e-mail, we would typically give a company's group of respondents 10 consecutive working days to answer the survey.

By June 2004, 847 of the 2050 boundary-spanning leaders of the companies had responded to the survey (a response rate of 41.3%) (see Table 1). This quite high response rate meant that our respondents reflected the profile and characteristics of the entire population of their organizations' "boundary-spanning" leadership cadre rather well. In addition, as will be shown in more detail in the next section, tests were conducted for the missing responses that were received and, based on either a pairwise deletion or an EM-algorithm,[22] these missing responses did not show any discernible patterns. It was therefore assumed that the missing values were non-informative, in other words, that the respondents probably missed those responses by mistake rather than because of any issue related to the specific statements of the survey.

Table 1: Number of Glue Test respondents

Surname	No. of respondents	No. of effective respondents
A	10	10
B	62	62
C	147	147
D	91	91
E	79	79
F[23]	200	193
G	111	111
H	23	23
I	31	31
J	62	62
K	38	38
Total	854	847

Developing a Statistical Model to Test the Hypotheses

During the June 2003 to June 2004 period, I together with statistics professor Olivier Renaud, examined the data I had gathered and had a series of discussions over the impending quantitative analyses. Then, during August to December 2004, Olivier designed a statistical model that I deemed highly satisfactory to analyze the data. The next step was for Olivier to carry out the entire set of quantitative analyses that were required in order to test the seven hypotheses and five propositions that I had elicited, which are shown in the first sections of this chapter. The statistical model that was developed is presented in the following subsections of this chapter, whereas the findings of the quantitative analyses will be shown in the next chapter.

Treatment of Missing Values

The first step for analyzing the data gathered is to examine whether any patterns exist in non-responses (or missing values). Over a total of 854 respondents, 7 individuals from company F had stopped answering after the initial sections on basic demographics and strategies.[23] These surveys certainly were not going to be useful for most of the statistical analyses that needed to be carried out. We resumed work with the remaining 847 surveys, which showed a very low rate of non-response — about 1.07% — suggesting that the treatment of missing values was not expected to influence the results of the statistical analyses in any significant way.

Figure 13 illustrates the pattern of the missing values. Each of the 847 lines corresponds to one respondent, and each of the 104 columns corresponds to one statement of the survey. The dark lines and squares in the graph represent the missing values. We can see, for example, three dark squares representing groups of respondents who did not answer the initial section of the survey on basic demographic data. Since these data are not vital for our quantitative analysis, this pattern of non-response is not harmful. The dark lines show that, except for a few statements missing here and there, the majority of missing values seem to reflect respondents that could not finish the survey or forgot to fill in one section. The graph clearly shows that the missing data follow a random pattern, not to be associated with any statement of the survey itself but rather to time constraints or oversights on the side of the respondents. However, with such a small rate of missing values as we have in our data gathered, even a non-random distribution of missing values would represent an insignificant problem.

Based on this analysis, we decided to make a correction for the proportion of missing values in the survey, and to apply this correction to all of the statistical

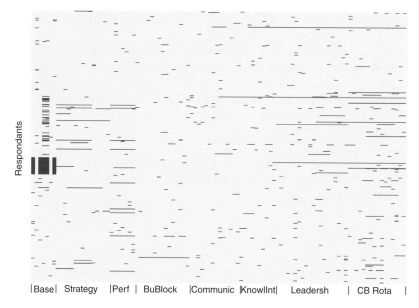

Figure 13: Each dark line or square represents missing responses. The grey space represents actual responses. The non-response rate is only 1.07%.

analyses we were about to carry out. We followed the usual guidelines for these types of corrections, suggesting to compute the equivalent number of respondents without including the missing values. In our case, this computation amounts to 847*(100%−1.07%)=838 equivalent number of respondents. This correction is a rather minuscule one as our quantitative results would be virtually the same as if we were using the full sample size of 847 respondents.

Exploring the Data

Graphs provide a very effective way to explore data, allowing us to visually capture the main patterns and to select the most appropriate statistical approaches for analysis. In order to explore our data graphically, we will look at Figure 13 once more to capture some obvious patterns. We will then plot all our respondents' answers together, regardless of which companies they belonged to. As a next step, we will explore whether we can see any differences between the overall patterns and any trends that may exist within the individual companies.

Figure 13 shows patterns of actual responses for the "Strategy" section of the survey that appears to provide strong support for Propositions 1 and 2. In fact, the gray space of Figure 13, representing the actual responses, suggests that the overwhelming majority of respondents systematically prioritized more than one "strategy" as well as to more than one "strategic approach to growth". A closer look at the original dataset confirmed this visual impression fully. We examined the responses to the following statement in the Glue Test: "Please think about the strategic priorities and approaches [to top-line growth] that your company *actually realized or achieved* during the past three years." As mentioned, the possible responses to this statement were structured on a 1-to-10 Likert scale in the survey, where 1 meant "no priority" and 10 meant "very high priority." Moreover, the respondents had three possible strategies to prioritize (delighting the customer, cost leadership and innovation), as well as two strategic approaches to top-line growth to rank (internal growth and external growth).

The original data showed that, out of 854 respondents, 850 prioritized more than one strategy and 818 prioritized more than one strategic approach to top-line growth. More specifically, regarding the three strategies, out of the 854 respondents, only 4 answered to two or three strategies with the value 1 (=no priority). Furthermore, only 76 answered to two or three strategies with the values 1, 2 or 3 (i.e. low priority). We went even further, and confirmed that only 308 answered to two or three strategies with the values 1, 2, 3, 4 or 5 (i.e. covering the entire lower half of the scale). This evidence demonstrates that 91% of the original 854 respondents gave moderate to high priority (i.e. 4, 5, 6, 7, 8, 9 or 10) to two or three strategies, and about two thirds of them gave a relatively high priority (i.e. 6, 7, 8, 9 or 10) to two or three strategies.

Likewise, regarding the two strategic approaches to top-line growth (internal or external), out of the original 854 respondents, only 36 answered to two approaches with the value 1 (=no priority), 196 answered to two approaches with the values 1, 2 or 3 (i.e. low priority), and 470 answered to two approaches with the values 1, 2, 3, 4 or 5 (i.e. covering the entire lower half of the scale). This evidences that 77% of the original 854 respondents gave moderate to high priority (i.e. 4, 5, 6, 7, 8, 9 or 10) to the two strategic approaches to growth, and 45% of them gave a relatively high priority (i.e. 6, 7, 8, 9 or 10) to the two strategic approaches to growth. This pattern of responses provides strong support for Propositions 1 and 2, suggesting that company managers tend to choose and implement balanced combinations of strategic options — what has been termed here as *blending* strategies and *blending* approaches to growth — rather than prioritize one alternative over all others.

We then deleted the seven respondents from company F whom had abandoned the survey very early,[23] and graphically explored the data stemming from the remaining 847 respondents. Figure 14 shows the correlations between the

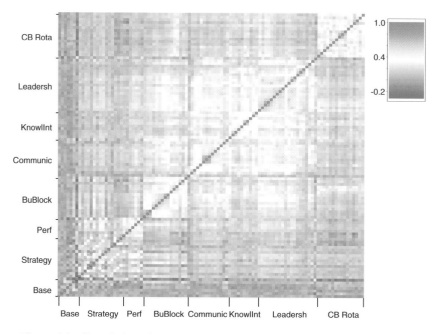

Figure 14: Correlations between all of the 104 survey statements. The latter have been grouped in eight categories. Each small square represents the value of a correlation between any two statements of the survey. The higher correlations between statements of the same category are evidence for the modelization that will be carried out.

answers of the 847 respondents to the 104 statements in our survey (10 "Base" statements about the individual's demographics, 15 "Strategy" statements about generic strategies and strategic approaches to growth, 75 statements concerning the five constructs of social capabilities and 7 statements concerning competitive business performance — "Perf").

In Figure 14, each small square represents the value of a correlation between any two statements of the survey. On the one hand, the rose spaces in the graph represent a correlation close to zero, meaning that the pairs of responses that are intersected within the rose-colored spaces are not linked at all. On the other hand, white - to blue-colored spaces represent a correlation close to 1, meaning that for each respondent, the answers to these two statements are very closely linked to one another. Figure 14 demonstrates that any pair of statements concerning the same construct/category in the survey shows a higher correlation than any pair of statements concerning different constructs. This is generally the case, although there are pairs of statements concerning different constructs of the survey that can nevertheless be highly correlated.

Let us zoom into Figure 14 to look at the relationship between the five social capabilities constructs and competitive business performance. This can be seen in Figure 15, showing in greater detail how any pair of statements concerning the same construct/category in the survey shows a higher correlation than any pair of statements concerning different constructs. This suggests that the 75 statements associated with the five constructs in the survey contain real information about the underlying "social capabilities". The same can obviously be concluded about the seven statements on performance vis-à-vis the underlying construct "competitive business performance."

The strength of the links between the different constructs can also be inferred from Figure 15. If the squares between statements of two different constructs are white to blue, this tends to show that the two constructs have strong links. In other words, respondents that greatly emphasized on the first construct tended to give as much importance to thsecond, and, conversely, there are respondents that placed very little emphasis in both constructs. In particular, we can see that the

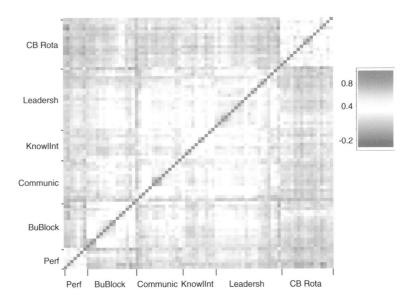

Figure 15: Correlation between the survey statements on the five "social capa-bilities" constructs and "competitive business performance."

strongest links are between statements regarding 'boundary-spanning leadership' and 'communication rituals'.

Of particular interest is the link between the statements concerning "competitive business performance" and the other constructs. Figure 15 already seems to indicate an important link amongst each other. This will be confirmed by the formal analysis shown in Chapter 5. At this point, it suffices to conclude that Figures 14 and 15 seem to show correlation patterns that are in accordance with our hypothesized relationships between *blending* strategies, *blending* approaches to top-line growth, the Common Glue and competitive performance.

Developing a Structural Equation Model

After our initial exploratory steps, we can proceed with a statistical analysis that will tell us formally if the data support our hypothesized links between predictive variables, as well as how important are these different variables to predict competitive business performance. The statistical question is how to treat the various statements linked to each given construct, given that each of these statements supposedly are related to the other constructs as well.

A simple approach would be, for example, to average the responses over the seven statements concerning business performance and call this average the "index of competitive business performance". The main drawback of this approach is that, by averaging out the data, we would not be taking advantage of all the information gathered through our survey. In fact, in the next chapter we will demonstrate that the approach we ended up choosing is far superior to this simple approach, both in the way it fits the data gathered as well as in the information and insights that our approach allowed us to obtain from the analysis.

This approach consists in modeling groups of statements in the survey around "latent" variables that are not to be measured directly. Under this approach, for example, the *true* "competitive business performance" variable is to be considered a "latent variable" and the value of the seven statements about performance in our survey are merely linked to this "latent variable". The same modeling approach can obviously be used for the remaining statements in the survey, and thus each social capability construct, for example, becomes a "latent variable" that is indirectly measured by 10–20 different statements in our survey.

The methodology that takes latent variables into account is called structural equation model (SEM) or linear structural relation (LISREL).[24] Factorial analysis is a special case of SEM, but the advantage of SEM is that we can use (unmeasured) latent variables in our empirical model and treat them as if they were being measured. We can therefore test and compare various different hypotheses about the relations between the latent variables (i.e. via linear regressions). An example of the type of model we will use is given in Figure 16. In the center of the figure, the six constructs are shown as ovals. They are our primary interest. We want to know whether the data support their existence as different constructs, and whether

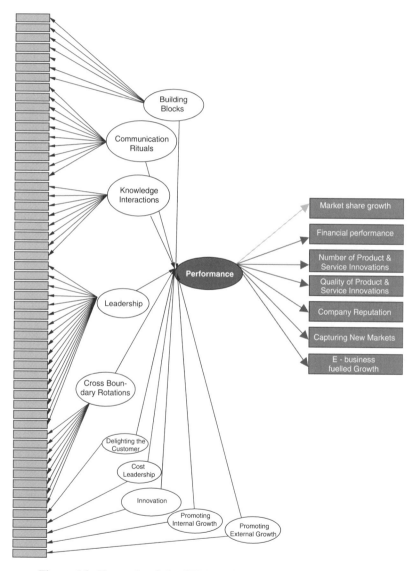

Figure 16: Example of the SEM model applied to the Glue Test.

the associations we postulated amongst them are correct. However, since we cannot measure them directly, we need to build/measure them indirectly through the survey statements. All the survey statements are on both sides of Figure 16, represented by rectangles. They are linked to the construct they are supposed to represent, but we need to formally check if the data support such links or whether one or several statements is/are in contradiction to the construction of the survey.

With an SEM approach, the essential information required from the data gathered is provided by the correlations or the covariances between all the survey statements (which were represented in Figures 14 and 15 by the colors). This information allows us to test the existence of the underlying latent variables and the relationships between them, in order to determine whether the underlying model is compatible with the observed covariances between the original survey statements. Thus the indices utilized to test the validity and reliability of such a model concern both the existence of the latent variables and the types of hypothesized relationships between them.

Thus, we designed an empirical model as follows:

- Each statement in the survey is related (though linear regression) to the underlying construct it is associated with: i.e. one of the five social capabilities constructs or "competitive business performance".
- The five latent variables representing the five social capabilities constructs are allowed to correlate freely, since we certainly do not expect these five social capabilities to be independent from one another.
- *All* of the five latent variables representing the five social capabilities — together with the "strategy" variables — are then used to predict "competitive business performance".

As mentioned, in this model a series of six latent variables (five for the social capabilities and one for "competitive business performance") are not measured directly but rather estimated together with all other parameters through a SEM approach.

Measuring the Blending Power of Organizations

By September 2004, we were ready to proceed with the formal quantitative assessment of our hypothesized relationships. We had attempted to capture the female-like blending power of organizations — *blending* strategies, *blending* approaches to top-line growth and the Common Glue — on a series of simple constructs that now needed to be validated numerically. In addition, the hypothesized relationships amongst these constructs needed to be tested: was the Common Glue the holistic, hologramic and evolutionary collective asset that managers had described? Was it to be associated with the internal approaches to growth and the female-like strategies of delighting the customer and innovation as these managers had argued? Equally importantly: what was the link between, on the one hand, *blending* strategies, *blending* approaches to top-line growth and the Common Glue, and, on the other hand, competitive business performance? Were all these elements together to be regarded as *the blending power of organizations* that drove superior competitive performance across cultural, functional and geographic boundaries?

With these questions in mind, we embarked in the quantitative analyses of the data following the method and statistical model we had developed. Our findings were pretty clear, statistically reliable and strongly supportive of the relationships we had hypothesized. All this is presented in detail in Chapter 5.

Notes and References

[1] Nahapiet, J. and S. Ghoshal (1998) "Social capital, intellectual capital, and the organizational advantage," *Academy of Management Review* **23**(2): 242–266; Also see Bourdieu, P. (1986) "The forms of capital." In: J.G. Richardson (Ed.), *Handbook of Theory and Research for the Sociology of Education*, Greenwood Publishing Group, New York, NY, pp. 241–258; Baker, W.E. (1990) "Market networks and corporate behavior," *American Journal of Sociology* **96**(3): 589–625 (1996).

[2] Burt, R.S. (1992) *Structural Holes: The Social Structure of Competition*, Harvard University Press, Cambridge, MA; Putnam, R.D. (1993) "The prosperous community: Social capital and public life," *American Prospect* **4**(13): 35–42; Nahapiet, J. and S. Ghoshal (1998) "Social capital, intellectual capital, and the organizational advantage," *Academy of Management Review* **23**(2): 242–266.

[3] Ghoshal, S. and P. Moran (1996) Value creation by firms. *Academy of Management Proceedings*: 41–45; Jacobs, J. (1965) *The Death and Life of Great American Cities*, Penguin Books, London; Fukuyama, F. (1995) *Trust*, The Free Press, New York, NY.

[4] Jewkes, J., D. Sawers and R.R. Still. (1958) *The Sources of Invention*, Macmillan, New York, NY. Henderson, R.M. and K.B. Clark (1990). Architectural innovation: The reconfiguration of existing product technologies and the failure of established firms. *Administrative Science Quarterly* **35**(1): 9–30; Stalk, G. (1988) "Time: The next source of competitive advantage," *Harvard Business Review* **66**(4): 41–51.

[5] Kogut, B. and U. Zander (1992) "Knowledge of the firm, combinative capabilities, and the replication of technology," *Organization Science* **3**(3): 383–397; Grant, R.M. (1996). "Towards a knowledge-based theory of the firm," *Strategic Management Journal* **17**(10): 109–122; Morosini, P. (1998) *Managing Cultural Differences: Effective Strategy and Execution Across Cultures in Global Corporate Alliances*, Pergamon, Oxford; Morosini, P., S. Shane and H. Singh (1998) "National Cultural Distance and

Cross-Border Acquisitions Performance," *Journal of International Business Studies* **29**(1): 137–158.

[6] DeHoff, K. and D. Neely (2004) "Innovation and Product Development — Clearing the New Performance Bar," Booz Allen Hamilton Report.

[7] Jonash, R.S. and T. Sommerlatte (1999) *The Innovation Premium: How Next Generation Companies are Achieving Peak Performance and Profitability*, Perseus Books Group, New York.

[8] Carlzon, J. (1987) *Moments of Truth*, Harper Perennial, New York.

[9] See for example Morosini, P. and U. Steger (Eds.), (2004) *Managing Complex Mergers*, Financial Times-Prentice Hall, U.K.

[10] Boisot, M.H. (1998) *Knowledge Assets: Securing Competitive Advantage in the Information Economy*, Oxford University Press, Oxford;. Brown, J.S. and P. Duguid. (1991) "Organizational learning and communities of practice: Toward a unified view of working, learning, and innovation," *Organization Science* **2**(1): 40–57; Kay, N M. (1979) *The Innovating Firm*, Macmillan, London.

[11] Norburn, D. and S. Birley (1988) "The top management team and corporate performance," *Strategic Management Journal* **9**(3): 225–237.

[12] Black, J.S., H.B. Gregersen and M.E. Mendenhall (1993) *Global Assignments: Successfully Expatriating and Repatriating International Managers*, Jossey-Bass, San Francisco; Also see Edstrom, A. and J.R. Galbraith (1977) "Transfer of managers as a coordination and control strategy in multinational organizations," *Administrative Science Quarterly* **27**: 248–263.

[13] Collins, J.C. and J.I. Porras (1996) "Building your company's vision," *Harvard Business Review* **74**(5): 65–77.

[14] Kaplan, R.S. and D.P. Norton (2001) *The Strategy-Focused Organization: How Balanced Scorecard Companies Thrive in the New Business Environment*, Harvard Business School Press Cambridge.

[15] Collis, D.J. (1994) "Research note: How valuable are organizational capabilities?" *Strategic Management Journal* **15**(8): 143–152; Zollo, M. and S.G. Winter (1999) "From organizational routines to dynamic capabilities," A working paper of the Reginald H. Jones Center, The Wharton School, University of Pennsylvania; Eisenhardt, K.E. and J.A. Martin. (2000) "Dynamic capabilities: What are they?" *Strategic Management Journal* **21**(10/11): 1105–1121.

[16] Marchand, D.A., W. Kettinger and J.D. Rollins (2001) *Information Orientation: The Link to Business Performance*, Oxford University Press, Oxford; Venkatraman, N. (1985) "Research on MIS planning: Some guidelines from strategic planning research," *Journal of Management Information Systems* **2**(2): 65–77; Venkatraman, N. and V. Ramanujam (1986) "Measurement of business performance in strategy research: A comparison of approaches," *Academy of Management Review* **11**(4): 801–814.

[17] Kettinger, W.J. and V. Grover. (1994) "Strategic information systems revisited: A study in sustainability and performance," *MIS Quarterly* **18**(1): 31–37.

[18] Cyert, R. M. and March, J. G. (1963) *A behavioral theory of the firm*. Prentice-Hall, Englewood Cliffs, NJ; Thompson, J.D. (1967) *Organizations in Action*, McGraw–Hill,

New York, NY; Child, J. (1972). "Organization structure, environment and performance: The role of strategic choice, "*Sociology* **6**: 2–21; Hambrick, D.C. and P.A. Mason. (1984) "Upper echelons: The organization as a reflection of its top managers," *Academy of Management Review* **9**(2): 193–206; Hrebiniak, L.G. and Joyce W.F. (1985) "Organisational adaptation: Strategic choice and environmental determinism," *Administrative Science Quarterly* **30**: 336–349; Priem, R.L. (1990) "Top management team group factors, consensus and firm performance," *Strategic Management Journal* **11**(6): 469–478; Schoemaker, P.J.H. (1992) "How to link strategic vision to core capabilities," *Sloan Management Review* **34**(1): 67–81.

[19] Meek, G.K. and S.M. Saudagaran (1990) "A survey or research on financial reporting in a transnational context," *Journal of Accounting Literature* **19**: 145–182; L.H. Radebaugh and S.J. Gray (1997) *International Accounting and Multinational Enterprises*, 4th ed., Wiley: New York, NY; Higgins, R. C. (1998) *Analysis for Financial Management,* 5th ed., Irwin/McGraw-Hill, Boston, MA; Hamilton, J. (1998) "Mastering global business 8: Accountants gather around different standards," *The Financial Times*, 20 March, p. 12.

[20] Bourgeois III, L.J. (1980) "Performance and consensus," *Strategic Management Journal* **1**(3): 227–248; Robinson, R.B. and J.A. Pearce. (1988) "Planned patterns of strategic behavior and their relationship to business-unit performance," *Strategic Management Journal* **9**(1): 43–60.

[21] Chan, Y.E, S.L Huff, D.W. Barclay and D.G. Copeland (1997) "Business strategic orientation, information systems strategic orientation, and strategic alignment," *Information Systems Research* **8**(2): 125–50.

[22] Dempster, A.P., N.M. Laird, and D.B. Rubin (1977) "Maximum likelihood from incomplete data via the EM Algorithm," *Journal of the Royal Statistical Society* **39**: 1–22.

[23] Amongst the 200 respondents of company F, seven quit very early in the process and did not answer any of the items we were interested in, so we eliminated them and used the answers of the remaining 193 respondents. In order to preserve the confidentiality of the data vis-à-vis the identities of the companies surveyed in my research, the ordering of companies A – K in Table 1 (as well as in Figures 23, 24, 27 and 28 in the following chapter 5), does NOT correspond to the ordering of the *same* companies in Figure 10. Thus, for example, the data of companies A, B, or K in Table 1 (or in Figures 23, 24, 27 and 28 in the following chapter 5), does not correspond to DaimlerChrysler, Allianz Dresdner or AVL. And so on.

[24] Long, J.S. (1988) *Covariance Structure Models: An Introduction to LISREL*, Sage, London. Bollen, K.A. (1989). *Structural Equations With Latent Variables*, Wiley, New York, NY.

Chapter 5

Testing the Link between Blending Power and Performance

> In God we trust; all others must bring data.
>
> W. Edwards Deming

During September to December 2004, a series of formal quantitative analyses were carried out on a sample of data that I had gathered over the previous 3 years from 847 respondents belonging to a highly diverse group of 11 multinational organizations. These analyses were geared to find out whether empirical support existed for the so-called 'social capabilities': a series of five organizational aspects that managers had described as interacting together to create a female-like blending power within organizations. This blending power was termed the Common Glue, and it was hypothesized that along with *blending* strategies and *blending* approaches to top-line growth, it drove superior competitive performance across cultural, organizational and geographic boundaries.

As we saw in the previous chapter, Figure 13 and the numerical analysis of the responses provided strong empirical support to Propositions 1 and 2 (see Figure 17), whereas Figure 14 suggested a series of actual links between the "social capabilities", "strategy" and "competitive performance" constructs. Our quantitative analyses was therefore carried out on two levels. First, we wanted to find support for the constituent elements of the Common Glue itself as well as its main characteristics, as described in Propositions 3–5 in Figure 17. Equally importantly, we wanted to find whether or not there was empirical support for the entire set of hypothesized relationships shown in Figure 18.

Empirical Support for the Blending Power of Organizations

We used the software LISREL version 8.54 to estimate the parameters of our model.[1] As stated in Hypothesis 1, strategies and strategic approaches to top-line growth, along with the five social capabilities are postulated to be important predictors of "competitive business performance". However, it would be unwise to include too many variables in the statistical model as it would render

Proposition 1 – *Blending strategies are combinations of the generic strategic options of: delighting the customer, cost leadership and innovation.*

Proposition 2 – *An organization's blending approach to top line growth is a combination of: external (i.e. via mergers, acquisitions and strategic alliances) and internal (i.e. organic) growth.*

Proposition 3 – *An organization's Common Glue is represented by the holistic interaction of five social capabilities: boundary-spanning leadership, company-wide building blocks, knowledge interactions, communication rituals, and cross-boundary rotations.*

Proposition 4 – *An organization's Common Glue is made up by five social capabilities which are, at the same time, distinct from one another but closely interrelated amongst themselves.*

Proposition 5 – *The strength of an organization's Common Glue is nurtured over time.*

Figure 17: Research propositions

the results less reliable and weak for interpretation purposes. We therefore chose the strategies and the strategic approaches to growth that were actually *realized* by the respondents' organizations over the 3-year period prior to their assessments. We did not expect the results to be very different if we chose, for example, the past strategic priorities that were *intended* or the future strategic priorities. In fact, if one looks closely at the correlations among the statements related to "strategy" (i.e. the three generic strategies of delighting the customer, cost leadership and innovation) and "strategic approaches to growth" (in other words internal and external approaches to top-line growth), in Figure 14 in Chapter 4, we can see three diagonals of very high correlations (highlighted in blue color). This signals that the three different groups of responses will give very close results.

We thus built an initial SEM model that aimed at fitting the data of the five different "strategies" and "strategic approaches to growth" to predict "competitive business performance". The model is depicted in Figure 19 and has a fit that is medium to the data (AIC = 704.96, RMSEA = 0.13, fit indices around 0.81). The lack of fit might be due to the disproportion in the number of statements related to each construct: seven for "competitive business performance" and only one for the "strategies and the strategic approaches to growth".[2]

Next we combined both the "strategies" and the strategic approaches to growth" and the "social capabilities" to see if together they can explain more of the variability of "competitive business performance". However, an initial model thus designed suffered from the fact that among the statements associated with the same "social capabilities" constructs, there were some groups of statements

H1 – The blending power of organizations

An organization's blending strategies and blending approaches to top line growth, together with its Common Glue, positively explain its level of competitive performance across cultural, organizational and geographic boundaries, and the strength of this link is greater than the links between each separate element and competitive performance

H2 – The Common Glue hypothesis

The stronger a firm's Common Glue the better its competitive performance; and the strength of this link is greater than the links between each separate social capability and competitive performance.

H3 – Generic strategies and competitive performance

3.a) Delighting the customer is positively correlated with competitive performance.
3.b) Cost leadership is positively correlated with competitive performance.
3.c) Innovation is positively correlated with competitive performance.

H4 – *Generic* strategies, social capabilities and performance

4.a) Innovation and delighting the customer have a stronger positive correlation with competitive performance than cost leadership does.
4.b) Innovation and delighting the customer have a stronger correlation with social capabilities than cost leadership does.

H5 – Strategic growth, social capabilities and performance

5.a) Internal growth has a stronger positive correlation with competitive performance than external growth.
5.b) Internal growth has a stronger correlation with social capabilities than external growth.

H6 – Link between *female* strategies and approaches to growth

Innovation and delighting the customer have a stronger positive correlation with internal growth than cost leadership does.

H7 – Link between social capabilities and performance

7.a) The stronger a firm's boundary-spanning leadership, the better its competitive performance.
7.b) The stronger a firm's company-wide building blocks, the better its competitive performance.
7.c) The stronger a firm's knowledge interactions, the better its competitive performance.
7.d) The stronger a firm's communication rituals, the better its competitive performance.
7.e) The stronger a firm's cross-boundary rotations, the better its competitive performance.

Figure 18: Research hypotheses.

that showed a higher correlation between each other than vis-à-vis other statements. In order to circumvent this problem, we grouped some questions together and computed an average index of similarity based on whether strong correlations existed between groups of statements.

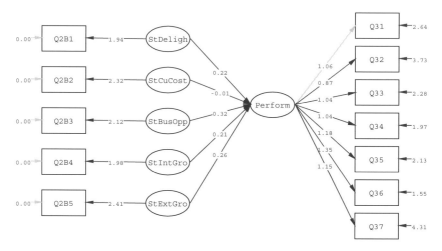

Figure 19: SEM model with the strategies and strategic approaches to growth as predictors of competitive business performance.

We then individually examined those groups of statements that showed a higher degree of index similarity, assessing the extent to which some of these statements were redundant vis-à-vis other survey statements and could thus be merged in the model.[3] This step has two major statistical advantages. First, by merging some "redundant" survey statements based on index similarity, we can significantly reduce the number of parameters that have to be estimated in the underlying model. Second, reducing the number of parameters that need to be estimated both normalizes and increases the reliability of the remaining variables in the model. After merging the "redundant" survey statements based on index similarity, 50 grouped-statements remained: 7 concerning "company-wide building blocks", 10 about "communication rituals", 8 regarding "knowledge interactions", 17 about "boundary-spanning leadership" and 8 about "cross-boundary rotations".

The new model is sketched in Figure 20. Each box represents either a statement or a group of statements in our empirical survey, and each latent variable is represented by an oval. Thus, in Figure 20, the three "strategies", two "strategic approaches to growth" and five "social capabilities" are represented by the vertically aligned oval boxes, and they are used as predictors of "competitive business performance" represented by the single oval box. An arrow from one box to another indicates a regression between the two variables, and the number on each of these connecting arrows represents the associated regression coefficient. The

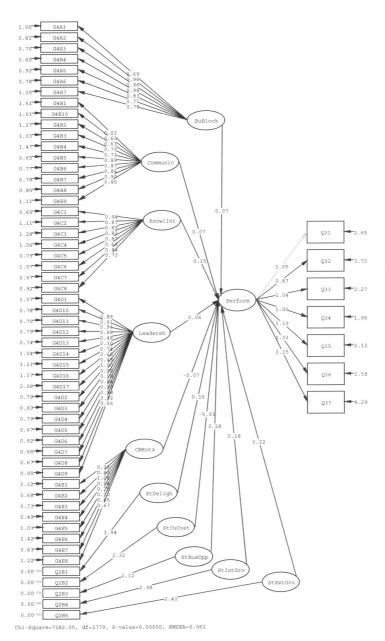

Figure 20: SEM linking "strategies", "strategic approaches to growth", "social capabilities" and "competitive business performance".

short arrows represent the error (or innovation) parameters of the regression and the specific value beside the short arrows gives the estimated variance.

Table 2 provides the statistics of the model in Figure 20. The model fit the data well, the RMSEA is 0.061 and the fit indices are all above 0.94, except for one that is at 0.89. This is evidence of a good fit since it is generally admitted that a fit index higher than 0.90 is evidence of a good model.[4] This model suggests that both the "social capabilities" as well as the "strategies" and "strategic approaches to growth" are all useful for the prediction of. "competitive business performance". We will demonstrate in the later sections of this chapter that if one uses only one of the two groups of constructs, the prediction becomes significantly poorer.

Trying All Possible Combinations of Predictive Variables

We wanted to further assess which possible combination of "strategies", "strategic approaches to growth" and "social capabilities", in addition to the one shown in Figure 20, were particularly useful for predicting "competitive business performance". In order to do this we performed additional analyses of the data following Mallows' Cp method.[5] This method is a very useful tool when we have numerous predictors (as in our case) for a given variable, such as: "competitive business performance". We thus want to know, based on the data, which subgroup of predictors are very good vis-à-vis the dependent variable. Mallows' Cp method

Table 2: Indices for the SEM including "strategies", "strategic approaches to growth", "social capabilities" and "competitive business performance".

Goodness of Fit Statistics
Degrees of freedom = 1,779
Normal theory weighted least squares chi-square = 7,382.05 ($P = 0.0$)
Root mean square error of approximation (RMSEA) = 0.061
90% confidence interval for RMSEA = (0.060; 0.063)
Model AIC = 7,730.05
Normed fit index (NFI) = 0.95
Non-normed fit index (NNFI) = 0.96
Parsimony normed fit index (PNFI) = 0.89
Comparative fit index (CFI) = 0.96
Incremental fit index (IFI) = 0.96
Relative fit index (RFI) = 0.94

explores *all* possible subgroups and rates them based on their predictive power compared to their sparsity (i.e. the number of "strategies", "strategic approaches to growth" and "social capabilities" that were in a given subgroup utilized to predict performance). On the basis of this method, we designed all 75 possible models that utilize one, two, three, all the way up to 10 variables that predict "competitive business performance". Each model was then ranked.[6]

The results of our Mallows' Cp analyses are shown in Figure 21 and should be interpreted as follows: each model is represented by one or several joined letters that correspond to the "social capabilities", and numbers 1–5 corresponding to the "strategies" and "strategic approaches to growth" that are used in this model to predict "competitive business performance". For example, the letters BLR14 represent the model that uses only "company-wide building blocks"(B), "boundary-spanning leadership"(L), "cross-boundary rotations" (R), "delighting the customer" (1) and "internal growth" (4) to predict "competitive business performance". The model CK235 uses only "communications rituals", "knowledge interactions", "cost leadership", "innovation" and "external growth", and so on. Mallows' Cp approach establishes that any model under

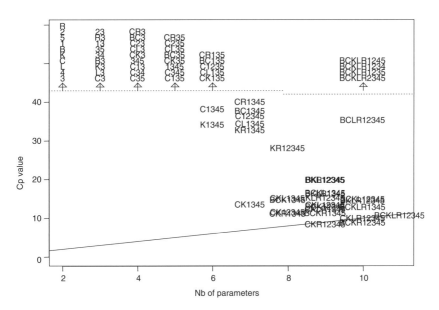

Figure 21: Mallows' Cp assessing the predictive power of 75 combinations of "strategies", "strategic approaches to growth", "social capabilities" vis-à-vis "competitive business performance".

the diagonal line (see Figure 21) can be considered as a good predictive model that should be kept. The best models obviously are the ones well under the diagonal line.

Figure 21 and Table 3 (in Appendix B) show that, besides the full model, very few others are ranked as being good ones. Apart from the full model (BCKLR12345, $Cp=11$, $p=11$), two models have a Cp below p (below the diagonal): CKR12345 ($Cp=8.7$, $p=9$) and BCKR12345 ($Cp=9.2$, $p=10$) and a few have a Cp close to p: CKR1345 ($Cp=11.5$, $p=8$), CK12345 ($Cp=11.8$, $p=8$), BCKR1345 ($Cp=11.6$, $p=9$), CKLR1345 ($Cp=12.6$, $p=9$), CKLR12345 ($Cp=10.3$, $p=10$), BCKLR1345 ($Cp=13.2$, $p=10$), BKLR12345 ($Cp=14.8$, $p=10$), BCKL12345 ($Cp=15.2$, $p=10$). Since among these models none is clearly superior to the others and no construct is systematically absent in all good models, we can conclude that we have a strong evidence supporting the full model with the five "strategies" and "strategic approaches to growth" and the five "social capabilities".

'Srategy' and 'Social Capabilities' Together Predict Performance

An additional group of analyses that is useful to carry out consists of formally assessing whether all or some of the "strategy" constructs (i.e. the "strategies" and the "strategic approaches to growth") add significantly to "social capabilities" for the prediction of competitive business performance (and conversely). The tests that will be utilized in this part of the analyses are known as likelihood ratio tests or ANOVA tables.

The different tests carried out are summarized in Table 4. Each line corresponds to a hypothesis and should be read as follows: the first column gives the basic or small model. For instance, on the first line it corresponds to BCKLR, i.e. the model with the five "social capabilities" but with neither "strategies" nor "strategic approaches to growth". The second column shows which constructs were added to the basic or small model. On the first line we read 12345, which means that all five "strategies" and "strategic approaches to growth" were added. The question is whether this addition increases significantly the predictive power of "competitive business performance". For this, the F value of the test is given on the third column, the degrees of freedom on the fourth column and its p Value on the fifth column. If the p Value is smaller than 0.05, there is evidence that the additional construct(s) improve(s) the prediction.

Table 4 shows very strong evidence (p Values very close to 0, i.e. 1 e-10 meaning, in engineering notation, a value of 0.0000000001) that using only the "social capabilities" or only some (or all) of the "strategies" and the "strategic approaches to growth" always weakens the predictive power vis-à-vis competitive business

Table 4: Likelihood ratio tests to assess the additional contribution of one of the two groups "social capabilities" and "strategies and strategic approaches to growth" to predict performance. The results are clear and both groups together are useful.

First constructs	Additional constructs	F value	test df	*p* Value
BCKLR	12345	56.24	5	$<1e-10$
12345	BCKLR	26.55	5	$<1e-10$
BCKLR	12	20.89	2	$1.3e-9$
12	BCKLR	44.58	5	$<1e-10$
BCKLR	123	65.97	3	$<1e-10$
123	BCKLR	32.86	5	$<1e-10$
BCKLR	45	86.29	2	$<1e-10$
45	BCKLR	37.79	5	$<1e-10$
BCKLR	13	99.06	2	$<1e-10$
13	BCKLR	33.30	5	$<1e-10$
BCKLR	2	5.13	1	0.02
2	BCKLR	60.05	5	$<1e-10$
BCKLR	4	87.92	1	$<1e-10$
4	BCKLR	42.87	5	$<1e-10$
BCKLR	5	80.12	1	$<1e-10$
5	BCKLR	59.77	5	$<1e-10$

performance. Conversely, when both "strategies" and "strategic approaches to growth" as well as "social capabilities" are utilized, this leads to better predictions of competitive business performance. In other words, both the "strategy" constructs *together* with the "social capabilities" constructs are stronger predictors of competitive business performance than any of those sets of constructs individually. This provides additional support for our Hypothesis 1, in Figure 18.

Addressing the 'Common Variance' Problem

The first important issue that this quantitative analysis must address is the so-called "common variance problem". Since the survey statements on "strategies", "strategic approaches to growth" and "social capabilities" were assessed by the same persons (and at the same time) than the statements on "competitive business performance", there is a risk of bias in our analysis. In other words, if there were "optimistic" respondents that tended to assess every statement with very high scores, or "pessimistic" ones that always gave low scores, then our analysis would be biased since any two variables would show a strong correlation not because there were actually linked but because of the effect of the optimistic and pessimistic respondents.

The first argument against common variance problems in our data is given by Figure 14 in Chapter 4. Indeed, if a common variance pattern existed, *all* the squares in the graph would be white to blue, since *all* correlations would be forced to be high. On the contrary, some correlations are close to zero showing that for these pairs of statements, there are neither "optimists" nor "pessimists" at work. There are even negative correlations in Figure 14 in Chapter 4, showing that for that particular pair of statements, people who tended to provide higher than average scores in one statement, also tended to give lower than average scores to the other statement.

A second argument against common variance problems in our analyses is given by the results of the Mallows' Cp analyses. If the correlations in our data were merely due to a response bias, all the models with only one variable (1,2,3,4,5,B, C, K, L and R in Figure 21 and Table 3 in Appendix B) would be the good models, i.e. close or below the diagonal. Also, the more variables you would add, the worse the model would become. The results of the Mallows' Cp analyses indicate exactly the opposite patterns: no model with one variable is good and only more complex models — in other words those with the broader set of variables representing the "blending power" of organizations — are below the diagonal.

A third argument against common variance problems in our model regards the SEM models that we tried. In Figure 22, for example, we have represented a model with only one latent variable (assembling all the statements of the "social capabilities" together) in order to predict "competitive business performance". This model has an AIC and fit indices by far worse than the model in Figure 25. This would not be the case if the response bias was high. Indeed, data with a high response bias would favor models with only one latent variable, which could be called "the degree of optimism of the respondent". The model of Figure 22 is a generalization of this model and it has been found to be statistically poor. For simplicity, the model in Figure 22 uses only the "social capabilities" (without the "strategies" and the "strategic approaches to growth") to predict performance. This model should therefore be compared with the model depicted in Figure 25. However, exactly the same conclusions can be reached with models that include the "strategies" and the "strategic approaches to growth".

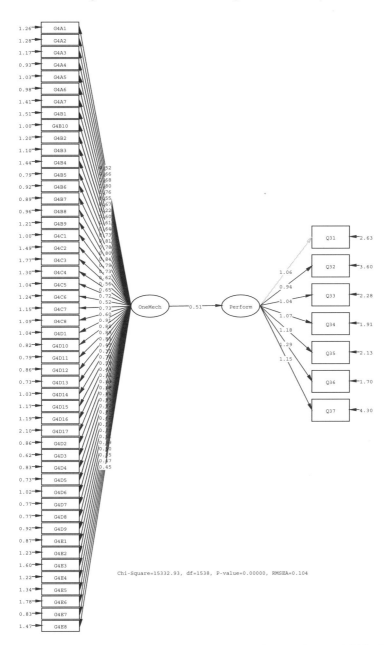

Figure 22: SEM model with only one latent variable for "social capabilities". All the indices show that this model is by far inferior to the model of Figure 20.

Sensitivity Analysis and Controls

To better understand the results of our analyses, and to further control the homogeneity of our results across the companies, we can represent graphically the relationship we found between, on the one hand, "social capabilities", "strategies" and "strategic approaches to growth" and, on the other hand, "competitive business performance". In Figure 23, each respondent is represented by its "blending power index" value (given by the standardized scores of each respondent to the latent variables given in Figure 20, so as to obtain the same scale as in the original survey questions) on the horizontal axis and its "competitive business performance" index value (a weighted average of his/her competitive performance assessments) on the vertical axis. If there were no links between the two, we would obviously have a widely scattered diagram. Instead, the points clearly show that there is a positive correlation between the two indices. We have superimposed the regression lines, one per company. It shows us the best prediction of "competitive business performance" for any given value of "blending power"

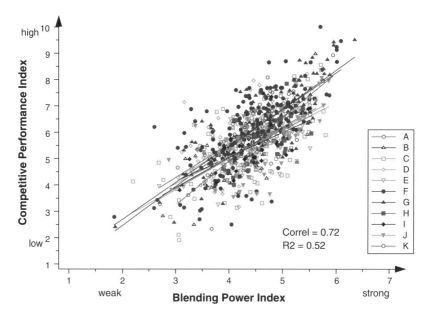

Figure 23: Scatter plot of the "blending power index" and "competitive business performance" for each respondent. The regression lines are given by companies and are satisfactorily close to one another.

index. Again, if these lines were horizontal, it would mean that there is no relationship between the two indices, which is clearly not the case.

Another very interesting insight stemming from Figure 23 is the possibility to assess whether there are differences in the pattern of responses across the different companies in our sample. Up till now, we have grouped all the respondents as if they were a homogeneous sample. But if we made the same plots as in Figure 23 separately for each company, we can see whether the response patterns in some companies contradict those that can be found in other companies, in which case it would mean that our findings could not be generalizable to the entire sample. Figure 24 shows the respondents per individual company and their respective regression lines. Although, as might be expected, the regression lines are not perfectly identical across the different companies, they all show the same pattern of positive correlation. It is extremely important that no company showed very different patterns from the others, i.e. like a flat regression line, all points concentrating in one corner of the graph, weird patterns.

This last point is crucial. In spite of the companies being from very different industries, different sizes, diverse geographic locations, cultures, organizational structures, etc. we still find that, in all cases, the *same* combination of "social capabilities", "strategies" and "strategic approaches to growth" is positively correlated with "competitive business performance".

Links between Strategies, Approaches to Growth, Social Capabilities and Performance

Let us now turn to the correlations between the predictive constructs that are given in Table 5. We see that the "strategies" and the "strategic approaches to growth" are positively correlated among each other in all but one case, the maximum level being being 49% for the correlation between StIntGro (internal approach to top-line growth) and StInnov (innovation strategy) and 40% between StIntGro and StDeligh (delighting the customer strategy). The lowest correlation is that between StExtGro (external approach to top-line growth) and StDeligh: −2%. These results provide support to Hypothesis 6 in Figure 18, which stated that 'innovation and delighting the customer have a stronger positive correlation with internal growth than cost leadership does.'

Table 5 also provides strong support for Hypotheses 4.b and 5.b, in Figure 18, demonstrating that innovation and delighting the customer *always* have stronger correlation levels with the five social capabilities than cost leadership does, and that internal growth has much stronger correlations with the five social capabilities than external growth does.

Table 6 gives the regression coefficients and their *t* Values. However, since at least some of the constructs are expected to be highly correlated, there are risks of multi-collinearity and we cannot interpret these coefficients directly. This issue will be addressed in more detail in the next sections of this chapter. The only value that is not affected by multi-collinearity in Table 6 is the R2, which gives the strength of the group of all predictors taken together for the prediction of "competitive business performance". The value of R2 is 0.52, which can be considered as quite high.

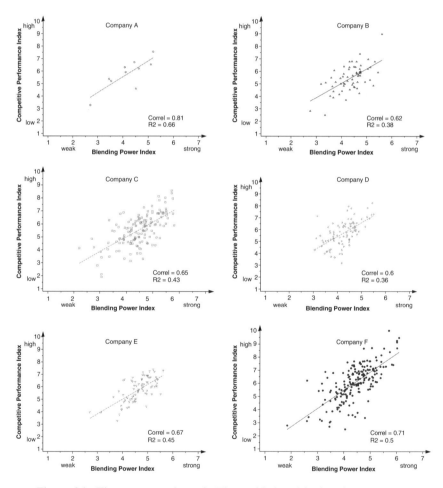

Figure 24: The same graphs as in Figure 23, but this time by company.

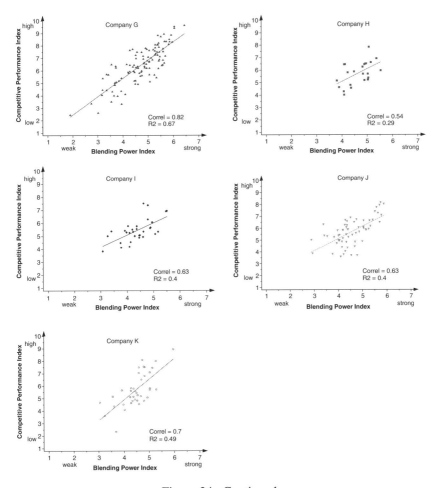

Figure 24: Continued.

We also look at the individual correlations between each of the predictive constructs and competitive business performance. The values are given in Table 7, showing that all the correlations coefficients are significant. All the correlations between "social capabilities" and competitive business performance are above 44%, except for CBRota (cross-boundary rotations), whereas the correlations between "strategies" and "strategic approaches to growth" and competitive business performance range from 18% to 56%.

Table 5: Correlations between and within the "strategies", "strategic approaches to growth" and "social capabilities".

	StDeligh	StCuCost	StInnov	StIntGro	StExtGro	BuBlock	Communic	KnowlInt	Leadersh	CBRota
StDelight	1.00									
StCuCost	0.17	1.00								
t-val	4.93									
StInnov	0.30	0.25	1.00							
t-val	9.42	7.59								
StIntGro	0.40	0.24	0.49	1.00						
t-val	13.54	7.49	18.66							
StExtGro	−0.02	0.11	0.29	0.11	1.00					
t-val	−0.72	3.33	9.02	3.07						
BuBlock	0.45	0.24	0.33	0.38	0.03	1.00				
t-val	14.68	6.68	9.72	11.67	0.88					
Communic	0.30	0.20	0.30	0.32	0.20	0.72	1.00			
t-val	8.93	5.54	8.67	9.35	5.53	32.23				
KnowlInt	0.22	0.14	0.29	0.26	0.21	0.51	0.68	1.00		
t-val	6.23	3.76	8.35	7.44	5.84	16.20	27.25			
Leadersh	0.29	0.25	0.32	0.33	0.18	0.68	0.90	0.68	1.00	
t-val	8.99	7.58	10.11	10.32	5.34	30.41	78.32	30.07		
CBRota	0.22	0.17	0.22	0.26	0.10	0.43	0.38	0.46	0.41	1.00
t-val	6.17	4.85	6.37	7.78	2.85	13.19	11.07	14.39	12.80	

Table 6: Regression between the constructs of the model in Figure 20.

$$\text{Perform} = 0.16*\text{StDeligh} - 0.034*\text{StCuCost} + 0.28*\text{StInnov} + 0.18*\text{StIntGro} + 0.22*\text{StExtGro} + 0.072*\text{BuBlock} + 0.068*\text{Communic}$$

t-val   4.39   − 1.05   6.78   4.55   6.27   1.19   0.61

$$+ 0.15*\text{KnowlInt} + 0.063*\text{Leadersh} - 0.067*\text{CBRota}, \quad \text{Errorvar.}= 0.48, \quad R2 = 0.52$$

         2.79   0.64   − 1.71   7.30

Table 7: Correlations between predictors of the model in Figure 20 and performance.

	StDeligh	StCuCost	StInnov	StIntGro	StExtGro	BuBlock	Communic	KnowlInt	Leadersh	CBRota
Perform	0.39	0.18	0.56	0.48	0.37	0.44	0.48	0.45	0.48	0.24
t-val	11.65	4.89	19.74	15.48	10.67	12.4	13.88	12.63	14.59	6.25

Table 7 provides support to Hypotheses 3 and 7 in Figure 18, demonstrating that all the "strategies" and the "social capabilities" are positively correlated with "competitive business performance". In addition, Table 7 gives positive support to Hypotheses 4.a and 5.a in Figure 18, showing that, on the one hand, innovation and delighting the customer have stronger correlations with competitive business performance than cost leadership does, and, on the other hand, internal approach to top-line growth has a stronger correlation with competitive business performance than external approach to growth does.

Empirical Support for the Common Glue

We now turn our attention to the five "social capabilities" constructs that might capture the Common Glue's organizational characteristics. In order to analyze these characteristics further, we developed an SEM with only the five "social capabilities" constructs and "competitive business performance". The results showed that the model fitted the data quite well[7] and is better than numerous variants we tried (normal theory weighted least squares chi-square = 16,357 for 3,224 degrees of freedom, root mean square error of approximation (RMSEA) of 0.070 and all fit indices above 0.90). However, once more, these statistics did suffer from the fact that among the statements associated with the same "social capabilities" constructs, there were some groups of statements that showed a higher correlation between each other than vis-à-vis other statements.

We circumvented this problem exactly as before, by grouping some questions together and computed an average index of similarity based on whether strong correlations existed between groups of statements. We then individually examined those groups of statements that showed a higher degree of index similarity, assessing the extent to which some of these statements were redundant vis-à-vis other survey statements and could thus be merged in the model. The new model that resulted after the elimination of redundant statements is sketched in Figure 25. As before, each box represents either a statement or a group of statements in our empirical survey, and each latent variable is represented by an oval. Thus, in Figure 25, the five "social capabilities" are represented by the vertically aligned oval boxes, and they are used as predictors of "competitive business performance" represented by the single oval box. An arrow from one box to another indicates a regression between the two variables, and the number on each of these connecting arrows represents the associated regression coefficient. The short arrows represent the error (or innovation) parameters of the regression and the specific value beside the short arrows gives the estimated variance.

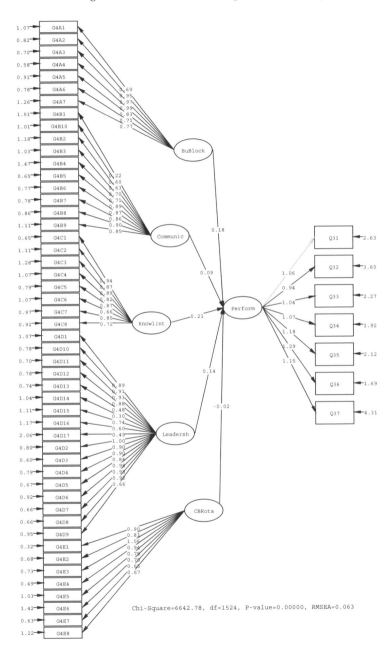

Figure 25: SEM linking "social capabilities" and "competitive business performance".

As shown in Table 8, the new model graphically represented in Figure 25 fits the data of the (grouped) survey statements much better than the initial model. In Table 8, note that the upper confidence limit of the RMSEA is 0.063, indicating a strong data fit for this model. Moreover, all but one fit indices are above 0.95, the latter being at 0.91. This is evidence of a good fit since, as mentioned, it is generally accepted that a fit index higher than 0.90 represents evidence of a good model. We further looked at the modification indices to find opportunities to modify the model slightly in order to improve it,[8] but concluded that no such small changes could significantly improve the model-data fit. Indeed, the residuals of the covariance matrix (shown in Appendix D) confirm that the residuals are zero-centered, bell-shaped and do not exhibit any outliers, which again indicates that the model fits the data quite well.

One of the main advantages of the SEM methodology is that different models can be designed with the same constructs in order to compare them and assess which model(s) fit(s) the data best. To compare the different models, one can either look at the individual indices of model-data fit or — more directly — at the akaike information criterion (AIC) value of each model. If the latter approach is chosen, the commonly accepted criterion stipulates that the smaller the AIC value of the model, the better its corresponding data fit compared to alternative (higher AIC) models.[9]

A competing model to the one represented in Figure 25 states that there are not five separate "social capabilities" constructs but only one. In such a model, all of the grouped survey statements represented on the left-hand side of Figure 25 are related to one single latent variable, which in turn explains "competitive

Table 8: Statistics for the fit of the model graphically represented in Figure 25.

Goodness of Fit Statistics
Degrees of freedom = 1,524
Normal theory weighted least squares chi-square = 6,642.78 (P = 0.0)
Root mean square error of approximation (RMSEA) = 0.063
90% confidence interval for RMSEA = (0.062; 0.065)
Model AIC = 6,900.78
Normed fit index (NFI) = 0.95
Non-normed fit index (NNFI) = 0.96
Parsimony normed fit index (PNFI) = 0.91
Comparative fit index (CFI) = 0.96
Incremental fit index (IFI) = 0.96
Relative fit index (RFI) = 0.95

business performance". We designed this alternative model and its graph can be found in Figure 22. The associated AIC value is 15,562.93, a much higher AIC value than the model represented in Figure 25 (AIC of 6,900.78; see Table 8). Indeed, when comparing two models, a difference of 10 can already be considered as strong evidence that the model with the smallest AIC is better. Here the difference is in thousands, indicating that there is no possible doubt that the model depicted in Figure 25 is by far superior. This proves that, in terms of fitting the underlying data, the model represented in Figure 25 (i.e. including five "social capabilities" constructs) is by far superior to the model with only one "social capability" construct.

Next, we looked at the correlation values between the five "social capabilities" to explore whether additional, alternative models could be thought of that included more than one — but less than five — "social capabilities" as predictors of "competitive business performance." The correlations matrix in Table 9 suggests that there are three particularly highly correlated "social capabilities": "communication rituals" (CommRit), "knowledge interactions" (KnowInt) and "boundary-spanning leadership" (Leadersh). We therefore built an alternative model that merged all of these three "social capabilities" into one, but kept everything else the same as in Figure 25. The resulting model with three "social capabilities" constructs predicting "competitive business performance" has an AIC value of 9,364.84. These results show that this model is far inferior to the model represented in Figure 25. Furthermore, these results suggest that "communication

Table 9: Correlations between the five "social capabilities" and the associated *t* Values.

	BuBlock	**CommRit**	**KnowInt**	**Leadersh**	**CBRota**
BuBlock	1.00				
CommRit	0.72	1.00			
t-val	32.33				
KnowInt	0.51	0.68	1.00		
t-val	16.23	27.24			
Leadersh	0.68	0.90	0.68	1.00	
t-val	30.51	78.36	30.07		
CBRota	0.43	0.38	0.46	0.41	1.00
t-val	13.17	11.07	14.39	12.80	

rituals", "knowledge interactions" and "boundary-spanning leadership" are to be regarded as three separate constructs, albeit correlated.

Another important alternative model is the following: if we were willing to simply average all the statements concerning a construct, this would be almost equivalent to forcing all loadings (weights) to be identical. We therefore have tried this model with these additional constraints and its AIC is 8,584.94. Again this value is so much higher than the AIC of the model in Figure 25 (6,900.78) that there remains absolutely no doubt that our approach is more suited to the responses observed than the simple averaging method.[10]

We tried other alternative models that combined the five "social capabilities" in different ways, and compared both the AIC values and various other components of these models (equality of the variances of the residuals, combined with equality of loadings, and so on). However, every other model we tried confirmed that the model represented in Figure 25 offered the best fit with the data. This is summarized in Table 10.

To conclude, our comparative analyses of the various alternative models to the model represented in Figure 25 suggest that all five "social capabilities" are to be considered as separate — albeit highly correlated — constructs. These results are clear from our analyses and provides strong support to Propositions 3 and 4 in Figure 17, stating that the Common Glue is made up by the holistic interaction of five social capabilities that are distinct from one another but highly interrelated among themselves. These findings also provide support for Hypothesis 2 in Figure 18, postulating a positive link between Common Glue and "competitive business performance", where the strength of that link is greater than that between each individual "social capability" and "competitive business performance".

After having shown that the data support the fact that the five different constructs we proposed are well defined, different, mutually correlated, and linked to the statements they are related to, we now turn to understanding better the relationships between the constructs. Our aim is to show that all five "social capabilities" are useful to predict "competitive business performance". The center part of Figure 25 shows the hypothesized regression model and the estimated coefficients. To be more precise, Table 11 shows the equation fitted for the model and the estimated coefficients as well as the associated t Values are given.

At first thought, we might expect the entire set of coefficients to be highly significant to support our hypothesis. However, we can see that a number of them are not significant (since their t Values are between -2 and 2).[11] This can however be explained by the moderate to strong correlations that exist between the five "social capabilities" constructs (see Table 9). Indeed, since we are using correlated constructs to explain "competitive business performance", all of these constructs tend to explain the same part of the dependent variable's variability,

Table 10: Summary of the AIC values for the different models tried. The basic model of Figure 25 has the lower, i.e. the best AIC.

Basic	One construct	3 constructs	Equal loadings	Only B	Only C	Only K	Only L	Only R
6,900.78	15,562.93	9,364.84	8,584.94	6,975.44	6,913.44	6,980.63	6,918.94	7,048.23

Table 11: Coefficients and *t* Values of the regression equation model.

Perform = 0.18*BuBlock + 0.090*CommRit + 0.21*KnowInt
t-val   2.85   0.72   3.42

+ 0.14*Leadersh − 0.022*CBRota,   Errorvar.= 0.72,   R2 = 0.28
t-val   1.22   − 0.49   7.52

thereby preventing each from showing its unique contribution to predicting the dependent variable and becoming much less significant as a result.

This well-known phenomenon is called multi-collinearity.[12] Another way to explain this is to get back to the definition of the significance of a coefficient in regression: a coefficient is significant if the model without the given construct, but with all other constructs, can explain much less of the variability of the "competitive business performance". Since the constructs are correlated, removing only one of them does not deteriorate enough the fit for the coefficient to be significant. This in fact corresponds quite well with the *hologramic* characteristics of the Common Glue that were described in Chapter 3. There we saw that, although each constituent social capability of the Common Glue was described as distinct from one another, it was also suggested that, when examined separately, each of them *included and delineated clearly all the essential elements of the remaining four social capabilities.*

Hologramic Properties of the Common Glue's Elements

Let us clarify from the outset that, as stated by Leser, "multi-collinearity is serious when emphasis lies on the estimation of individual parameters in the relationship, but less serious when the objective of prediction of the dependent variable is stressed."[13] Individual parameters would be of prime interest if we wanted to select one single construct that best predicted "competitive business performance", or if our objective was to compare their underlying regression coefficients.[14] However, both the concepts behind the very definition of "social capabilities" as well as our comparative analyses of the data clearly suggest that we cannot do such a selection. Nevertheless, if our goal is limited to showing that all five "social capabilities" as a whole can be used to predict "competitive business performance", then multi-collinearity is not really a problem. Since both the R2 and our model as a whole are quite stable, our treatment of multi-collinearity is consistent with Cramer's observations that "even though regression coefficients may have large standard errors (in the face of multi-collinearity], the predictions [of the underlying model) may be very stable."[15] This will be confirmed by a sensitivity analysis further on in this chapter.

One of the most important indices for assessing the severity of multi-collinearity is called the (maximal) condition number index. Within the context of our model, this index is defined as the square root of the ratio between the largest and the smallest eigenvalue of the *standardized* covariance matrix of the five "social capabilities"[16] In the case of our model, the condition number index is equal 5.99, which is considered as mild multi-collinearity. As stated by Mansfield and Helms, the consequences of multi-collinearity are — among others — that "the estimates are often large and may have signs that disagree with known theoretical properties of the variables [...] The estimates have large variances."[17] One consequence of these large variances is of course that the resulting t Values are small,[18] which is clearly the case in our model (see Table 11). In our case, we also have a sign change: CBRota is hypothesed to be positively related to "competitive business performance" and the next analysis shows that it is the case. However, due to multi-collinearity, its regression coefficient given in Table 11 is negative. This all means that we have to analyze the relationship between the constructs more in detail, since multi-collinearity prevents us from directly interpreting the regression coefficients given in Table 11.

The first step is to estimate the correlation between each of the five "social capabilities" and "competitive business performance" as well as the associated t Values. These estimates are necessary: (i) in order to verify that the non-significance of the coefficients in Table 11 is not due to an absence of a link between the five mechanisms and performance (but due to multi-collinearity) and (ii) in order

Table 12: Correlations (and t-values) of each "social capability" and "competitive business performance".

	BuBlock	CommRit	KnowInt	Leadersh	CBRota
Perform	0.44	0.48	0.45	0.48	0.24
t-val	12.40	13.96	12.64	14.63	6.25

to test hypothesis 1 (see Section 2). Table 12 shows the results of this analysis, demonstrating that, considered separately from the rest, each "social capability" is correlated with "competitive business performance" (abbreviated as "perform" in Table 12), and all five correlation values are strongly significant. This demonstrates our first assertion that each "social capability" is linked to and has an important predictive power on "competitive business performance".

It is clear that, were the "social capabilities" independent of each other, their regression coefficients[19] would be exactly the same as those shown in Table 11. Instead, the regression line in Table 11 gives one negative coefficient and all t Values are non-significant. On the one hand, this comparison between the results obtained in Tables 11 and 12 demonstrates that the non-significance of the underlying coefficients is not due to an absence of a link between the five "social capabilties" and "competitive business performance". Rather, it confirms that these mechanisms are separate but not independent constructs and that there exists an associated problem of multi-collinearity. On the other hand, the results in Table 12 provide additional support for our Hypothesis 7 in Figure 18 that each "social capability", considered separately from the rest, is positively linked to "competitive business performance".

Further evidence in support of Hypothesis 7 is provided by the following analyses: if, in the model represented in Figure 25, we remove four of the five links connecting each "social capability" to "competitive business performance" and subsequently estimate the parameters of the resulting new model, the remaining link (from one mechanism to performance) becomes positive and strongly significant. This remains true for each of the five "social capabilities", demonstrating that, considered independently of the rest, each mechanism is strongly and positively linked to performance. More precisely, for the model with only the link from BuBlock (company-wide building blocks), the significance of the regression coefficient is 9.92 and the AIC of the model is 6,975.44. For CommRit these values are respectively 10.63 and 6,913.44, for KnowInt, 10.08 and 6,980.63, for Leadersh, 10.44 and 6,918.94 and finally for CBRota (cross-boundary rotations), they are 6.28 and 7,048.23 (see Table 10). Note that the AICs show that these models are interesting for proving evidence of multi-collinearity, and for showing that all "social capabilities" are strongly related to "competitive business performance", but that these models are not good models and we should stick to the model given in Figure 25.

The data shown in Tables 9, 11 and 12 clearly demonstrate that the five "social capabilities" are well defined and separate constructs but, as expected, not independent of one another. On the contrary, these mechanisms are moderately to highly correlated between each other, pointing to the existence of multi-collinearity that prevents the underlying regression coefficients from being significant and precludes us from interpreting the value of these coefficients. Indeed, we have based our analyses so far on assessing the global fit of our model as a whole, as given by the AIC and RMSEA criteria, which have both provided quite satisfactory data for our model represented in Figure 25. These results provide strong support for our "Common Glue" Hypothesis 2 in Figure 18 that all five "social capabilities" *together* are positively linked to "competitive business performance."

Trying All Possible Combinations of Social Capabilities

As in the previous section, we wanted to further assess whether any given combination of "social capabilities" was particularly useful for predicting "competitive business performance". We therefore performed additional analyses of the data following Mallows' Cp method. Because, as mentioned, this tool explores *all* possible subgroups and rates them, based on their predictive power compared to their sparsity, Mallows' Cp is useful both to circumvent the possible problem of multi-collinearity (and to understand the results of the regression) and to select what appears to be the best model, or more generally a handset of good models. Based on this method, we designed and ranked all of the 24 possible models that utilize one, two, three, four or five of the "social capabilities" to predict "competitive business performance".

Figure 26 and Table 13 (in Appendix B) show that, out of the 24 models examined, besides the full model BCKLR (Cp=6.00, p=6), there are five other models that are clearly superior to the rest: BCK (Cp=6.20, p=4), BKL (Cp=7.57, p=4), BCKL (Cp=4.13, p=5), BCKR (Cp=8.17, p=5) and BKLR (Cp=9.26, p=5). A second point worth highlighting is that the model that retains *all five* "social capabilities" — BCKLR — is among the best models. A third point to note is that *all* models with a single "social capability" as predictor of "competitive business performance" are well above the diagonal line in Figure 26. This provides further support to our Common Glue Hypothesis 2 in Figure 18 suggesting that there is a positive link between all five "social capabilities" *together* and "competitive business performance", and that this link is stronger than any links between each separate social capability and performance. These results also provide additional confirmation that the model represented in Figure 25 is indeed a good one. Another point to note in Figure 26 is that company-wide building blocks (B) and knowledge interactions (K) are two social capabilities that are present in all of the six best models selected according to the Mallows' Cp criteria. This would appear to suggest that these two "social capabilities" *together* are especially strong predictors of "competitive business performance".

All the analyses carried out so far show that the hypotheses we have postulated in Figure 18 are strongly supported by the data. However, to further strengthen our findings, we will show that these findings also hold when looking at each

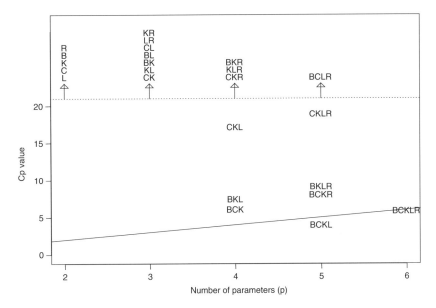

Figure 26: Mallows' Cp assessing the predictive power of 24 combinations of "social capabilities" vis-à-vis performance.

company separately, and that there is no other explanation (variable) to the links we have established. These further analyses are called controls, and will be developed in the next section.

Controlling for the 'Common Variance' Problem

The way in which the "common variance problem" was addressed in our previous analyses obviously applies here as well. In particular, the second set of arguments offered were related to the results of the Mallows' Cp. If the correlation were simply due to a response bias, all the models with only one variable (B, C, K, L and R in Figure 26 and Table 13 in Appendix B) would be the good models and we would see them close or below the diagonal line in Figure 26. In addition, the more variables one would add, the worse the weaker the model would become. However, as before, the results of the Mallows' Cp indicate that the data behave exactly in the opposite way.

The third argument against "common variance" in our data regarded the series of SEM models that we tried, and this applies here as well. As previously mentioned,

Figure 22, representing the model with only one latent variable (in other words, putting all the statements of the "social capabilities" together) to predict "competitive business performance", has an AIC and fit indices by far worse than the model with the five "social capabilities". This would not be the case if the response bias was high, in which case we would expect models with only one latent variable to be the best ones.

Sensitivity Analyses Across the Different Companies

The findings above are quite robust, since they were based on respondents stemming from 11 companies that are highly diverse from the viewpoint of the industries and geographies they operate in, their national and corporate cultures, organizational dimensions and other important characteristics. In order to further strengthen our findings we carried out the same analyses for each separate company. Since these kind of models require a large number of respondents, we will stick to the four companies for which we have the higher number of responses. They are called "C", "D", "F" and "G" and have, respectively, 147, 91, 193 and 111 respondents. Fitting the same model as shown in Figure 25 for each separate company gives us a RMSEA of 0.079 for "C", 0.071 for "D", 0.069 for "F" and 0.076 for "G". We cannot compare the chi-square tests or the AIC since these depend on the number of respondents. Due to multi-collinearity, we cannot expect the regression coefficients to be close, nor can they be interpreted. By contrast, R2 is an interesting measure that is not perturbed by multi-collinearity. The value of the R2 is 46% for "C", 36% for "D", 30% for "F" and 47% for "G". These values are slightly higher than those stemming from the analysis with all respondents (28%), but stay reasonably close. The higher values of the R2 are both due to the smaller number of respondents utilized here and perhaps also to some specific characteristics of some of the companies/areas of business. However, if the latter was the case, this has a mild influence on our results since the R2 are not very different. The non-normed fit index (NNFI) has moved from 0.96 (for the data with all 11 companies) to 0.93 for "C", 0.87 for "D", 0.95 for "F" and 0.92 for "G". Once more, this shows that there is a very mild difference between companies, if any.

These findings are robust in relation to different groupings of statements as well. We tried three types of groupings: no grouping, the grouping we have just presented, and an even more important grouping with an additional division in half the number of grouped statements. Again, due to multi-collinearity, the regression coefficients differ, but the R2 of the regression remains remarkably stable: in all three cases it is R2=28% for the full data. The chi-square statistics and the AIC statistics cannot be compared since they also depend on the number of variables utilized, which is different in every case. The RMSEA is 0.070 without grouping,

0.063 with grouping and 0.068 with increased grouping. The NNFI is 0.94 without grouping, 0.96 with grouping and 0.97 with increased grouping (refer to Appendix E). All these statistics remain remarkably stable and provide further evidence of the robustness of our model.

Controlling the Results Across the Different Companies

Similar to our previous analyses, we represented graphically the relationship we found between "social capabilities" and "competitive business performance". In Figure 27, each respondent is represented by a point giving his/her Common Glue strength assessment on the horizontal axis and his/her "competitive business performance" assessment on the vertical axis. The graphic patterns of the points clearly show that there is a correlation between these two indices. As before, we superimposed the individual companies' regression lines, confirming that there clearly is a relationship between these two concepts across every single company in our sample.

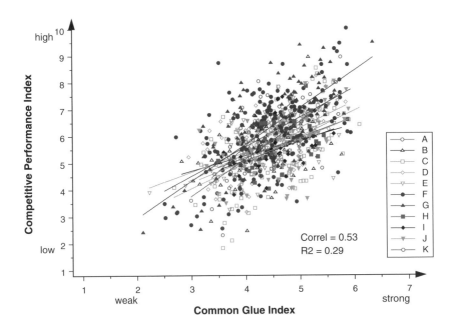

Figure 27: Scatter plot of the value of "social capabilities" (the Common Glue Index) and "competitive business performance" for each respondent. The regression lines are given by company and are satisfactorily close to one another.

From our previous analyses we saw that another very interesting insight stemming from the data is to check whether any substantial differences in response patterns exist across the 11 different companies. If this was the case, it would obviously mean that this part of our findings could not be generalized to all companies, but that we should rather treat each of them separately. Figure 28 shows the plot of responses per each individual company with its respective regression line. As before, let us note that, although we would not expect the individual companies'

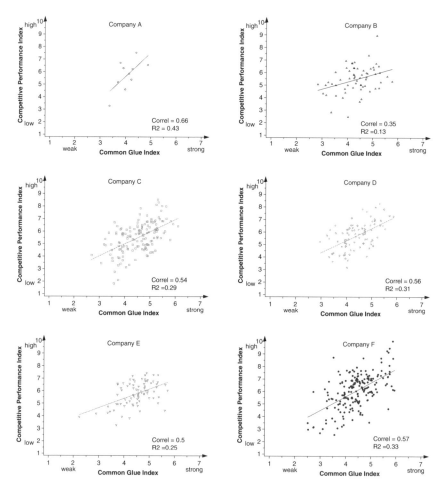

Figure 28: The same graphs as in Figure 27, but this time by company.

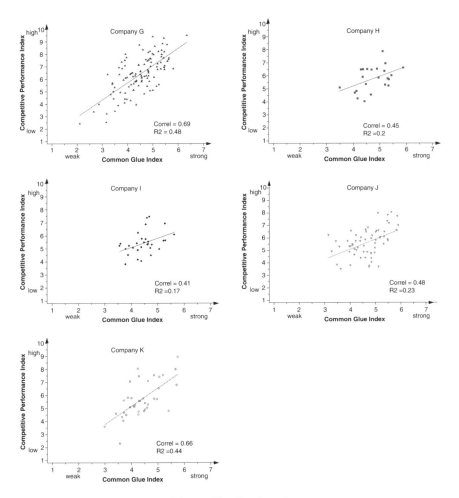

Figure 28: Continued

regression lines to be identical, it is extremely important that no company shows a very different pattern from the others.

This latter point has already been highlighted as being crucially important, as it shows that the patterns of relationships we found between Common Glue and competitive business performance, hold across every single difference represented by the sample of companies: different industry or service sectors, different sizes, diverse national and corporate cultures, different organizational structures, management styles, corporate histories and identities, etc. Our quantitative results show that, across *all* these organizational differences, the Common Glue remains a good predictor of "competitive business performance".

Evolutionary characteristics of the Common Glue

We gathered information on one company's Common Glue over time, which is worth analyzing further to formally test its evolutionary characteristics. Different groups of company managers belonging to the same seniority cadre, were assessed in eight different occasions over the 22 months elapsed between July 2001 and May 2003. During that period, this leading global automotive company experienced very profound transformations throughout the entire organization, including a large-scale "merger of equals" with a leading US-based automaker. It is therefore of interest to incorporate these longitudinal aspects into the analyses.

Figure 29 shows the weighted average of both Competitive Performance and the Common Glue indices stemming from the assessments by each group of respondents in each of the eight sessions carried out between July 2001 and May 2003. By comparing the general shapes of both curves, we can observe that they show roughly the same behavior: first the curves go down from July 2001 to mid-2002,

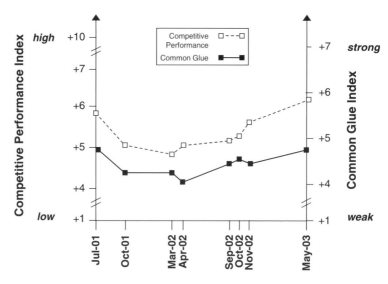

Figure 29: Auto company example: Common Glue and Competitive Performance over time.

and then the tendency reverses and both curves slowly but firmly go up again until the last measure carried out in May 2003.

To formally analyze these patterns we performed the following statistical analysis. Since both index scales cannot be compared directly, the only important information we can examine is whether the two curves reach their minimum points at roughly the same time. If this were to be true, we can state that, over time, the competitive performance index varies together with the Common Glue index. This would provide support to the evolutionary characteristics of the Common Glue vis-à-vis its positive effects in competitive performance, as articulated in Proposition 5 in Figure 17, together with Hypothesis 2 in Figure 18. If our analyses led to discovering that the relationship between these two indices is untrue, then we would have to assume a more complex and unknown relationship at work.

In order to test the above, we developed a model for the time dependence of both the competitive performance and the Glue indices. Figure 29 suggests that a quadratic model could provide a reasonable fit by adjusting a parabola to both curves. However, a closer look at the graph indicates that the "downhill" part of these curves (July 2001 to mid-2002) is somewhat steeper the "uphill" part (mid-2002 to May 2003), indicating that a logarithmic transformation of the time variable could improve the fit of the model to the data. The statistical analyses support this impression and indeed the logarithmic transformation improves the fit.[20] We therefore adopted the analytical model based on the logarithm of the time variable. The two curves are estimated as:

$$\text{Competitive Performance} = 51.56 - 27.94 \, \text{logTime} + 4.22 \, \text{logTime}^2 + \text{error}$$

$$\text{Common Glue} = 23.31 - 11.44 \, \text{logTime} + 1.73 \, \text{logTime}^2 + \text{error}$$

As we know, the minimum of a parabola is reached at $-b/(2a)$. For Competitive Performance this means a minimum at $-(-27.94)/(2*4.22) = 3.31$ in logTime or $\exp(3.31) = 27.51$. In other words, the minimum of the Competitive Performance index is reached between March and April 2002. A similar calculus computation for the Common Glue index gives a minimum at $-(-11.44)/(2*1.73) = 3.30$ in logTime or $\exp(3.30) = 27.17$, again between March and April 2002. If, in addition, we compute the difference between these two minimum values we obtain $27.51 - 27.17 = 0.34$ month. This means that the two minima are just about 10 days apart!

Since our interest here regards a complex quantity (the difference of exponential of ratio of quadratic regression coefficients), it is virtually impossible to obtain a test of significance and a *p* Value for this difference by following classical methods. However, it is possible to obtain a confidence interval for this difference, computed in months, by using a simulation technique called bootstrap, or Monte-Carlo simulation.[21] The basic idea is to test how certain we are about the difference computed as being 0.34 month. This is done by resampling 1,000 times the respondent's value and to see what values are obtained with these "new" samples.[22]

The 95% confidence interval for the difference in month is (−4.29; 5.23). This means that there is 95% of chance that the minimum of the two curves is about within 5 months. The first implication is that this difference covers the "no difference" value, which is 0. This is evidence that the hypothesis of a simultaneous time influence on both Competitive Performance and Common Glue indices is tenable. Secondly, since the value 0 is almost in the middle of the confidence interval, and not just at the edge, this strengthens the hypothesis of a simultaneous time influence. Thirdly, the confidence interval goes from −4.3 months to 5.2 months. In other words, even if the minima are not attained exactly at the same time, this shows that they are anyway quite close to one another and therefore there is strong evidence that time had a similar effect on both Competitive Performance and Common Glue. These results provide support to the evolutionary characteristics of the Common Glue vis-à-vis competitive performance, as articulated in Proposition 5 in Figure 17, together with Hypothesis 2 in Figure 18.

By contrast, if one looks at the "strategies" and "strategic approaches to growth", they do not follow similar patterns over time at all. Figure 30 shows the

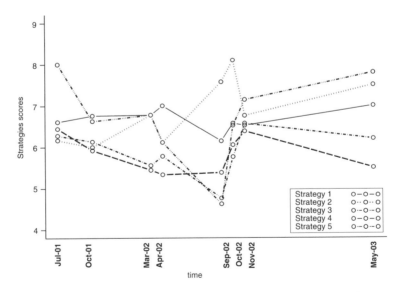

Figure 30: Auto company example: Strategies and strategic approaches to top-line growth over time.

five "strategies" and "strategic approaches" scores over the different sessions. It is normal that these curves are less smooth than the curves for the Competitive Performance and Common Glue indices, since they are based on only one score per person. However, they do not follow even slightly the same patterns, as we previously saw in the case of the Common Glue and the Competitive Performance indices. We therefore conclude that there is an evolutionary phenomenon shared over time between the Common Glue and the Competitive Performance indices, that is completely absent in the case of "strategies" and "strategic approaches to growth".

The Crucial Link Between Blending Power and Performance

In this chapter, we presented strong empirical support for all of our propositions and hypotheses in Figures 17 and 18. Hence, the *blending power* of organizations — *blending* strategies and *blending* approaches to top-line growth, together with the Common Glue — can be regarded as strong, positive and reliable predictors of "competitive business performance". The strength of this link is greater than the links between each separate element and "competitive business performance". Moreover, the strength of this link — formally tested using hard data stemming from 847 respondents — holds across every possible difference represented by each of the 11 companies in our sample: different industry or service sectors with very diverse technological paradigms at work, different company sizes, diverse national and corporate cultures, different professional cultures and mindsets, different organizational structures, functional arrangements, management styles, corporate histories and identities, and so on. Equally importantly, the fact that these statistical findings are based on data gathered over a relatively long time period — April 2001 to June 2004 — suggests that our empirical results also hold across a series of important macroeconomic phenomena that took place over those years, i.e. different stages of global macroeconomic growth, the introduction of the Euro in most countries within the European Union, and so on.

In addition, we found strong empirical support that internal approaches to top-line growth as well as strategies focusing on delighting the customer and innovation, have a stronger correlation with "competitive business performance" than either external approaches to growth or cost leadership strategies. Similarly, these strategies and strategic approaches to growth show a stronger correlation with "social capabilities" than either external approaches to growth or cost leadership strategies. This does not mean that the latter strategies and external approaches to growth are detrimental to organizational performance, or that the respondents in our sample refrained systematically from adopting them within their organizations.

Rather, these findings place all these strategies and strategic approaches to top-line growth within the broader context of organizations balancing — *blending* — these strategic options properly, harmoniously and wisely at every point of time and depending on context. These findings also highlight the crucial interplay between an organization's Common Glue, its orientations to organizational innovation and customer delight, its internal approaches to organizational growth and its attainment of sustainable competitive performance across organizational, cultural, geographic and professional boundaries of any kind.

Equally importantly, our empirical results show strong support for the Common Glue as a holistic, hologramic and evolutionary organizational asset that constitutes a solid, reliable and positive predictor of "competitive business performance" over time. Again, these results were shown to be empirically strong against a very diverse array of competing hypotheses and explanatory models as well as throughout the same diversity of companies that we utilized in the first part of our formal analyses. Not only each of the five "social capabilities" described by the managers in their interviews (boundary-spanning leadership, company-wide building blocks, knowledge interactions, communication rituals and cross-boundary rotations) were actually found to exist as distinct but interrelated realities within organizations, but, *together*, they were also found to have a strong and positive link with competitive business performance. The strength of this link was greater than the links between each separate social capability and competitive business performance. As before, the strength of this link holds across every possible difference represented by each of the 11 companies in our sample as well as across a series of important global macroeconomic phenomena that took place during the 38-month data-gathering period.

Our quantitative findings reinforce strongly what we had discovered during the qualitative phase of our research. The blending power of organizations — bringing their 'male' and 'female' characteristics together at both the strategic and transformational levels — seems to be *what* drives superior competitive performance across organizational, cultural, geographic and professional boundaries of any kind. These discoveries have very obvious and major implications to all organizations operating in our increasingly interconnected world, and hints at some profound additional insights that go well beyond the organizational arena. I will reflect on some of these implications in the next chapter.

Notes and References

[1] Jöreskog, K.G. and D. Sörbom (1999). *LISREL 8: User's Reference Guide*, 2nd ed., Scientific Software International: Chicago, IL. SSI – Scientific Software International. 2004. LISREL 8.54, http://www.ssicentral.com.

[2] To fit a model with latent variable(s) with only one manifest variable, we need to fix a supposed reliability to the regression between them (see Jöreskog and Sörbom, 1999). Here we have fixed it to 100%, but if we fix them to 30%, the AIC happens to be identical, and the model is very similar.

[3] These very high correlations can be readily seen by closely inspecting Figure 14 in chapter 4. A more formal way of doing this is provided by the so-called modification indices that can be computed on top of a SEM model. A high modification index between (the error of) two statements indicates that the proposed model does not incorporate all the correlations observed between the responses to these two statements.

[4] It is generally accepted that RMSEA upper confidence limit values smaller than 0.080 are indicative of good model-data fit (Jöreskog and Sörbom, 1999). Although a chi-square test could be regarded as a more stringent test of model-data fit than RMSEA, this type of test presupposes normality of the variables under examination (Long, J.S. (1988). *Covariance Structure Models: An Introduction to LISREL*, Sage, London). However, a chi-square test is not suitable to our statistical model, as the underlying variables stem from 7- or 10-point scale survey statements that do not follow a continuous, normal (bell-shaped) distribution.

[5] Mallows, C.L. (1973). "Some comments on CP", *Technometrics* 15: 661–675. Ripley, B.D. (1996). *Pattern Recognition and Neural Networks,* Cambridge University Press, Cambridge.

[6] Up to now the methods used were able to deal with the missing data without having to replace them. The Cp method however need full data and we therefore have to use a replacement mechanism. We used a model based replacement algorithm called expectation-maximization (EM) algorithm (Dempster et al., 1977). The models fitted in the above stay extremely stable whether we use the replaced case or not. Given the small number of missing values, this was anticipated. On the basis of the full data, we computed the scores of each respondent on each of the latent variable. Finally, the Cp analysis was fed with these scores.

[7] In exploratory graphs, we have used the correlation of the statements since its interpretation is much more natural. However, for the statistical analysis *per se,* we have used the covariances, since it has been shown in Cudek and Jöreskog and Sörbom that it provides (much more) correct inferences. Cudeck, R. (1989) "Analysis of correlation structures with covariance structure models," *Psychological Bulletin* 105 (2): 316–329. Jöreskog, K.G. and D. Sörbom. (1999) *LISREL 8: User's Reference Guide*, 2nd ed., Scientific Software International, Chicago, IL

[8] Jöreskog, K.G. and D. Sörbom. (1999). *LISREL 8: User's Reference Guide*, 2nd ed., Scientific Software International, Chicago, IL.

[9] Jöreskog, K.G. and D. Sörbom. 1999. *LISREL 8: User's Reference Guide*, 2nd ed., Scientific Software International: Chicago, IL., Akaike, H. (1981) "Likelihood of a model and information criteria". *Journal of Econometrics* 16, 3–14. Ripley, B.D. (1996). *Pattern Recognition and Neural Networks*. Cambridge University Press, Cambridge.

[10] In this case we can even make a test that compares the two models, since they are nested. The statistic is the difference of the chi-square values, here 1786.16 and this is compared

with a chi-square distribution with the difference of the two models degrees of freedom (here 51). The p Value is extremly close to zero ($p<1e-10$), meaning that the constrained model is not sufficient to explain the data.

[11] For individual companies, since the number of respondents is lower than the total number of respondents, the effect of multi-collinearity is even more severe and none of the coefficients are significant.

[12] A classic example of multi-collinearity is given by Morrison (1983), where the price of gold is predicted based on the exchange rate of dollars into German marks and Swiss francs. Although the two exchange rates were correlated (0.87 and 0.84 respectively) with the price of gold, the regression coefficients were not significant using the Scheffé multiple comparison test. Such a test reveals that multi-collinearity in this example stems from the extremely high (0.95) correlation between the two exchange rates. Of course, when only one of the exchange rates was used, the significance of the regression coefficient became very strong. For a good introductory text on multi-collinearity see Cramer (1985), Belinfante and Coxe (1982) and Mansfield and Helms (1982). Silvey (1969) gives a very good mathematical background to multi-collinearity, whereas Schink and Chiu (1969) take more of an econometrical orientation. Cassel et al. (2000) and Jagpal (1982) offer some special approaches to treating multi-collinearity in the context of SEMs. (Morrison, D.F. (1983). *Applied Linear Statistical Methods,*. Prentice-Hall Inc., Englewood Cliffs, NJ; Cramer, E.M. (1985). "Multi-collinearity." *Encyclopedia of Statistical Sciences* 1(5): 639–643; Belinfante, A. and K. Coxe (1982). Multicollinearity and ridge regression. *ASA Proceedings of the Statistical Computing Section*; 165–175; Mansfield, E.R. and B.P. Helms (1982). "Detecting multi-collinearity," *The American Statistician* 36: 158–160; Silvey, S.D. (1969). "Multi-collinearity and imprecise estimation," *Journal of the Royal Statistical Society*, Series B, Methodological 31: 539–552; Schink, W.A. and J.S.Y. Chiu (1969). "A simulation study of multi-collinearity and autocorrelation on estimates of parameters," *Journal of Financial and Quantitative Analysis* 1(2): 36–67; Cassel, C.M., P. Hackl and A.H. Westlund (2000). "On measurement of intangible assets: A study of robustness of partial least squares," *Total Quality Management* 11(7): 897–907; Jagpal, H.S. (1982). "Multicollinearity in structural equation models with unobservable variables," *Journal of Marketing Research* 19(4): 431–439.

[13] Leser, C.E.V. (1969). *Economic Techniques and Problems,* Griffin, London, p. 113.

[14] See: Webster, T. J. (2001). "A principal component analysis of the U.S. news & world report tier rankings of colleges and universities," *Economics of Education Review* 20(3): 235–244, for a series of statistical examples where a comparison between regression coefficients is of prime interest and where multi-collinearity therefore perturbs the statistical selection process.

[15] Cramer, E.M. (1985). "Multi-collinearity,". *Encyclopedia of Statistical Sciences* 1(5): 639–643.

[16] See: Belsley, D.A., E. Kuh and R.E. Welsch (1980). *Regression Diagnostics: Identifying Influential Data and Sources of Collinearity,* Wiley, Chichester; Chowdhary, U. (2000). "Correlates of apparel significance among older men and women," *Journal of Consumer*

Studies & Home Economics 24(3): 150–159. In those cases where severe multi-collinearity exists, the value for other eigenvalues may also be of interest (Erkel-Rousse, H. 1995. Detection of multicollinearity in an ordinary linear model: Some elements of an informed use of the Belsley, Kuh and Welsch indicators. *Revue de Statistique Appliquee – CERESTA* 43(4): 19–42; Willan, A.R. and D.G. Watts (1978). "Meaningful multicollinearity measures," *Technometrics* 20(4): 407–41; The *standardized* covariance matrix is central to estimating both the regression coefficients and their variability. When the (maximal) condition number index is large, the associated matrix is said to be ill-conditioned, causing a problem of multicollinearity as a result.

[17] Mansfield, E.R. and B.P. Helms (1982). "Detecting multicollinearity," *The American Statistician* 36: 158–160.

[18] Morton, T.G. (1977). "Factor analysis, multicollinearity, and regression appraisal models," *The Appraisal Journal* 45(4): 578–588.

[19] For a regression with only one explanatory variable (and one explained variable), the correlation between the two variables and its significance are the same as the regression coefficient when both variables are standardized, which is the case here.

[20] The time unit here is months. For convenience, we considered the beginning of year 2000 as the origin, i.e. the month number 1 is January 2000. So July 2001 is month 19, and May 2003 is month 46.

[21] See for example: Davison, A. C. and Hinkley, D. V. (1997). *Bootstrap Methods and their Application*, Cambridge University Press, Cambridge, UK; Efron, B. and Tibshirani, R. (1993). *An Introduction to the Bootstrap*, Chapman & Hall, London.

[22] More precisely, we resampled the respondents and computed the statistic that is the difference of the exponentials. We then computed the bias corrected and accelerated (BCa) confidence interval, which is a golden standard for statistics that may be asymmetric (see: Davison and Hinkley, 1997). We also computed the estimator conditional on the distribution of the times, that is by resampling within each time period, but the results are very similar: 95% CI $= (-4.24; 5.30)$.

Chapter 6

Getting Ready for the Journey

The [male and the female] will embrace in such a way that never
again will they be separable one from another. Then indeed will
the spirit unite with the body in perfect harmony…

Jean Cooper[1]

The best way to help mankind is through the perfection of yourself.

Krishna

Over the previous chapters I have described how the blending power of organizations can direct diversity to unleashing performance across boundaries of every
kind. And we saw that it takes a very special journey to fulfill this promise. A
transformational journey fit for leaders possessing strong *boundary-spanning*
character traits of: tolerance, walk-the-talk, wholeness, patience and a giver's
mentality. An open-ended organizational journey of relentless dedication to follow challenging *blending* strategies and approaches to growth, and, at the same
time, to nurture a strong Common Glue for driving organizational cohesiveness
and co-operation across all sorts of divides. I found evidence that, by undertaking
this journey, organizations can harmoniously blend their 'male' and 'female'
characteristics together, and in doing so transcend their cultural and organizational boundaries in order to drive sustainable competitive performance. These
findings have potentially radical implications for management research and practice, as well as over a number of other relevant dimensions in our increasingly
interconnected world. Let us start with the former.

The idea that *blending* strategies and *blending* approaches to top-line growth
can be seen as crucial predictors of competitive performance, broadens the debate
from the pursuit of specific generic strategies, to the issue of wisely *balancing*
both co-operative and competitive strategies and tactical options within a complex milieu. At the *strategic* level this, means adopting a view where customers
become centerpiece for strategy formulation, with suppliers, complementors,
allies and the like constantly helping organizations come up with strategic value
propositions that delight customers while at the same time obtaining cost advantages driven by innovation and knowledge sharing. At the *tactical* level, *blending*
strategies highlight that certain transactional and game-theoretical pundits portraying the strategic landscape of organizations as a battlefield where a series of
competitive choice outcomes are exercised mechanistically between utilitarian

and opportunistic agents, may have over-simplified the playing field a bit. Instead, these theorists might find greater predictive insights by looking at strategies and tactics as integrative forms of co-operative and competitive options, developed by organizations that operate as social actors within well-established, diverse and complex communities. Researching the conditions of collaborative behavior and co-operative choice outcomes between these organizations may crucially complement the positioning, utilitarian and opportunistic perspectives that have been developed from the transactional and tactical viewpoints.

Likewise, the Common Glue perspective opens new vistas for management research across the entire range of theories that, in the past, have emphasized rather mechanistically on transactional, optimizing or relational aspects in order to explain *what* is it that drives the competitive performance of organizations across cultural, functional and professional boundaries. We will elicit some of the most obvious paths for further research that come to mind. The Common Glue implies that *transactional* viewpoints — emphasizing the role of organizational settings in minimizing transaction costs — might evolve toward embracing those aspects of organizations that manifestly makes them organic and transformational entities driving social learning and innovation. The optimizing *resource-based* theories might enrich their predictive power vis-à-vis organizational performance by looking in greater detail at those resources and *social* capabilities that allow organizations to continuously change, transform, adapt and grow out of their internal and external boundaries. The *relational* perspectives may broaden their views of firms as constituting a series of economically efficient contracts, and look at organizational knowledge as a *socially* constructed and dynamic phenomenon that can be transformed in ways that go well beyond what any contract can capture. These are just some of the initial insights a 'female' theory of the Common Glue can bring in order to enrich further our current theories of organizational performance.

The Scientific Journey

Equally important, to my view, the Common Glue suggests a *blending* journey of sorts for researchers that, both within and outside the management field, have looked in a fragmented way at the various aspects that drive organizational performance across boundaries. The Common Glue highlights the enormous potential inherent in all these fields, of *blending* their insights together in an open-ended interdisciplinarian journey toward designing a new epistemology of socially constructed knowledge, both within — and amongst — organizations. Such a journey would challenge researchers in highly diverse disciplines — ranging from strategic management, finance, leadership, and knowledge management, to cultural anthropology, psychology and genetics — to bring out their 'female' professional sides in order to nurture the kind of professional collaboration across scientific divides that is so obviously needed to address complex issues such as the attainment of organizational performance across boundaries. Such an effort would unveil many further aspects of this latter issue that have been only initially charted in this book.

For example, some of the companies examined in this research illustrate quite spectacularly that systematically overlooking the strength of an organization's social capabilities vis-à-vis its international growth initiatives, might be leading to deeply flawed financial performance analyses and valuations. Thus, after its alliance with Nissan was publicly announced on March 1999, Renault's share price fell and three separate rating agencies issued negative reviews of the company's debt. However, almost exactly 5 years later in March 2004, Renault's original US$ 5.4 billion investment in Nissan was worth US$ 18.4 billion. This made Renault's 36.6 % stake in Nissan (which Renault increased to 44.4 % in 2003), worth more than the total market value of the French carmaker itself. Nissan's head of Europe (and former Renault executive) Patrick Pelata called it: *"the biggest return on investment in the history of the automotive industry."*.[2] By contrast, the May 1998 "merger of equals" between Daimler Benz and Chrysler was heralded as "a merger made in heaven" by many analysts whom were proved wrong just eighteen months later, when the company had catastrophically lost half the market value it had at the announcement of the deal[3]. In light of examples like this, financial researchers and analysts together with strategic management pundits might find it compelling to look at the obvious connections between the strength of an organization's social capabilities — i.e. measured via instruments such as the Glue Test© — and its financial valuation. It could very well be that certain organizations with leadership cadres possessing strong social capabilities for international growth — and potential investors in those organizations as well — are being unfairly penalized by financial analysts whom do not yet incorporate those aspects systematically into their assessments. Conversely, organizations that are weak in social capabilities nevertheless might be getting strong endorsements from the financial community that do not reflect some of those organizations' fundamental drawbacks for successful international growth.

From a complementary perspective, cross-cultural psychologists as well as cross-cultural management researchers might find it alluring to combine many decades of attention into what makes "another" culture different from one's own, with an enquiry into what it takes for an individual of any race to make her/his introspective search for attaining higher levels of tolerance a successful one. Behavioral scientists and management researchers can examine under which conditions highly heterogeneous teams can successfully craft a common language and instill within its members a mutual understanding for innovative cross-functional work. Linguists, semiologists and knowledge management researchers can investigate further how the social use of language can lead to profound, meaningful and transformational conversations between people of very diverse psychological, cultural and social experiences. Together with cultural anthropologists, historians and leadership pundits, these researchers could also investigate further into the social paradigm of the *Pacha-Yacha* or *collective reciprocity* which under the golden covenant of *giving first in order to receive,* led the most ancient civilization of Peru to unique levels of enlightened social co-operation and organizational achievements that are stunning in their sustainability and harmony with the surrounding environment. It could be of significance if today's researchers could dwell into these kinds of ancient sources to examine what can be learned there that might be useful to address our current challenges of driving organizational performance in ways that are sustainable over the long-run. In short, all these disciplines could — and should — build on each other's wealth of knowledge to delineate with ever greater clarity all aspects of this female-like business paradigm that purports the blending power of organizations. That remarkable transformational power that has been termed the Common Glue and which has revealed itself as a crucial predictor of organizational performance across cultural, functional and professional boundaries.

The Individual Journey

The Common Glue also charts a journey of sorts for leaders, employees and for all kinds of professionals alike that live and work within today's increasingly multicultural and interconnected world. The Common Glue tenets suggests that these individuals might benefit from going through a personal journey of self-introspection in order to strengthen their innate *boundary-spanning* character traits further. This might prove both invaluable and necessary to help them transcend any internal barries that might be constraining their full-potential at any level, i.e. cultural stereotypes, gender assumptions, professional mindsets, personal beliefs, generational values and so on. In doing this, these individuals might find that hurdles for introspective work might have risen deep inside them, and turned into mental models that operate in barely conscious and unsuspected ways that nevertheless pervasively influence how they view the world around them. Attaining awareness of our mental models in order to select what ought to remain and discard what is not likely to be useful for cross-cultural interactions, clearly constitutes a most daunting and formidable journey of self-assessment. One that requires a profound intelligence — both body and mind — on the individual as well as great doses of courage, resilience and humility. And one that usually requires help from others as well — a trusted friend, a wise coach, a nurturing organizational milieu — who can guide and support the individual throughout her/his long-lasting journey of introspective transformation. However, the upside of this journey is correspondingly grand. It is about these individuals gaining the admirable faculty to reach out to others transcending any differences of space and culture, and the thrilling gift to *blend* diversity into valuable wholeness. This is a challenge fit for will-be heroes of our own times, for remarkable individuals who are willing to help the rest of us transcend the barriers that separate us all. And a demanding test of generosity on those individuals who are ready to live by Krishna's dictum that: *the best way to help mankind is through the perfection of yourself.*

The Organizational Journey

For organizations operating within today's complex milieu, the challenge entails nothing less than going through a long-lasting and relentless journey to nurturing an ever stronger Common Glue for superior competitive performance across boundaries. By helping multinational organizations address this challenge over the past few years, I have learned that it really is about following a self-devised path of enlightened action through, where pinning down the *what-to-do* at the outset of the journey constitutes a necessary but comparatively easy part. Although I have already provided some obvious hints on Chapter 3, the *how* to carry out the organizational journey to nurturing a strong Common Glue will be the subject of a forthcoming book[4]. To the end, the theme of this volume ought to remain: the unveiling of *what* is it that *really* drives the competitive performance of organizations across cultural, organizational and geographic boundaries of any kind. Accordingly, let us suggest *what* is it that organizations often need to do in order to set out properly their Common Glue journeys. In this area, although in the end every organization I looked at developed their Common Glues in their own unique ways, they all tended to pursue the following sequence:

(1) Assess how strong is your organization's Common Glue at the start of the journey.
(2) Revisit the mission of your organization and place it as close as possible to the end customer.
(3) Imagine an exciting "company-wide business case" strongly linked to the mission of your organization, as the first destination of the journey.
(4) Identify your organization's boundary-spanning leadership team.
(5) Launch your organization's "company-wide business case" within a compelling communications event (as a minimum involving the company's entire boundary-leadership cadre) to 'kick-off' the journey.

(6) Get to work establishing a few building blocks and implementing the "company-wide business case."

In carrying out this journey I have found that organizations benefit enormously from establishing adequate measurements and milestones from the outset. In fact, when properly organized, these measurements and milestones themselves become part of the common language that the organization is intent on creating over time. For example, two such measurement tools that proved invaluable to support the Common Glue journeys of the organizations I followed are: the Glue Test©, helping organizations make the intial assessment in point 1 above and afterward monitor the level of strength of the Common Glue that is nurtured over time, and the Morosini and Næss Leadership Assessment©, that supports organizations appraise the *boundary-spanning* character traits within their key managerial cadres. Moreover, the creation and roll out of a series of communication events among the organization's *boundary-spanning* leadership cadre — i.e. to design a challenging "company-wide business case" they all fell passionate about and to foster true learning and innovation throughout the entire organization — are crucial steps to providing an initial and unstoppable momentum to this long-lasting journey.

The Journeys Beyond

A high-ranking female executive of Portuguese nationality that participated in my research told me something very simple that I have been unable to forget. Referring to the Common Glue trek, her organization — a leading Iberian electrical utility — was going through in 2005, she remarked that: *this Common Glue journey is about creating indestructible bondings the same way a family grows them: by sticking together through happy times as well as through testing experiences.* This, in fact, encapsulates quite well the practical dimension of this female business paradigm. A paradigm based on simple — not simplistic — tenets that grow out of very basic human experiences of socialization that all cultures share — and have shared since immemorial times. On the one hand, this makes it a rather *natural* paradigm of action for men and women of every race and creed.

On the other hand, this suggests that the applicability of the Common Glue theory can reach well beyond the internal organizational settings into which it was born. One very visible example of this concerns the economic performance of industrial clusters. Industrial clusters have rapidly moved to the top of the economic policy agenda in developed and developing countries alike. From northern Italy to Silicon Valley and Bangalore to Southern Brazil, voluminous research during the last two decades of the 20th century has shown that clusters provide unusually efficient and effective ways of creating regional economic growth and employment. Companies that belong to these clusters — large or small, global or local — can also achieve scale economies, specialized knowledge and continuous innovations that often underpin world-class competitive advantages across a wide array of industries. Regarding what drives the economic performance results of industrial clusters, it has been noted that:

> A broad array of existing empirical evidence […] suggests that *both* the degree of knowledge integration and the scope of competition are co-evolving factors that are crucial to explain the economic performance of industrial clusters [This evidence] suggests that firms in industrial clusters that present a high degree of knowledge integration and compete globally innovate more, present stronger growth patterns, adapt to changing environmental conditions more rapidly and have a more sustainable economic performance than firms in less integrated clusters that tend to compete within strictly local geographic boundaries[5].

In the same work, it was highlighted that the Common Glue's constituent social capabilities are *precisely* what drive the level of knowledge integration of industrial clusters, leading to the differences in economic performance that can be observed between them[5]. The notion of a strong Common Glue driving the economic performance of industrial clusters, turns social capabilities into a paradigm that potentially applies to the relationships between any given set of organizations, be them: allies, competitors, complementors, suppliers, customers, educational and research partners, interest groups, political and cultural associations, national and supra-national regulators, and so on. Amongst other things, this suggests that the tenets of the Common Glue theory of organizational performance may apply fully to an extremely broad array of *inter-organizational* phenomena.

And perhaps to global-scale phenomena as well. As I was finishing writing this book in early February 2005, the media continued to bring news of unrest, injustice and outright wars being fought everywhere along racial, cultural and religious divides. The dawn of the 21st century in fact seemed to signal that the human race might have grown enormously its scientific knowledge and technological ingenuity, but not so its wisdom. Thus, while surrounded by powerful communications technology and other extraordinary artifacts our recent ancestors could have hardly dreamt about, thinkers from all parts of the planet were seriously debating in early 2005, the very survival of modern civilization from all sorts of real as well as perceived threats. It all sounded rather familiar and quite regrettable. A portentous civilization successfully enduring every test but its own fear, rising above every challenge but its own deeply engrained cultural constraints.

Against this background, it would be of great significance if the ideas developed in this volume provide a doses of hope and reassurance to all those individuals and organizations that — from so many different perspectives — continue to actively work at bringing the human race together across linguistic, racial, religious, political and socioeconomical divides. Those remarkable people and supra-national institutions that continue to patiently craft the universal commonalities that may ensure our peaceful and sustainable viability for generations to come. May they find in the tenets of the Common Glue some inspiration to strengthen their own *boundary-spanning* leadership traits and those of others like them, as well as an overarching framework of ideas to help them build a common language and nurture a mutual understanding on a global scale.

Notes and References

[1] Cooper, J.C. (1990) *Chinese Alchemy — The Taoist Quest for Immortality,* Sterling Publishing Company, New York.

[2] Morosini, P. (2005) "Nurturing successful alliances across boundaries", In: *The Handbook of Strategic Alliances,* O. Shenkar (Ed.), Sage, London.

[3] Morosini, P. (2004) "Are mergers and acquisitions about creating value?" In: *Managing Complex Mergers,* P. Morosini and U. Steger (Eds.), Financial Times-Prentice Hall, UK.

[4] Morosini, P. (2005) *The Path of Wiracocha.* For more information about this publication, please contact the author at: piero.morosini@commonglue.com

[5] Morosini, P. (2004) "Industrial clusters, knowledge integration and performance", *World Development* 32 (2): 305-326.

Epilogue

Who are you?
Where are you?
What do you intend?
Answer me!
Let me see you!
Is in the heavens
or down in the shades
or in the outside world
that I will find you?

Ancient Kichua hymn to the the mysterious One Principle

The Peruvian city of Puno lies in the Western shores of the Titicaca lake, at 3,810 m (12,500 ft) above sea level. From there, it takes a short car ride to cross the border into Bolivia. It is an unusual border, with no customs, no guards and hardly any roadsigns informing the visitor that a different country has been entered. Only an endless multitude of people crossing the border in both directions, continuously throughout the day and into the night. But then, I thought, it has always been this way in this part of the world, named the *Alto Perú* — the Peruvian Highlands — by the first Spanish Conquistadores who ventured there on the 16th century. The name turned out to be most appropriate for this majestic region of magical beauty, as the Titicaca lake had been the cradle of the Kichua people, the creators of the *Tawantinsuyu* — the Inka empire — one the largest organized states ever built by any civilization.

The old car took me to my destination before the end of that sunny winter morning. I was about to enter the Kalasasaya temple, a strange and arresting megalithic structure within the ancient city of Tiwanaku, 20 k away from the Bolivian side of the Titicaca lake. As I walked through the temple's vast courtyard I saw the cyclopean stones of what had been a massive harbor wharf called the *Puma Punku*. Weighing between 100 and 470 tons, these stones had been transported from distant quarries over rugged mountainous terrain all the way to Tiwanaku. The mysterious ancient technology that allowed for such an extraordinary feat of engineering had vanished together with the city inhabitants over 14,000 years ago, seemingly as a result of a cataclysmic earthquake that devastated the entire region. I also saw the elegant entrance of the Kalasasaya temple, a masterpiece of stonework and symmetric harmony, with a grand trapezoidal gate accessible through an imposing set of steps. Through the temple's entrance one could see, far away in the distance, the carved sculpture of a strange individual of regal and divine presence.

But I found what I was looking for somewhere else in the Kalasasaya temple. I knew I had reached my destination when I finally glanced at the enigmatic figure at the top of the 3-meter high ancient gateway made up of a single block of andesite rock. I was looking at the 17,000-year-old face of Tunapa Wiracocha Wajinqira, the wise man of this strange land, the *Amauta* who had first taught the ancient Peruvians about the Harmonic Fusion of the Two Great Powers. When I finally saw him, I paused and marveled at the implausible set of circumstances that makes a man's message cross the millennia effortlessly to reach another man's mind. Like millions before me, I had come from very far to thank Tunapa Wiracocha in his own land, and to solicit guidance for the road ahead. I therefore murmured his message, and the ancient Kichua words sounded strangely familiar against the rarified atmosphere of the Andean highlands:

Apu Kon Ti-Ti Illa Tecsi Kailla Wiracocha Pachayachachi Kuruna Camac

The sun was reaching its zenith. The place was calm and peaceful and only the wind could be heard as it made its way softly through the magnificent Andean mountains.

- *Rimayñi!* (Answer me!) I pleaded.

And listened attentively to the wind.

Milan, February 7th, 2005

STATISTICAL APPENDICES

Appendix A

References in Figure 12, Chapter 4

Adler, N.J., 1991. International Dimensions of Organizational Behavior. Kent, Boston, MA.

Allen, D., Alvarez, S., 1998. Empowering expatriates and organizations to improve repatriation effectiveness. Human Resource Planning 21(4), 29–39.

Almeida, P., Song, J., Grant., R.M., 2002. Are firms superior to alliances and markets? An empirical test of cross-border knowledge building. Organization Science 13(2), 147–161.

Atkinson, A.A., Waterhouse., J.H., 1997. A stakeholder approach to strategic performance measurement. Sloan Management Review 38(3), 25–37.

Bannister, B.D., Higgins, R.B., 1991. Strategic capability, corporate communications and strategic credibility. Academy of Management Proceedings 2–6.

Barnard, C.I., 1938. The Functions of the Executive. Harvard University Press, Cambridge, MA.

Barney, J.B., 1986. Organizational culture: can it be a source of sustained competitive advantage? Academy of Management Review 11(3), 656–665.

Barney, J.B., Hansen, M.H., 1994. Trustworthiness as a source of competitive advantage. Strategic Management Journal 15(8), 174–189.

Bartlett, C.A., 1986. Building and managing the transnational: The new organizational challenge. In: Porter, M. (Ed.), Competition in Global Industries. Harvard Business School Press, Boston, MA.

Bartlett, C.A., Ghoshal, S., 1989. Managing Across Borders: The Transnational Solution. Harvard Business School Press, Boston, MA.

Bartlett, C.A., Ghoshal, S., 1990. The mu ltinational corporation as an interorganizational network. Academy of Management Review 15(4), 603–625.

Bartlett, C.A., Ghoshal, S.,1992. What is a global manager? Harvard Business Review 70(5), 124–132.

Bartlett, C.A., Ghoshal, S., 1994. Changing the role of top management: beyond strategy to purpose. Harvard Business Review 72(6), 79–88.

Bartlett, C.A., Ghoshal, S., 2002. Building competitive advantage through people. Sloan Management Review 43(2), 34–41.

Baruch, Y., Altman, Y., 2002. Expatriation and repatriation in MNCs: a taxonomy. Human Resource Management 41(2), 239–260.

Beck, J.E., 1988. Expatriate management development: realizing the learning potential of the overseas assignment. Academy of Management Proceedings 112–116.

Beechler, S., Taylor, S., Boyacigiller, N., Levy., O., 1999. Building global mindset for competitive advantage: A conceptual integration of global mindset, international human resource management and organizational performance in multinational corporations.

International Management Division, Academy of Management Division, Academy of Management Annual Meeting, Chicago, IL.

Bennis, W., Nanus, B., 1985. Leaders: The Strategies for Taking Charge. Harper & Row, New York, NY.

Bennis, W.G., Thomas, R.J., 2002. Crucibles of leadership. Harvard Business Review 80(9), 5–11.

Black, J.S., 1991. Coming home: the relationship of expatriate expectations with repatriation adjustment and job performance. Academy of Management Proceedings, 95–99.

Black, J.S., Stephens, G.K., 1989. The influence of the spouse on American expatriate adjustment in overseas assignments. Journal of Management 15(4), 529–544.

Black, J.S., Gregersen, H.B., Mendenhall, M.E., 1993. Global Assignments: Successfully Expatriating and Repatriating International Managers. Jossey-Bass, San Francisco, CA.

Bloom, M., Milkovich, G.T., 1999. An SHRM perspective on international compensation and reward systems. In: Wright, P.M., Dyer, L.D., Boudreau, J.W., Milkovich, G.T., (Eds.), Strategic Human Resources Management: Research in Personnel and Human Resources Management. JAI Press, Stamford, CT.

Bolt, J.F., 1985. Tailor executive development to strategy. Harvard Business Review 63(6), 168–176.

Bonache, J., Brewster, C., 2001. Knowledge transfer and the management of expatriation. Thunderbird International Business Review 43(1), 145–168.

Bonache, J., Brewster, C., Suutari, V., 2001. Expatriation: a developing research agenda. Thunderbird International Business Review 43(1), 3–20.

Bourgeois III, L.J., 1980. Performance and consensus. Strategic Management Journal 1(3), 227–248.

Boyd, B.K., Salamin, A., 2001. Strategic reward systems: a contingency model of pay system design. Strategic Management Journal 22(8), 777–792.

Brandt, W.K., Hulbert, J.M., 1976. Patterns of communication in the multinational corporation: an empirical study. Journal of International Business Studies 7(1), 57–64.

Brewster, C., 1991. The Management of Expatriates. Kogan Press, London.

Brown, J.S., Duguid, P., 1991. Organizational learning and communities of practice: toward a unified view of working, learning, and innovation. Organization Science 2(1), 40–57.

Burt, R.S., 1992. Structural Holes: The Social Structure of Competition. Harvard University Press, Cambridge, MA.

Caligiuri, P., Philips, J., Lazarova, M., Tarique, I., Burgi, P., 2001. The theory of met expectations applied to expatriate adjustment: The role of crosscultural training. International Journal of Human Resource Management 12(3), 357–372.

Campion, M.A., Cheraskin, L., 1994. Career-related antecedents and outcomes of job rotation. Academy of Management Journal 37(6), 1518–1542.

Chakravarthy, B.S., Lorange, P., 1991. Managing the Strategy Process: A Framework for a Multibusiness Firm. Prentice-Hall International Inc, Englewood Cliffs, NJ.

Chandler Jr., A.D., 1991. The functions of the HQ unit in the multibusiness firm. Strategic Management Journal 12(8), 31–50.

Chesbrough, H.W., Teece, D.J., 1996. When is virtual virtuous? Organizing for innovation. Harvard Business Review 74(1), 65–73.

Chew, I.K.H., Chong, P., 1999. Effects of strategic human resource management on strategic vision. International Journal of Human Resource Management 10(6), 1031–1045.

Collins, J.C., Porras, J.I., 1991. Organization vision and visionary organizations. California Management Review 34(1), 30–52.

Collins, J.C., Porras, J.I., 1996. Building your company's vision. Harvard Business Review 74(5), 65–77.

Conger, J.A., 1991. Inspiring others: the language of leadership. Academy of Management Executive 5(1), 31–45.

Conner, J., 2000. Developing the global leaders of tomorrow. Human Resource Management 39(2/3), 147–158.

Daft, R.L., 1983. Organization Theory and Design. West, New York, NY.

Daft, R.L., Lengel, R.H., 1986. Organizational information requirements, media richness and structural design. Management Science 32(5), 554–571.

Davenport, T.H., Prusak, L., 1998. Working Knowledge: How Organizations Manage What They Know. Harvard Business School Press, Boston, MA.

Davenport, T.H., De Long, D.W., Beers, M.C., 1998. Successful knowledge management projects. Sloan Management Review 39(2), 43–57.

Davidson Frame, J., 1987. Managing Projects in Organizations. Jossey-Bass, San Francisco, CA.

Davis, J.H., Schoorman, D.F., Mayer, R.C., Hoon Tan, H., 2000. The trusted manager and business unit performance: Empirical evidence of a competitive advantage. Strategic Management Journal 21(5), 563–576.

Day, G.S., 1999. Creating a market-driven organization. Sloan Management Review 41(1), 11–22.

De Meyer, A., 1991. Tech talk: how managers are stimulating global R&D communication. Sloan Management Review 32(3), 49–58.

Dess, G.G., 1987. Consensus on strategy formulation and organizational performance: competitors in a fragmented industry. Strategic Management Journal 8(3), 259–278.

Doz, Y.L., 1991. The international leadership challenges: Becoming a global corporation. In: Barlinn, S. (Ed.), Innovation, Integration and Strategic Processes: A Managerial Approach. Bedriftsokonomens Forlag, Oslo.

Doz, Y.L., Prahalad, C.K., 1986. Controlled variety: a challenge for human resource management in the MNC. Human Resource Management 25(1), 55–72.

Drucker, P.F., 2001. The Essential Drucker. Harper Business, New York, NY.

Eccles, R.G., 1991. The performance measurement manifesto. Harvard Business Review 69(1), 131–137.

Edstrom, A., Galbraith, J.R., 1977. Transfer of managers as a coordination and control strategy in multinational organizations. Administrative Science Quarterly 22(2), 248–263.

Eisenhardt, K.M., 1985. Control: organizational and economic approaches. Management Science 31(2), 134–149.

Evans, P.A.L., 1992a. Developing leaders and managing development. European Management Journal 10(1), 1–9.

Evans, P.A.L., 1992b. Management development as glue technology. Human Resource Planning 15(1), 85–106.

Evans, P.A.L., 1993. Dosing the glue: applying human resource technology to build the global organization. In: Shaw, B., Kirkbide, P. (Eds.), Research in Personnel and Human Resources Management, vol. 3. JAI Press, Greenwich.

Evans, P.A.L., Pucik, V., Barsoux, J.L., 2002. The Global Challenge: Frameworks for International Human Resource Management. McGraw-Hill, Boston, MA.

Feldman, D.C., 1991. Repatriate moves as career transitions. Human Resource Management Review 1(3), 163–178.

Ferner, A., Edwards, P., Sisson, K., 1995. Coming unstuck? In search of the "corporate glue" in an international professional services firm. Human Resource Management 34(3), 343–362.

Flamholtz, E., 1979. Organizational control systems as a managerial tool. California Management Review 22(2), 50–59.

Forster, N., 2000. Expatriates and the impact of cross-cultural training. Human Resource Management Journal 10(3), 63–78.

Frost, T.S., Birkinshaw, J.M., Ensign, P.C., 2002. Centers of excellence in multinational corporations. Strategic Management Journal 23(11), 997–1018.

Fulmer, R.M., Gibbs, P.A., Goldsmith, M., 2000. Developing leaders: how winning companies keep on winning. Sloan Management Review 42(1), 49–59.

Galford, R., Drapeau, A.S., 2003. The enemies of trust. Harvard Business Review 81(2), 5–11.

Galunic, D.C., Weeks, J., 1999. Managing knowledge at Booz Allen & Hamilton: Knowledge on-line and off. Case No. 09/1999-4846, INSEAD, Fontainebleau.

Galunic, D.C. Rodan, S., 1998. Resource recombinations in the firm: knowledge structures and the potential for Schumpeterian innovation. Strategic Management Journal 19(12), 1193–1202.

Ghoshal, S., 1987. Global strategy: an organizing framework. Strategic Management Journal 8(5), 425–440.

Ghoshal, S., Bartlett, C.A., 1988. Creation, adoption, and diffusion of innovations by subsidiaries of multinational corporations. Journal of International Business Studies 19(3), 365–388.

Ghoshal, S., Bartlett, C.A., 1996. Rebuilding behavioral context: a blueprint for corporate renewal. Sloan Management Review 37(2), 23–36.

Ghoshal, S., Nohria, N., 1989. Internal differentiation within multinational corporations. Strategic Management Journal 10(4), 323–338.

Ghoshal, S., Korine, H., Szulanski, G., 1994. Interunit communication in multinational corporations. Management Science 40(1), 96–110.

Gittell, J.H., 2000. Paradox of coordination and control. California Management Review 42(3), 101–117.

Goold, M., Quinn, J.J., 1990. The paradox of strategic controls. Strategic Management Journal 11(1), 43–58.

Govindarajan, V., Gupta, A.K., 2001. Building an effective global business team. Sloan Management Review 42(4), 63–71.

Granovetter, M., 1976. The strength of weak ties. American Journal of Sociology 78(3), 1360–1380.

Granovetter, M., 1985. Economic action and social structure: the problem of embeddedness. American Journal of Sociology 91(3), 481–510.

Grant, R.M., 1996a. Prospering in dynamically-competitive environments: organizational capability as knowledge integration. Organization Science 7(4), 375–387.

Grant, R.M., 1996b. Towards a knowledge-based theory of the firm. Strategic Management Journal 17(10), 109–122.

Grant, R.M., 1997. Knowledge-based view of the firm: implications for management practice. Long Range Planning 30(3), 450–454.

Gratton, L., Ghoshal, S., 2002. Integrating the enterprise. Sloan Management Review 44(1), 31–38.

Gregersen, H.B., Morrison, A., Black, J.S., 1998. Developing leaders for the global frontier. Sloan Management Review 40(1), 21–32.

Grover, V., Davenport, T.H., 2001. General perspectives on knowledge management: fostering a research agenda. Journal of Management Information Systems 18(1), 5–21.

Gupta, A.K., Govindarajan, V., 1991. Knowledge flows and the structure of control within multinational corporations. Academy of Management Review 16(4), 768–792.

Gupta, A.K., Govindarajan, V., 1999. Feedback-seeking behavior within multinational corporations. Strategic Management Journal 20(3), 205–222.

Gupta, A.K., Govindarajan, V., 2000. Knowledge flows within multinational corporations. Strategic Management Journal 21(4), 473–496.

Hambrick, D.C., 1980. Strategic awareness within top management teams. Academy of Management Proceedings 12–16.

Hambrick, D.C., 1987. The top management team: key to strategic success. California Management Review 30(1), 88–108.

Hambrick, D.C., Mason, P.A., 1984. Upper echelons: the organization as a reflection of its top managers. Academy of Management Review 9(2), 193–206.

Hamel, G., Prahalad, C.K., 1994. Competing for the Future. Harvard Business School Press, Boston, MA.

Hansen, M.T., 1999. The search-transfer problem: the role of weak ties in sharing knowledge across organizational subunits. Administrative Science Quarterly 44(1), 82–111.

Hansen, M.T., 2002. Knowledge Networks: explaining effective knowledge sharing in multiunit organizations. Organization Science 13(3), 232–248.

Hansen, M.T., Nohria, N., Tierney, T., 1999. What's your strategy for managing knowledge? Harvard Business Review 77(2), 106–116.

Harris, H., Brewster, C., 1999. An integrative framework for pre-departure preparation. In: Brewster, C., Harris, H. (Eds.), International HRM: Contemporary Issues in Europe. Routledge, London.

Harvey, M., 1989. Repatriation of corporate executives: an empirical study. Journal of International Business Studies 21(2), 131–144.

Harvey, M., Novicevic, M.M., 2002. The coordination of strategic initiatives within global organizations: the role of global teams. International Journal of Human Resource Management 13(4), 660–676.

Hedlund, G., 1994. A model of knowledge management and the N-form corporation. Strategic Management Journal 15(5), 73–90.

Hinds, P., Kiesler, S., 1995. Communication across boundaries: work, structure, and use of communication technologies in a large organization. Organization Science 6(4), 373–393.

Hofstede, G., 1980. Culture's Consequences: International Differences in Work-related Values. Sage, Newbury Park, CA.

Huselid, M.A., 1995. The impact of human resource management practices on turnover, productivity, and corporate financial performance. Academy of Management Journal 38(3), 635–672.

Iaquinto, A.L., Fredrickson, J.W., 1997. Top management team agreement about the strategic decision process: a test of some of its determinants and consequences. Strategic Management Journal 18(1), 63–76.

Jago, A.G., 1982. Leadership: perspectives in theory and research. Management Science 28(3), 315–336.

Jones, G.R., George, J.M., 1998. The experience and evolution of trust: implications for cooperation and teamwork. Academy of Management Review 23(3), 531–546.

Kaplan, R.S., Norton, D.P., 1992. The balanced scorecard – measures that drive performance. Harvard Business Review 70(1), 71–79.

Kaplan, R.S., Norton, D.P., 1996. Linking the balanced scorecard to strategy. California Management Review 39(1), 53–79

Kaplan, R.S., Norton, D.P., 2001. The Strategy-Focused Organization: How Balanced Scorecard Companies Thrive in the New Business Environment. Harvard Business School Press, Boston, MA.

Knez, M., Simester, D., 2002. Making across-the-board incentives work. Harvard Business Review 80(2), 16–17.

Kogut, B., Zander, U., 1992. Knowledge of the firm, combinative capabilities, and the replication of technology. Organization Science 3(3), 383–397.

Kogut, B., Zander, U., 1993. Knowledge of the firm and the evolutionary theory of the multinational corporation. Journal of International Business Studies 24(4), 625–645.

Kogut, B., Zander, U., 1996. What do firms do? Coordination, identity, and learning. Organization Science 7(5), 502–518.

Kotter, J.P., 1990. What leaders really do. Harvard Business Review 79(11), 103–111.

Kotter, J.P., Heskett, J.L., 1992. Corporate Culture and Performance. Free Press, New York, NY.

Kouzes, J.M., Posner, B.Z., 1987. The Leadership Challenge: How to Get Extraordinary Things Done in Organizations. Jossey-Bass, San Francisco, CA.

Kraimer, M.L., 1997. Organizational goals and values: a socialization model. Human Resource Management Review 7(4), 425–447.

Lachman, R., Nedd, A., Hinings, B., 1994. Analyzing cross-national management and organizations: a theoretical framework. Management Science 40(1), 40–55.

Larwood, L., Falbe, C.M., 1995. Structure and meaning of organization vision. Academy of Management Journal 38(3), 740–769.

Lazarova, M., Caligiuri, P., 2001. Retaining repatriates: the role of organizational support practices. Journal of World Business 36(4), 389–401.

Lencioni, P.M., 2002. Make your values mean something. Harvard Business Review 80(7), 5–9.

Levinthal, D.A., March, J.G., 1993. The myopia of learning. Strategic Management Journal 14(8), 95–112.

Lieberson, S., O'Conner, J.F., 1972. Leadership and organizational performance: a study of large corporations. American Sociology Review 37(2), 117–130.

Liebeskind, J.P., 1996. Knowledge, strategy and the theory of the firm. Strategic Management Journal 17(10), 93–108.

Lombardo, M.M., Eichinger, R.W., 1997. HR's role in building competitive edge leaders. Human Resource Management 36(1), 141–146.

Lovas, B. Ghoshal., S., 2000. Strategy as guided evolution. Strategic Management Journal 21(9), 875–896.

March, J.G., Simon, H.A., 1958. Organizations. Wiley , New York, NY.

Marschan, R., Welch, D., Welch, L., 1997. Language: the forgotten factor in multinational management. European Management Journal 15(5), 591–598.

Marschan-Piekkari, R., Welch, D., Welch, L., 1999. Adopting a common corporate language: IHRM implications. International Journal of Human Resource Management 10(3), 377–390.

Martinez, J.I., Jarillo, J.C., 1989. The evolution of research on coordination mechanisms in MNCs. Journal of International Business Studies 20(3), 489–514.

Maznevski, M.L., Chudoba, K.M., 2000. Bridging space over time: global virtual team dynamics and effectiveness. Organization Science 11(5), 473–492.

Mendenhall, M., Oddou, G., 1985. The dimensions of expatriate acculturation. Academy of Management Review 10(1), 39–47.

Mendenhall, M.E., Stahl, G.K., 2000. Expatriate training and development: where do we go from here? Human Resource Management 39(2/3), 251–266.

Meyer, C., 1994. How the right measures help teams excel. Harvard Business Review 72(3), 95–103.

Milkovich, G.T., Newman, J.M., Milkovich, C., 1996. Compensation. McGraw-Hill/Irwin, Homewood.

Moran, P., Galunic, D.C., 1999. Social capital and productive resource exchange: structural and relational embeddedness and managerial performance. Proceedings of Academy of Management Meetings, Business Policy and Strategy Track, Chicago, IL.

Moran, P., Ghoshal, S., 1996. Value creation by firms. Academy of Management Proceedings 41–45.

Morosini, P., 1998. Managing Cultural Differences: Effective Strategy and Execution Across Cultures in Global Corporate Alliances. Pergamon, Oxford.

Morosini, P., 2004. Competing on social capabilities. In: Chowdhury, S. (Ed.), Next Generation Business Handbook. Wiley, New York, pp. 248–271.

Murray, F.T., Murray, A.H., 1986. SMR Forum: global managers for global businesses. Sloan Management Review 27(2), 75–80

Nahapiet, J., Ghoshal, S., 1998. Social capital, intellectual capital, and the organizational advantage. Academy of Management Review 23(2), 242–266

Nobel, R., Birkinshaw, J., 1998. Innovation in multinational corporations: control and communication patterns in international R&D. Strategic Management Journal 19(5), 479–496.

Noel, J.L., Charan, R., 1988. Leadership development at GE's Crotonville. Human Resource Management, 27(4), 433–448.

Nohria, N., Ghoshal, S., 1994. Differentiated fit and shared values: alternatives for managing headquarters-subsidiary relations. Strategic Management Journal 15(6), 491–502.

Nonaka, I., 1991. The knowledge-creating company. Harvard Business Review 69(1), 96–104.

Nonaka, I., 1994. A dynamic theory of organizational knowledge creation. Organization Science 5(1), 14–37.

Nonaka, I., Toyama, R., Nagata, A., 2000. A firm as knowledge-creating entity: a new perspective on the theory of the firm. Industrial & Corporate Change 9(1), 1–20.

O'Reilly, C., 1989. Corporations, culture, and commitment: motivation and social control in organizations. California Management Review 31(4), 9–25

Ortega, J., 2001. Job rotation as a learning mechanism. Management Science 47(10), 1361–1370.

Pascale, R., 1985. The paradox of "corporate culture": reconciling ourselves to socialization. California Management Review 27(2), 26–41.

Prahalad, C.K., 1983. Developing strategic capability: an agenda for top management. Human Resource Management 22(3), 237–254.

Pucik, V., 1992. Globalization and human resource management. In: Pucik, V., Tichy, N.M., Barnett, C.K. (Eds.), Globalizing Management: Creating and Leading the Competitive Organization. Wiley, New York, NY.

Pucik, V., 1997. Human resources in the future: an obstacle or a champion of globalization? Human Resource Management 36(1), 163–167.

Pucik, V., Saba, T., 1998. Selecting and developing the global versus the expatriate manager: a review of the state-of-the-art. Human Resource Planning 21(4), 40–54.

Raynor, M.E., 2001. Lead from the center. Harvard Business Review 79(5), 92–100.

Rosenzweig, P., Gilbert, X., Malnight, T., Pucik. V., 2001. Accelerating International Growth. Wiley, Chichester.

Rotemberg, J.J., Saloner, G., 1993. Leadership style and incentives. Management Science 39(11), 1299–1318.

Roth, K., Ricks, D.A., 1994. Goal configuration in a global industry context. Strategic Management Journal 15(2), 103–120.

Schein, E.H., 1977. Increasing organizational effectiveness through better human resource planning and development. Sloan Management Review 19(1), 1–20.

Schein, E.H., 1992. Organizational Culture and Leadership. Jossey-Bass, San Francisco, CA.

Schein, E.H., 1996. Three cultures of management: the key to organizational learning. Sloan Management Review, 38(1), 9–20.

Schneier, C.E., Shaw, D.G., Beatty, R.W., 1991. Performance measurement and management: a tool for strategy execution. Human Resource Management 30(3), 279–302.

Schoemaker, P.J.H., 1992. How to link strategic vision to core capabilities. Sloan Management Review 34(1), 67–81.

Schuler, R.S., Fulkerson, J.R., Downing, P.J., 1991. Strategic performance measurement and management in multinational corporations. Human Resource Management 30(3), 365–392.

Sihler, W.H., 1971. Toward better management control systems. California Management Review 14(2), 33–39.

Simon, H., 1993. Strategy and organizational evolution. Strategic Management Journal 14(8), 131–142.

Simons, R., 1991. Strategic orientation and top management attention to control systems. Strategic Management Journal 12(1), 49–62.

Simons, R., 1994. How new top managers use control systems as levers of strategic renewal. Strategic Management Journal 15(3), 169–190.

Simons, T., 2002. Behavioral integrity: the perceived alignment between managers' words and deeds as a research focus. Organization Science 13(1), 18–35.

Singh, H., Zollo, M., 1998. The impact of knowledge codification, experience trajectories and integration strategies on the performance of corporate acquisitions. Academy of Management Best Paper Proceedings.

Spencer, J.W., 2003. Firms' knowledge-sharing strategies in the global innovation system: empirical evidence from the flat panel display industry. Strategic Management Journal 24(3), 217–234.

Stahl, G.K., Miller, E.L., Tung, R.L., 2002. Toward a boundaryless career: a closer look at the expatriate career concept and the perceived implications of an international assignment. Journal of World Business 37(3), 216–227.

Stephens, G.K., Black, J.S., 1991. The impact of spouse's career orientation on managers during international transfers. Journal of Management Studies 28(4), 417–428.

Stonich, P.J., 1981. Using rewards in implementing strategy. Strategic Management Journal 2(4), 345–352.

Subramaniam, M., Venkatraman, N., 2001. Determinants of transnational new product development capability: testing the influence of transferring and deploying tacit overseas knowledge. Strategic Management Journal 22(4), 359–378.

Sullivan Jr., C.H., Smart, J.R., 1987. Planning for information networks. Sloan Management Review 28(2), 39–44.

Sussman, L., Ricchio, P., Belohlav, J., 1983. Corporate speeches as a source of corporate values: an analysis across years, themes and industries. Strategic Management Journal 4(2), 187–196.

Szulanski, G., 1996. Exploring internal stickiness: impediments to the transfer of best practice within the firm. Strategic Management Journal 17(10), 27–43.

Takeuchi, H., Nonaka, I., 1986. The new new product development game. Harvard Business Review 64(1), 137–146.

Taylor, S., Beechler, S., 1996. Toward an integrative model of strategic international human resource management. Academy of Management Review 21(4), 959–985.

Teece, D. J., 2000. Strategies for managing knowledge assets: the role of firm structure and industrial context. Long Range Planning 33(1), 35–54.

Teece, D. J., Pisano, G., Shuen, A., 1997. Dynamic capabilities and strategic management. Strategic Management Journal 18(7), 509–533.

Teece, D., Rumelt, R., Dosi, G., Winter, S., 1994. Understanding corporate coherence: theory and evidence. Journal of Economic Behavior and Organization 23(1), 1–30.

Thomas, A.B., 1988. Does leadership make a difference to organizational performance? Administrative Science Quarterly 33(3), 388–400.

Tsai, W., 2000. Social capital, strategic relatedness and the formation of intraorganizational linkages. Strategic Management Journal 21(9), 925–939.

Tsai, W., Ghoshal, S., 1998. Social capital and value creation: the role of intrafirm networks. Academy of Management Journal 41(4), 464–476.

Tung, R.L., 1981. Selection and training of personnel for overseas assignments. Columbia Journal of World Business 16(1), 68–78.

Tung, R.L., 1988. Career issues in international assignments. Academy of Management Executive 2(3), 241–244.

Tushman, M.L., 1977. Communications across organizational boundaries: special boundary roles in the innovation process. Administrative Science Quarterly 22(4), 587–605.

Van den Bosch, F.A.J., van Wijk, R., 2001. Creation of managerial capabilities through managerial knowledge integration: a competence-based perspective. In: R. Sanchez (Ed.), Knowledge Management and Organizational Competence. Oxford University Press, Oxford.

Vancil, R.F., Green, C.H., 1984. How CEOs use top management committees. Harvard Business Review 62(1), 65–73.

Venkatraman, N., Ramanujam, V., 1986. Measurement of business performance in strategy research: a comparison of approaches. Academy of Management Review 11(4), 801–814.

Von Krogh, G., Nonaka, I., Aben, M., 2001. Making the most of your company's knowledge: a strategic framework. Long Range Planning 34(4), 421–440.

Webber, S.S., 2002. Leadership and trust facilitating cross-functional team success. Journal of Management Development 21(3–4), 201–214.

Wenger, E.C., Snyder, W.M., 2000. Communities of practice: the organizational frontier. Harvard Business Review 78(1), 139–145.

Wissema, J.G., Brand, A.F., Van der Pol, H.W., 1981. The incorporation of management development in strategic management. Strategic Management Journal 2(4), 361–377.

Yan, A., Guorong, Z., Hall, D.T., 2002. International assignments for career building: a model of agency relationships and psychological contacts. Academy of Management Review 27(3), 373–391.

Zaleznik, A., 1977. Managers and leaders: are they different? Harvard Business Review 55(3), 67–78.

Zander, U., Kogut, B., 1995. Knowledge and the speed of transfer and imitation of organizational capabilities: an empirical test. Organization Science 6(1), 76–92.

Zollo, M., Winter, S.G., 2002. Deliberate learning and the evolution of dynamic capabilities. Organization Science 13(3), 339–351.

Appendix B

Mallows' Cp Data (Chapter 5)

Table 3: Value of the Cp for all submodels of Figure 21 in Chapter 5.

Model No.	Cp	Nb param (p)	Label
1	430.5	2	3
2	614.5	2	4
3	643.9	2	L
4	679.2	2	C
5	700.8	2	K
6	755.9	2	B
7	796.6	2	1
8	800.8	2	5
9	970.5	2	2
10	977.0	2	R
11	242.4	3	C3
12	245.3	3	L3
13	254.7	3	K3
14	313.6	3	B3
15	315.0	3	34
16	321.1	3	35
17	324.0	3	13
18	400.0	3	R3
19	402.1	3	23
20	162.9	4	C35
21	176.4	4	C34
22	186.5	4	C13
23	194.7	4	345
24	201.3	4	CK3
25	229.1	4	CL3
26	231.3	4	C23
27	233.4	4	BC3
28	242.0	4	CR3
29	82.1	5	C135
30	85.6	5	C345

Table 3: Continued.

Model No.	Cp	Nb param (p)	Label
31	118.6	5	1345
32	130.3	5	CK35
33	142.0	5	BC35
34	151.0	5	CL35
35	153.8	5	C235
36	162.9	5	CR35
37	34.5	6	K1345
38	38.5	6	C1345
39	55.2	6	CK135
40	75.7	6	CL135
41	77.1	6	C1235
42	78.8	6	BC135
43	84.0	6	CR135
44	13.8	7	CK1345
45	33.0	7	KR1345
46	34.7	7	CL1345
47	36.7	7	C12345
48	38.0	7	BC1345
49	40.3	7	CR1345
50	11.5	8	CKR1345
51	11.8	8	CK12345
52	15.0	8	BCK1345
53	15.4	8	CKL1345
54	28.4	8	KR12345
55	8.7	9	CKR12345
56	11.6	9	BCKR1345
57	12.6	9	CKLR1345
58	13.3	9	BCK12345
59	13.7	9	CKL12345
60	15.6	9	KLR12345
61	16.6	9	BKLR1345
62	16.8	9	BCKL1345
63	20.1	9	BKR12345
64	20.2	9	BKL12345
65	9.2	10	BCKR12345
66	10.3	10	CKLR12345

Table 3: Continued.

Model No.	Cp	Nb param (*p*)	Label
67	13.2	10	BCKLR1345
68	14.8	10	BKLR12345
69	15.2	10	BCKL12345
70	35.6	10	BCLR12345
71	48.9	10	BCKLR2345
72	49.9	10	BCKLR1235
73	108.9	10	BCKLR1234
74	116.0	10	BCKLR1245
75	11.0	11	BCKLR12345

Table 13: Cp values for all the possible models, graphed in Figure 26 in Chapter 5. A Cp close to or even less than p is evidence of a good model.

Model No.	Cp	Nb param (*p*)	Label
1	59.03	2	L
2	76.67	2	C
3	90.85	2	K
4	124.20	2	B
5	259.79	2	R
6	24.87	3	CK
7	24.90	3	KL
8	28.71	3	BK
9	37.99	3	BL
10	47.48	3	CL
11	57.32	3	LR
12	90.02	3	KR
13	6.20	4	BCK
14	7.57	4	BKL
15	17.26	4	CKL
16	26.03	4	CKR
17	26.80	4	KLR
18	30.58	4	BKR
19	4.13	5	BCKL
20	8.17	5	BCKR

Table 13: Continued.

Model No.	Cp	Nb param (p)	Label
21	9.26	5	BKLR
22	19.04	5	CKLR
23	32.78	5	BCLR
24	6.00	6	BCKLR

Appendix C

Full Covariance Matrix of the Data

The type of model used in this work is called structural equation model (SEM) or linear structural relation (LISREL). The data that are given to the model is a summary of all the data gathered, called the covariance matrix. This matrix gives all the information on the correlations between two survey questions. In this appendix, we provide the interested reader the full covariance matrix, so that he can reproduce the results given in the book. The coding is as follows: Q31 to Q37 are the seven survey questions on "competitive business performance", G4A1 to G4A7 are the grouped survey questions on BuBlock, G4B1 to G4B10 are the grouped survey questions on CommRit, G4C1 to G4C8 are the grouped survey questions on KnowInt, G4D1 to G4D17 are the grouped survey questions on Leadersh and G4E1 to G4E8 are the grouped survey questions on CBRota.

Covariance Matrix

	Q31	Q32	Q33	Q34	Q35	Q36	Q37	G4A1	G4A2	G4A3	G4A4	G4A5
Q31	3.76											
Q32	2.11	4.48										
Q33	0.89	0.58	3.35									
Q34	0.82	0.97	1.52	3.05								
Q35	1.12	1.08	1.00	1.43	3.53							
Q36	1.41	0.91	1.40	1.17	1.73	3.36						
Q37	1.59	1.28	1.30	1.10	0.73	1.72	5.62					
G4A1	0.11	0.13	0.35	0.37	0.69	0.35	0.12	1.54				
G4A2	0.18	0.28	0.30	0.40	0.79	0.50	0.02	0.76	1.72			
G4A3	0.36	0.48	0.37	0.45	0.78	0.45	0.15	0.68	1.06	1.63		
G4A4	0.40	0.52	0.43	0.48	0.74	0.63	0.35	0.66	0.92	1.09	1.57	
G4A5	0.23	−0.01	0.52	0.49	0.64	0.52	0.36	0.55	0.76	0.64	0.75	1.60
G4A6	0.16	0.08	0.35	0.33	0.55	0.36	0.15	0.45	0.66	0.59	0.62	0.74
G4A7	0.07	0.07	0.48	0.43	0.75	0.51	0.14	0.48	0.58	0.60	0.71	0.78
G4B1	0.06	−0.03	0.08	0.01	0.10	0.04	−0.10	0.23	0.24	0.33	0.23	0.10
G4B10	0.33	0.40	0.26	0.23	0.51	0.36	0.14	0.44	0.71	0.64	0.65	0.58
G4B2	0.26	0.24	0.46	0.39	0.30	0.35	0.40	0.35	0.22	0.37	0.40	0.44
G4B3	0.29	0.34	0.24	0.28	0.40	0.31	0.35	0.33	0.32	0.43	0.49	0.42
G4B4	0.27	0.07	0.31	0.49	0.68	0.49	0.24	0.48	0.50	0.45	0.52	0.70
G4B5	0.42	0.52	0.35	0.49	0.70	0.51	0.60	0.36	0.48	0.49	0.62	0.42
G4B6	0.38	0.40	0.39	0.46	0.66	0.44	0.52	0.43	0.42	0.53	0.62	0.47
G4B7	0.45	0.52	0.41	0.53	0.75	0.49	0.40	0.48	0.74	0.82	0.87	0.57
G4B8	0.38	0.26	0.37	0.49	0.45	0.45	0.61	0.37	0.48	0.58	0.64	0.55
G4B9	0.34	0.38	0.34	0.42	0.55	0.50	0.43	0.38	0.43	0.51	0.56	0.44

	Q31	Q32	Q33	Q34	Q35	Q36	Q37	G4A1	G4A2	G4A3	G4A4	G4A5
G4C1	0.42	0.17	0.49	0.48	0.56	0.62	0.72	0.42	0.41	0.34	0.50	0.62
G4C2	0.42	0.15	0.38	0.43	0.38	0.43	0.72	0.33	0.23	0.22	0.40	0.52
G4C3	0.30	0.14	0.55	0.35	0.31	0.44	0.28	0.39	0.23	0.25	0.36	0.40
G4C4	0.42	0.34	0.38	0.35	0.41	0.30	0.32	0.31	0.37	0.40	0.41	0.39
G4C5	0.29	0.33	0.55	0.57	0.60	0.54	0.63	0.36	0.37	0.34	0.52	0.63
G4C6	0.41	0.36	0.33	0.35	0.34	0.35	0.35	0.29	0.25	0.32	0.38	0.32
G4C7	0.28	0.09	0.51	0.43	0.29	0.46	0.52	0.34	0.33	0.34	0.45	0.56
G4C8	0.33	0.35	0.43	0.38	0.29	0.35	0.52	0.31	0.24	0.30	0.37	0.43
G4D1	0.38	0.30	0.55	0.51	0.67	0.48	0.64	0.44	0.65	0.58	0.73	0.88
G4D10	0.18	0.17	0.44	0.55	0.45	0.49	0.33	0.38	0.52	0.56	0.63	0.63
G4D11	0.41	0.34	0.39	0.62	0.59	0.59	0.74	0.38	0.44	0.51	0.67	0.54
G4D12	0.44	0.49	0.38	0.59	0.65	0.59	0.66	0.42	0.46	0.47	0.61	0.47
G4D13	0.22	0.18	0.27	0.31	0.37	0.29	0.15	0.29	0.30	0.32	0.36	0.31
G4D14	0.11	0.10	0.14	0.15	0.12	0.21	0.25	0.14	0.23	0.21	0.22	0.18
G4D15	0.25	0.22	0.20	0.23	0.47	0.36	0.37	0.29	0.50	0.47	0.61	0.54
G4D16	0.13	0.07	0.20	0.43	0.56	0.44	0.33	0.27	0.35	0.41	0.47	0.35
G4D17	0.46	0.65	0.10	0.31	0.17	0.17	0.92	0.15	0.03	0.16	0.23	0.11
G4D2	0.37	0.48	0.55	0.66	0.72	0.59	0.71	0.43	0.58	0.59	0.77	0.74
G4D3	0.30	0.27	0.49	0.57	0.65	0.58	0.42	0.43	0.55	0.56	0.66	0.77
G4D4	0.31	0.38	0.41	0.56	0.57	0.53	0.43	0.39	0.51	0.56	0.66	0.64
G4D5	0.27	0.31	0.38	0.48	0.49	0.41	0.37	0.37	0.53	0.51	0.62	0.58
G4D6	0.45	0.40	0.44	0.59	0.67	0.61	0.57	0.39	0.50	0.54	0.67	0.54
G4D7	0.34	0.30	0.39	0.50	0.49	0.46	0.59	0.38	0.56	0.62	0.72	0.54
G4D8	0.46	0.56	0.41	0.54	0.72	0.55	0.42	0.41	0.54	0.61	0.74	0.48
G4D9	0.22	0.20	0.40	0.36	0.35	0.33	0.36	0.32	0.27	0.34	0.42	0.44
G4E1	0.18	0.12	0.18	0.37	0.41	0.26	0.22	0.23	0.37	0.29	0.36	0.62
G4E2	−0.05	−0.12	0.14	0.25	0.21	0.16	−0.03	0.16	0.32	0.20	0.21	0.42
G4E3	0.18	0.09	0.24	0.41	0.45	0.28	0.24	0.30	0.44	0.35	0.39	0.65
G4E4	0.09	−0.12	0.21	0.27	0.32	0.26	0.17	0.18	0.33	0.21	0.26	0.55
G4E5	0.35	0.29	0.29	0.41	0.35	0.33	0.50	0.16	0.24	0.19	0.34	0.50
G4E6	−0.17	−0.47	0.36	0.25	0.26	0.19	−0.07	0.12	0.21	0.09	0.15	0.51
G4E7	0.19	0.13	0.29	0.32	0.31	0.21	0.23	0.24	0.32	0.28	0.32	0.47
G4E8	0.21	0.21	0.16	0.29	0.39	0.23	0.33	0.23	0.31	0.27	0.31	0.48

	G4A6	G4A7	G4B1	G4B10	G4B2	G4B3	G4B4	G4B5	G4B6	G4B7	G4B8	G4B9
G4A6	1.28											
G4A7	0.86	1.85										
G4B1	0.12	0.13	1.56									
G4B10	0.56	0.54	0.19	1.36								
G4B2	0.27	0.46	0.46	0.32	1.57							
G4B3	0.29	0.37	0.32	0.36	0.64	1.51						
G4B4	0.42	0.49	0.10	0.43	0.55	0.49	1.98					
G4B5	0.35	0.51	0.11	0.48	0.53	0.62	0.62	1.44				
G4B6	0.31	0.52	0.18	0.41	0.56	0.58	0.54	0.85	1.52			
G4B7	0.50	0.55	0.20	0.63	0.54	0.52	0.55	0.76	0.82	1.52		
G4B8	0.41	0.63	0.11	0.46	0.48	0.62	0.63	0.79	0.84	0.81	1.66	
G4B9	0.36	0.37	0.19	0.51	0.47	0.66	0.54	0.82	0.79	0.62	0.70	1.84
G4C1	0.39	0.43	0.27	0.36	0.52	0.42	0.72	0.52	0.51	0.50	0.58	0.42
G4C2	0.26	0.35	0.23	0.32	0.51	0.41	0.69	0.31	0.40	0.39	0.49	0.39

	G4A6	G4A7	G4B1	G4B10	G4B2	G4B3	G4B4	G4B5	G4B6	G4B7	G4B8	G4B9
G4C3	0.20	0.26	0.45	0.34	0.57	0.44	0.53	0.28	0.33	0.37	0.35	0.42
G4C4	0.30	0.27	0.25	0.35	0.52	0.36	0.52	0.44	0.51	0.57	0.53	0.53
G4C5	0.44	0.49	0.23	0.44	0.56	0.44	0.66	0.50	0.52	0.50	0.54	0.39
G4C6	0.28	0.26	0.25	0.32	0.39	0.38	0.47	0.33	0.36	0.31	0.33	0.49
G4C7	0.29	0.36	0.29	0.35	0.59	0.50	0.68	0.52	0.51	0.45	0.59	0.53
G4C8	0.28	0.36	0.29	0.31	0.56	0.49	0.44	0.37	0.43	0.42	0.43	0.35
G4D1	0.60	0.64	0.14	0.52	0.47	0.53	0.58	0.68	0.64	0.67	0.77	0.65
G4D10	0.38	0.55	0.14	0.58	0.61	0.59	0.56	0.71	0.66	0.63	0.76	0.71
G4D11	0.40	0.53	0.07	0.42	0.53	0.57	0.60	0.79	0.67	0.67	0.80	0.72
G4D12	0.39	0.51	0.05	0.45	0.40	0.54	0.59	0.80	0.66	0.67	0.71	0.77
G4D13	0.26	0.30	0.21	0.27	0.25	0.31	0.40	0.37	0.37	0.35	0.38	0.48
G4D14	0.16	0.24	0.14	0.27	0.17	0.21	0.18	0.17	0.15	0.24	0.22	0.25
G4D15	0.43	0.54	0.04	0.44	0.26	0.33	0.38	0.68	0.55	0.56	0.62	0.53
G4D16	0.33	0.42	0.03	0.29	0.19	0.36	0.44	0.48	0.43	0.38	0.52	0.54
G4D17	0.07	0.04	−0.04	0.15	0.31	0.31	0.25	0.53	0.48	0.33	0.41	0.48
G4D2	0.51	0.67	0.05	0.48	0.52	0.57	0.67	0.80	0.68	0.70	0.96	0.72
G4D3	0.46	0.56	0.13	0.46	0.44	0.50	0.65	0.63	0.66	0.64	0.70	0.66
G4D4	0.35	0.45	0.17	0.48	0.52	0.62	0.56	0.67	0.64	0.60	0.71	0.67
G4D5	0.31	0.52	0.14	0.48	0.46	0.58	0.55	0.70	0.64	0.63	0.70	0.69
G4D6	0.33	0.55	0.20	0.46	0.54	0.63	0.57	0.89	0.83	0.70	0.85	1.06
G4D7	0.44	0.54	0.09	0.49	0.47	0.63	0.55	0.85	0.73	0.74	0.83	0.83
G4D8	0.38	0.55	0.10	0.44	0.41	0.61	0.55	0.90	0.75	0.70	0.74	0.85
G4D9	0.27	0.38	0.22	0.34	0.57	0.43	0.52	0.43	0.49	0.52	0.52	0.57
G4E1	0.35	0.31	0.05	0.36	0.28	0.18	0.43	0.29	0.28	0.35	0.29	0.26
G4E2	0.31	0.28	0.05	0.25	0.21	0.15	0.29	0.22	0.20	0.22	0.24	0.15
G4E3	0.38	0.37	0.11	0.41	0.31	0.22	0.41	0.27	0.29	0.32	0.26	0.22
G4E4	0.31	0.29	0.06	0.32	0.21	0.17	0.31	0.17	0.19	0.24	0.23	0.16
G4E5	0.31	0.26	0.17	0.32	0.34	0.24	0.31	0.29	0.34	0.28	0.29	0.27
G4E6	0.23	0.39	0.14	0.21	0.27	0.10	0.50	0.12	0.18	0.19	0.15	0.06
G4E7	0.34	0.35	0.12	0.35	0.35	0.24	0.48	0.31	0.33	0.34	0.28	0.31
G4E8	0.36	0.23	0.08	0.27	0.29	0.21	0.31	0.27	0.29	0.29	0.28	0.23

	G4C1	G4C2	G4C3	G4C4	G4C5	G4C6	G4C7	G4C8	G4D1	G4D10	G4D11	G4D12
G4C1	1.53											
G4C2	1.01	1.87										
G4C3	0.86	0.99	2.08									
G4C4	0.73	0.72	0.90	1.73								
G4C5	0.86	0.66	0.77	0.63	1.55							
G4C6	0.50	0.40	0.66	0.65	0.68	1.51						
G4C7	0.74	0.64	0.64	0.63	0.70	0.61	1.68					
G4C8	0.58	0.58	0.59	0.57	0.59	0.52	0.86	1.45				
G4D1	0.60	0.49	0.34	0.49	0.61	0.37	0.65	0.53	1.86			
G4D10	0.53	0.52	0.46	0.50	0.58	0.43	0.72	0.56	0.82	1.61		
G4D11	0.66	0.56	0.38	0.51	0.56	0.41	0.63	0.47	0.73	0.83	1.57	
G4D12	0.54	0.44	0.31	0.53	0.51	0.40	0.52	0.40	0.66	0.73	1.01	1.55
G4D13	0.44	0.38	0.44	0.53	0.41	0.42	0.43	0.30	0.34	0.39	0.44	0.53
G4D14	0.26	0.25	0.23	0.35	0.24	0.29	0.21	0.25	0.23	0.27	0.27	0.28
G4D15	0.39	0.32	0.13	0.37	0.37	0.22	0.34	0.27	0.72	0.58	0.69	0.73
G4D16	0.46	0.42	0.26	0.30	0.44	0.31	0.47	0.28	0.48	0.56	0.64	0.53

	G4C1	G4C2	G4C3	G4C4	G4C5	G4C6	G4C7	G4C8	G4D1	G4D10	G4D11	G4D12
G4D17	0.37	0.33	0.21	0.39	0.29	0.28	0.26	0.25	0.28	0.35	0.59	0.50
G4D2	0.65	0.56	0.31	0.50	0.71	0.40	0.67	0.56	1.08	0.89	1.02	0.86
G4D3	0.57	0.48	0.41	0.52	0.58	0.40	0.65	0.51	1.01	0.88	0.77	0.74
G4D4	0.62	0.47	0.52	0.50	0.60	0.40	0.74	0.57	0.84	1.01	0.77	0.68
G4D5	0.49	0.46	0.37	0.42	0.43	0.37	0.55	0.48	0.75	0.75	0.75	0.69
G4D6	0.62	0.51	0.49	0.64	0.57	0.45	0.65	0.47	0.74	0.86	0.89	0.89
G4D7	0.55	0.39	0.34	0.53	0.50	0.42	0.62	0.43	0.78	0.89	0.95	0.84
G4D8	0.49	0.37	0.25	0.50	0.45	0.36	0.49	0.38	0.75	0.79	0.87	0.86
G4D9	0.62	0.52	0.67	0.79	0.56	0.59	0.67	0.55	0.52	0.67	0.60	0.57
G4E1	0.47	0.38	0.36	0.39	0.49	0.25	0.36	0.32	0.56	0.41	0.35	0.28
G4E2	0.28	0.20	0.13	0.12	0.32	0.10	0.24	0.23	0.44	0.25	0.20	0.15
G4E3	0.40	0.37	0.30	0.24	0.47	0.20	0.29	0.34	0.60	0.37	0.31	0.28
G4E4	0.31	0.29	0.32	0.22	0.41	0.14	0.25	0.22	0.44	0.28	0.21	0.21
G4E5	0.45	0.47	0.46	0.35	0.51	0.36	0.43	0.37	0.56	0.38	0.38	0.34
G4E6	0.33	0.36	0.30	0.15	0.34	0.20	0.40	0.32	0.39	0.29	0.22	0.17
G4E7	0.38	0.34	0.30	0.30	0.45	0.24	0.41	0.37	0.49	0.39	0.28	0.28
G4E8	0.40	0.30	0.33	0.27	0.43	0.26	0.30	0.31	0.46	0.35	0.31	0.29

	G4D13	G4D14	G4D15	G4D16	G4D17	G4D2	G4D3	G4D4	G4D5	G4D6	G4D7	G4D8
G4D13	0.97											
G4D14	0.44	1.13										
G4D15	0.33	0.23	1.66									
G4D16	0.33	0.34	0.55	1.54								
G4D17	0.16	0.09	0.40	0.28	2.30							
G4D2	0.41	0.26	0.75	0.57	0.55	1.79						
G4D3	0.37	0.24	0.67	0.55	0.32	1.00	1.42					
G4D4	0.41	0.25	0.53	0.52	0.43	0.88	0.99	1.60				
G4D5	0.37	0.22	0.64	0.44	0.40	0.76	0.76	0.78	1.38			
G4D6	0.49	0.31	0.75	0.55	0.56	0.89	0.80	0.86	0.90	1.88		
G4D7	0.38	0.23	0.78	0.57	0.49	0.95	0.85	0.84	0.89	1.08	1.61	
G4D8	0.43	0.18	0.74	0.57	0.46	0.89	0.78	0.78	0.84	0.92	0.99	1.52
G4D9	0.48	0.28	0.43	0.35	0.36	0.57	0.54	0.58	0.56	0.66	0.59	0.61
G4E1	0.22	0.17	0.30	0.28	0.18	0.40	0.50	0.42	0.28	0.29	0.34	0.29
G4E2	0.12	0.07	0.22	0.17	0.08	0.29	0.38	0.28	0.25	0.20	0.26	0.20
G4E3	0.21	0.15	0.29	0.29	0.05	0.42	0.52	0.43	0.28	0.22	0.27	0.27
G4E4	0.15	0.07	0.17	0.12	−0.01	0.27	0.44	0.31	0.21	0.17	0.22	0.14
G4E5	0.25	0.13	0.28	0.23	0.25	0.38	0.48	0.45	0.31	0.32	0.31	0.24
G4E6	0.16	0.17	0.07	0.21	−0.16	0.24	0.41	0.27	0.29	0.15	0.12	0.07
G4E7	0.27	0.18	0.23	0.26	0.06	0.35	0.46	0.40	0.30	0.28	0.28	0.27
G4E8	0.14	0.10	0.23	0.17	0.20	0.35	0.40	0.42	0.32	0.29	0.29	0.29

	G4D9	G4E1	G4E2	G4E3	G4E4	G4E5	G4E6	G4E7	G4E8
G4D9	1.38								
G4E1	0.35	1.12							
G4E2	0.24	0.74	1.36						
G4E3	0.26	0.95	0.86	1.86					

	G4D9	G4E1	G4E2	G4E3	G4E4	G4E5	G4E6	G4E7	G4E8
G4E4	0.27	0.86	0.84	1.11	1.38				
G4E5	0.34	0.69	0.51	0.75	0.63	1.59			
G4E6	0.22	0.54	0.77	0.65	0.63	0.54	1.90		
G4E7	0.34	0.55	0.54	0.61	0.52	0.65	0.71	1.05	
G4E8	0.32	0.60	0.49	0.77	0.55	0.63	0.30	0.52	1.67

Appendix D

Standardized Residuals of the SEM

In this appendix, we show the standardized residuals of the model given in Figure 25 (Chapter 5). The stem and leaf plot show that the residuals have a normal (bell-shaped) distributon, as requested in the conditions for structural equation models.

	Q31	Q32	Q33	Q34	Q35	Q36	Q37	G4A1	G4A2	G4A3	G4A4	G4A5
Q31	–											
Q32	11.57	–										
Q33	−2.87	−4.42	–									
Q34	−4.67	−0.35	6.95	–								
Q35	−2.04	−0.35	−3.69	2.99	–							
Q36	0.79	−4.35	1.24	−4.54	4.18	–						
Q37	3.63	1.57	1.18	−1.38	−6.99	3.16	–					
G4A1	−2.82	−1.82	0.61	0.79	4.86	−0.56	−2.48	–				
G4A2	−3.63	−1.34	−2.04	−0.68	4.52	−0.62	−5.11	3.98	–			
G4A3	−1.34	1.09	−1.12	0.05	4.45	−1.70	−3.88	0.80	7.25	–		
G4A4	−1.00	1.48	−0.39	0.25	3.85	1.28	−1.75	−1.07	−1.34	8.07	–	
G4A5	−2.17	−4.29	2.15	1.57	3.19	0.75	−0.67	−0.58	−1.12	−6.94	−3.69	–
G4A6	−2.66	−2.82	0.50	−0.10	3.04	−0.81	−2.54	−1.30	−0.40	−4.41	−4.61	6.04
G4A7	−3.68	−2.77	1.67	0.91	4.66	1.04	−2.52	−1.35	−4.87	−5.32	−2.43	4.20
G4B1	−0.68	−1.51	−0.36	−1.45	−0.32	−1.30	−2.23	2.55	1.92	3.79	1.55	−0.70
G4B10	0.32	1.63	−0.61	−1.18	2.59	−0.16	−2.21	3.46	7.73	6.06	6.38	5.72
G4B2	−0.80	−0.50	2.10	1.04	−0.77	−0.58	0.63	0.87	−5.04	−1.71	−1.45	1.53
G4B3	−0.89	0.39	−1.52	−1.21	0.01	−1.91	−0.31	−0.42	−4.02	−1.43	−0.40	0.03
G4B4	−1.08	−2.69	−0.54	1.72	3.47	0.63	−1.40	2.50	0.26	−1.08	0.21	5.83
G4B5	−0.54	1.67	−1.62	0.71	3.32	−0.71	1.41	−2.19	−3.95	−4.24	−0.82	−3.38
G4B6	−0.89	0.14	−0.60	0.24	2.72	−1.66	0.54	−0.10	−4.80	−2.29	−0.03	−1.42
G4B7	0.24	1.67	−0.37	1.50	4.19	−0.71	−0.88	1.42	4.21	6.44	8.03	1.35
G4B8	−1.03	−1.80	−1.21	0.60	−0.83	−1.83	1.34	−1.94	−3.56	−1.42	−0.18	0.32
G4B9	−1.23	−0.01	−1.21	−0.28	0.96	−0.36	−0.43	−1.06	−3.60	−2.09	−1.24	−1.59
G4C1	−0.38	−2.89	0.93	0.64	1.05	1.53	2.90	2.31	−1.08	−3.41	0.79	5.72
G4C2	0.02	−2.44	−0.38	0.15	−1.12	−1.13	2.79	0.41	−4.14	−4.77	−0.94	3.13
G4C3	−1.46	−2.47	1.79	−1.11	−2.12	−1.13	−1.72	1.49	−3.89	−3.96	−1.92	0.50
G4C4	0.40	−0.06	0.07	−0.58	−0.37	−2.68	−1.07	0.58	−0.56	0.02	0.07	1.02
G4C5	−1.85	−0.43	2.26	2.63	2.27	0.63	2.16	1.19	−1.32	−2.24	2.27	6.25
G4C6	1.33	0.97	0.31	0.51	−0.17	−0.42	0.17	1.31	−1.50	−0.09	1.17	0.89
G4C7	−1.62	−3.20	1.71	0.45	−2.29	−0.38	0.98	0.89	−1.72	−1.87	0.54	4.53
G4C8	−0.16	0.64	1.43	0.59	−1.41	−1.05	1.75	1.36	−2.53	−1.27	0.06	3.03
G4D1	−0.95	−1.17	1.54	0.94	2.30	−0.94	1.60	0.53	1.79	−0.18	3.33	8.54
G4D10	−4.12	−2.96	−0.10	1.42	−1.09	−1.13	−1.91	−1.29	−1.76	−1.18	0.24	2.93
G4D11	−0.94	−1.02	−1.19	2.41	0.99	0.28	2.63	−1.63	−4.44	−3.13	0.99	0.38
G4D12	0.02	1.24	−0.84	2.35	2.45	0.83	2.14	0.10	−2.88	−3.00	0.53	−0.81
G4D13	−0.42	−0.54	0.53	1.23	1.75	−0.14	−1.45	1.79	−0.35	0.19	1.20	1.23

	Q31	Q32	Q33	Q34	Q35	Q36	Q37	G4A1	G4A2	G4A3	G4A4	G4A5
G4D14	−0.58	−0.47	−0.17	−0.03	−0.69	0.35	1.00	0.08	0.78	0.24	0.51	0.35
G4D15	−1.66	−1.28	−2.38	−2.25	0.75	−1.44	−0.40	−1.18	0.38	−0.43	2.64	2.75
G4D16	−2.31	−2.39	−1.41	1.89	3.10	0.96	−0.03	−0.20	−0.87	0.26	1.49	0.28
G4D17	2.24	4.10	−1.55	0.78	−1.22	−1.49	5.55	−1.39	−5.03	−3.10	−1.99	−3.00
G4D2	−1.91	0.39	0.88	2.52	2.37	−0.31	1.77	−0.94	−1.73	−1.87	2.63	4.33
G4D3	−2.50	−1.81	0.66	2.06	2.40	0.37	−0.93	0.19	−1.11	−1.21	1.43	7.23
G4D4	−2.10	−0.30	−0.57	1.63	1.04	−0.36	−0.76	−0.79	−1.99	−0.96	1.51	3.22
G4D5	−2.42	−0.92	−0.61	0.95	0.27	−1.96	−1.10	−0.73	−0.49	−1.56	1.48	2.71
G4D6	−0.58	−0.45	−0.60	1.46	1.71	0.09	0.37	−1.71	−3.31	−2.76	0.09	−0.50
G4D7	−2.33	−1.73	−1.51	0.09	−0.95	−2.51	0.59	−2.00	−2.08	−0.71	1.65	−0.29
G4D8	−0.18	1.95	−0.71	1.29	3.25	−0.42	−1.03	−0.71	−1.69	0.10	3.64	−1.15
G4D9	−1.68	−1.25	1.12	0.49	−0.40	−1.24	−0.04	0.22	−3.99	−2.61	−0.88	1.63
G4E1	−0.90	−1.25	−0.85	2.73	2.94	−0.45	−0.48	−1.05	0.15	−2.73	−0.95	8.95
G4E2	−3.92	−3.95	−1.12	0.57	−0.48	−1.83	−3.04	−1.93	−0.51	−3.96	−4.11	3.15
G4E3	−1.25	−1.75	−0.39	2.03	1.99	−0.84	−0.57	−0.40	0.10	−2.41	−1.78	5.93
G4E4	−2.32	−4.50	−0.45	0.43	0.71	−0.80	−1.15	−2.51	−1.44	−5.21	−4.39	5.70
G4E5	1.98	1.35	1.34	3.18	1.85	1.43	3.04	−1.32	−1.50	−2.71	0.29	4.87
G4E6	−4.05	−6.55	2.33	0.92	0.72	−0.39	−2.44	−1.69	−1.47	−3.97	−3.09	4.94
G4E7	0.31	−0.33	2.20	2.75	2.10	0.09	0.60	1.31	1.48	0.31	1.26	6.33
G4E8	0.49	0.61	−0.13	1.58	2.59	0.29	1.45	0.58	0.74	−0.23	0.42	4.79

	G4A6	G4A7	G4B1	G4B10	G4B2	G4B3	G4B4	G4B5	G4B6	G4B7	G4B8	G4B9
G4A6	–											
G4A7	9.96	–										
G4B1	0.21	0.13	–									
G4B10	7.15	4.64	1.25	–								
G4B2	−1.28	2.34	6.95	−1.40	–							
G4B3	−1.73	−0.53	3.91	−1.61	5.67	–						
G4B4	1.19	1.70	−1.28	0.05	2.40	−0.07	–					
G4B5	−3.25	0.36	−2.81	−2.09	−1.17	−0.12	−0.44	–				
G4B6	−4.05	0.75	−0.37	−3.92	0.37	−0.75	−2.14	3.73	–			
G4B7	1.86	1.71	0.08	4.20	0.01	−2.71	−1.92	−0.37	2.90	–		
G4B8	−1.39	3.00	−2.50	−2.46	−2.61	−0.03	−0.35	−0.28	2.65	1.44	–	
G4B9	−1.95	−2.12	−0.14	0.10	−1.67	1.93	−1.60	2.18	1.83	−3.96	−2.18	–
G4C1	1.51	1.44	2.81	−0.62	3.07	−0.64	5.98	−1.37	−1.13	−1.43	0.27	−3.07
G4C2	−1.17	0.09	1.82	−0.84	2.86	−0.07	5.11	−5.48	−2.76	−2.95	−0.85	−2.42
G4C3	−2.64	−1.53	5.62	−0.46	3.84	0.46	1.82	−6.30	−4.36	−3.47	−4.09	−1.75
G4C4	0.05	−0.92	2.49	0.46	3.67	−0.65	2.47	−1.42	0.80	2.38	0.83	1.38
G4C5	3.23	3.09	2.08	2.29	4.63	0.86	5.20	−0.81	0.26	−0.30	0.23	−2.57
G4C6	1.11	0.04	3.09	1.24	2.52	1.61	3.13	−1.72	−0.66	−1.80	−1.60	2.32
G4C7	−0.46	0.55	3.39	0.15	5.09	2.38	5.39	0.39	0.47	−0.97	1.86	0.92
G4C8	0.63	1.49	3.86	0.35	6.04	3.68	1.86	−1.85	0.12	−0.13	−0.26	−1.56
G4D1	4.24	3.53	−0.82	1.15	−0.73	−0.55	0.28	−0.75	−1.37	−0.49	1.66	−0.75
G4D10	−1.64	1.44	−1.09	2.78	2.81	0.76	−0.61	−0.48	−1.63	−2.41	0.84	0.53
G4D11	−1.61	0.87	−3.04	−2.43	0.01	−0.47	0.07	1.72	−2.13	−1.71	1.61	0.31
G4D12	−0.98	1.09	−3.19	−0.57	−2.73	−0.29	0.91	3.56	−0.85	−0.14	0.08	2.86
G4D13	0.77	1.23	3.03	0.39	−0.44	0.40	2.46	−0.59	−0.08	−0.61	−0.17	3.43

	G4A6	G4A7	G4B1	G4B10	G4B2	G4B3	G4B4	G4B5	G4B6	G4B7	G4B8	G4B9
G4D14	0.50	1.76	1.79	3.07	0.11	0.69	-0.27	-2.26	-2.53	0.21	-0.62	0.69
G4D15	1.87	2.94	-2.29	1.09	-3.66	-3.24	-1.99	2.68	-0.75	-0.21	0.76	-0.79
G4D16	1.03	2.04	-1.86	-0.71	-3.54	-0.45	1.09	-0.16	-0.97	-2.34	1.06	1.95
G4D17	-3.25	-3.49	-2.30	-2.19	0.63	0.01	-0.99	3.10	2.21	-1.03	0.25	1.93
G4D2	0.88	3.12	-3.77	-1.44	-1.18	-1.36	0.80	0.31	-2.98	-2.45	5.18	-1.11
G4D3	0.81	2.15	-1.43	-0.84	-2.03	-2.13	2.15	-3.92	-1.69	-2.31	-1.09	-0.96
G4D4	-2.43	-0.54	-0.18	0.04	0.35	1.76	-0.23	-1.67	-2.04	-3.15	-0.41	-0.42
G4D5	-3.02	1.74	-0.79	0.90	-0.49	1.62	0.25	1.09	-0.68	-0.85	0.71	1.62
G4D6	-3.79	0.60	-0.02	-1.77	-0.45	0.48	-1.22	3.56	1.98	-1.70	1.85	8.18
G4D7	-1.07	0.54	-2.89	-1.24	-2.49	0.57	-2.08	2.68	-0.98	-0.68	1.64	2.67
G4D8	-1.97	1.41	-2.38	-1.63	-3.20	0.95	-1.12	6.46	1.27	-0.58	-0.06	4.64
G4D9	-1.40	0.72	1.94	-0.50	5.13	0.62	2.37	-3.15	-0.66	0.23	-0.31	1.86
G4E1	2.36	0.27	-0.58	4.36	1.69	-1.57	4.53	-0.31	-0.63	1.72	-0.32	-0.87
G4E2	1.48	0.00	-0.41	1.44	0.20	-1.67	1.35	-1.61	-1.79	-1.22	-1.09	-2.54
G4E3	1.30	0.25	0.37	3.60	1.08	-1.28	2.14	-2.28	-1.53	-0.68	-2.27	-2.40
G4E4	0.69	-0.48	-0.39	2.55	-0.29	-1.96	1.07	-4.42	-3.39	-1.89	-2.47	-3.37
G4E5	2.02	0.18	2.07	3.22	3.33	0.87	1.87	0.81	2.06	0.81	0.79	0.58
G4E6	0.41	2.73	1.47	1.10	1.87	-1.64	5.05	-2.36	-0.92	-0.71	-1.61	-2.83
G4E7	4.25	3.26	1.61	5.46	4.98	1.68	6.83	2.57	3.33	3.69	1.56	2.46
G4E8	3.46	0.16	0.34	2.37	2.54	0.66	2.29	0.98	1.41	1.53	1.06	0.31

	G4C1	G4C2	G4C3	G4C4	G4C5	G4C6	G4C7	G4C8	G4D1	G4D10	G4D11	G4D12
G4C1	–											
G4C2	8.06	–										
G4C3	0.96	5.63	–									
G4C4	-1.42	0.26	4.72	–								
G4C5	2.27	-3.57	-0.35	-2.85	–							
G4C6	-5.02	-5.09	1.90	3.32	3.70	–						
G4C7	-2.37	-3.15	-3.28	-2.06	-1.43	1.65	–					
G4C8	-4.55	-1.55	-1.80	-0.60	-1.60	1.24	8.59	–				
G4D1	0.78	-0.80	-3.95	-0.02	2.03	-0.57	3.12	2.15	–			
G4D10	-1.51	-0.45	-2.02	-0.22	1.13	0.56	4.89	2.86	0.55	–		
G4D11	1.88	0.14	-4.35	-0.36	0.01	-0.36	2.26	0.14	-3.38	-0.90	–	
G4D12	-0.62	-1.96	-4.96	1.04	-0.38	0.06	0.27	-0.94	-3.84	-2.57	7.98	–
G4D13	4.18	2.37	3.70	7.10	3.76	5.87	4.18	1.76	-2.77	-1.67	-0.12	4.43
G4D14	1.81	1.75	1.13	4.25	1.55	3.87	0.94	2.67	-1.01	-0.23	-0.33	0.48
G4D15	-2.21	-2.51	-6.39	-0.99	-1.59	-2.47	-1.87	-2.25	1.72	-3.07	0.04	2.61
G4D16	1.97	1.35	-2.18	-0.73	1.95	0.90	2.71	-0.54	-1.35	0.39	2.44	0.15
G4D17	1.10	0.57	-1.30	1.94	0.04	1.11	-0.31	0.20	-3.09	-2.18	3.28	1.77
G4D2	0.46	-0.86	-6.34	-1.22	3.03	-1.13	2.31	1.79	6.73	-0.51	3.60	-0.57
G4D3	-0.18	-1.58	-3.56	0.43	1.20	-0.27	3.52	1.90	7.91	2.45	-3.53	-2.58
G4D4	1.21	-1.59	-0.74	-0.12	1.75	-0.22	5.45	3.32	1.31	7.54	-3.17	-4.31
G4D5	-1.59	-1.04	-3.35	-1.19	-2.05	-0.21	1.64	1.92	0.10	-0.73	-1.77	-2.18
G4D6	-0.14	-1.72	-2.21	2.08	-0.33	0.12	1.96	-0.34	-4.02	-1.06	-0.97	1.12
G4D7	-2.31	-4.69	-5.89	-0.27	-2.21	-0.57	1.54	-1.61	-3.18	-0.17	1.60	-0.72
G4D8	-3.24	-4.57	-7.39	-0.33	-2.97	-1.37	-1.04	-2.16	-2.41	-2.40	0.20	2.14
G4D9	5.38	2.83	5.82	9.93	4.48	7.08	7.08	5.68	-1.84	2.38	-0.69	-0.37

	G4C1	G4C2	G4C3	G4C4	G4C5	G4C6	G4C7	G4C8	G4D1	G4D10	G4D11	G4D12
G4E1	2.83	0.63	−0.37	1.36	4.28	−0.65	0.30	0.64	6.24	2.22	0.15	−1.31
G4E2	−2.10	−3.13	−4.47	−4.54	−0.40	−3.77	−1.92	−1.31	3.19	−1.43	−2.89	−3.79
G4E3	−1.63	−1.24	−2.79	−3.33	1.10	−2.78	−2.85	−0.42	4.18	−0.59	−2.23	−2.33
G4E4	−2.95	−2.29	−1.61	−3.39	0.90	−3.64	−3.12	−2.53	2.22	−1.97	−4.20	−3.37
G4E5	2.86	3.36	2.80	1.31	4.62	2.71	2.99	2.66	5.54	2.09	2.12	1.50
G4E6	0.56	1.38	0.23	−1.99	1.25	−0.25	2.31	1.81	2.39	0.64	−0.90	−1.45
G4E7	3.08	2.09	0.74	1.40	5.34	1.18	4.09	4.35	6.14	4.02	0.88	1.42
G4E8	2.51	0.56	0.94	0.41	3.33	1.13	0.72	1.71	3.99	2.06	1.04	1.12

	G4D13	G4D14	G4D15	G4D16	G4D17	G4D2	G4D3	G4D4	G4D5	G4D6	G4D7	G4D8
G4D13	–											
G4D14	10.00	–										
G4D15	−0.75	0.29	–									
G4D16	1.38	4.13	2.70	–								
G4D17	−1.67	−1.21	0.73	−0.25	–							
G4D2	−2.67	−1.40	0.32	−0.92	1.51	–						
G4D3	−2.80	−1.03	−0.06	0.22	−3.26	4.66	–					
G4D4	−0.65	−0.61	−4.33	−0.61	−0.29	−0.67	7.91	–				
G4D5	−1.58	−1.02	0.67	−2.33	−0.19	−3.38	0.14	1.12	–			
G4D6	0.78	0.57	0.67	−1.14	1.67	−3.19	−3.86	−0.67	2.75	–		
G4D7	−3.94	−2.14	2.01	−0.65	0.42	−0.87	−1.69	−1.52	2.93	4.79	–	
G4D8	−0.47	−3.33	2.12	0.46	0.26	−1.22	−2.80	−2.34	2.84	0.72	4.18	–
G4D9	5.76	2.58	−1.73	−1.24	0.89	−2.91	−2.21	−0.43	0.10	0.37	−2.11	0.08
G4E1	1.60	1.77	0.67	1.56	−0.06	1.03	5.94	2.92	−0.81	−2.11	−0.68	−1.70
G4E2	−1.06	−0.89	−0.65	−0.78	−1.55	−1.15	1.95	−0.56	−1.05	−2.98	−1.97	−2.92
G4E3	0.00	0.42	−0.69	0.53	−2.53	−0.38	3.23	0.81	−2.01	−4.23	−3.63	−3.24
G4E4	−0.92	−1.13	−2.67	−2.64	−3.57	−2.91	2.64	−0.98	−3.48	−5.15	−4.45	−6.25
G4E5	2.73	0.93	1.03	0.85	1.55	1.48	4.69	3.83	1.15	0.43	0.31	−0.93
G4E6	0.56	1.79	−2.45	0.71	−4.34	−0.84	3.23	0.31	1.01	−2.30	−3.03	−3.76
G4E7	4.59	2.77	0.96	2.51	−1.44	2.32	6.70	4.32	2.21	0.61	0.72	0.66
G4E8	0.30	0.43	0.60	0.08	1.06	1.47	3.34	3.63	1.92	0.39	0.47	0.71

	G4D9	G4E1	G4E2	G4E3	G4E4	G4E5	G4E6	G4E7	G4E8
G4D9	–								
G4E1	3.19	–							
G4E2	0.51	−0.07	–						
G4E3	−0.55	−0.22	−1.09	–					
G4E4	0.45	1.93	3.89	6.78	–				
G4E5	2.99	1.22	−4.50	−2.01	−3.78	–			
G4E6	0.68	−4.52	6.24	−2.98	−1.04	0.51	–		
G4E7	4.46	−2.34	0.12	−3.97	−5.93	6.38	8.46	–	
G4E8	2.93	−0.20	−2.11	1.89	−3.53	3.49	−3.80	3.07	–

Stemleaf Plot

```
- 7 | 40
- 6 | 964332
- 5 | 995322110000
- 4 | 98877666555555444444433333222111100000000000
- 3 | 999999998888888877776666666655555444444444333332222222222222211111111100+09
- 2 | 999999999999988888888888877777777766666666555555555555555555555444444444444+77
- 1 | 99999999999999988888888888888887777777777777777777777777777766666666666666+62
- 0 | 999999999999999999999999999888888888888888888888888877777777777777777777+96
  0 | 1111111111111111111111111111111111111112222222222222222222222333333333333333+79
  1 | 000000000000000000000111111111111111111111111111112222222222222222222333333333+36
  2 | 000000000001111111111111111111122222222223333333333333333333344444444444444455555+56
  3 | 000000000111111111111112222222222233333333333334445555556666666777777888899999
  4 | 000111222222222223333344555555666667777889999
  5 | 0011122344555666777778888999
  6 | 00011222344457788
  7 | 001112235799
  8 | 001125569
  9 | 9
 10 | 00
 11 | 6
```

Appendix E

Goodness-of-Fit Statistics for Three Grouping Models

In this appendix, we give the goodness-of-fit statistics for three models. The three models compared vary on the type of grouping for the survey statements. The first set of results is in the case of 'No grouping'. The second is in the case of the grouping we have presented and the third is for an even more important grouping with about an additional division in half in the number of grouped statements.

No grouping

Perform = 0.17*BuBlock + 0.14*Communic + 0.22*KnowlInt
+ 0.10*Leadersh − 0.028*CBRota, Errorvar.= 0.72, $R^2 = 0.28$

Degrees of Freedom = 3224
Normal Theory Weighted Least-Squares $\chi^2 = 16357.97$ ($P = 0.0$)
Root Mean Square Error of Approximation (RMSEA) = 0.070
90% Confidence Interval for RMSEA = (0.069 ; 0.071)
Model AIC = 16715.97

Normed Fit Index (NFI) = 0.93
Non-Normed Fit Index (NNFI) = 0.94
Parsimony Normed Fit Index (PNFI) = 0.90
Comparative Fit Index (CFI) = 0.95
Incremental Fit Index (IFI) = 0.95
Relative Fit Index (RFI) = 0.93

Selected grouping

Perform = 0.18*BuBlock + 0.090*Communic + 0.21*KnowlInt
+ 0.14*Leadersh − 0.022*CBRota, Errorvar.= 0.72, $R^2 = 0.28$

Degrees of Freedom = 1524
Normal Theory Weighted Least-Squares $\chi^2 = 6642.78$ ($P = 0.0$)
Root Mean Square Error of Approximation (RMSEA) = 0.063
90% Confidence Interval for RMSEA = (0.062; 0.065)
Model AIC = 6900.78

Normed Fit Index (NFI) = 0.95
Non-Normed Fit Index (NNFI) = 0.96
Parsimony Normed Fit Index (PNFI) = 0.91
Comparative Fit Index (CFI) = 0.96
Incremental Fit Index (IFI) = 0.96
Relative Fit Index (RFI) = 0.95

Further grouping

Perform = 0.15*BuBlock + 0.081*Communic + 0.24*KnowlInt
       + 0.15*Leadersh − 0.034*CBRota, Errorvar.= 0.72 , $R^2 = 0.28$

Degrees of Freedom = 335
Normal Theory Weighted Least-Squares $\chi^2 = 1632.29$ ($P = 0.0$)
Root Mean Square Error of Approximation (RMSEA) = 0.068
90% Confidence Interval for RMSEA = (0.065; 0.071)
Model AIC = 1774.29

Normed Fit Index (NFI) = 0.97
Non-Normed Fit Index (NNFI) = 0.97
Parsimony Normed Fit Index (PNFI) = 0.86
Comparative Fit Index (CFI) = 0.97
Incremental Fit Index (IFI) = 0.97
Relative Fit Index (RFI) = 0.96

Index